MW01105478

Volume One

Trends in the
Judiciary

Interviews with Judges Across the Globe

International Police Executive Symposium Co-Publications

Dilip K. Das, *Founding President-IPES*

Interviews with Global Leaders in Policing, Prisons, and Courts Series

PUBLISHED

Trends in the Judiciary: Interviews with Judges Across the Globe, Volume One
By Dilip K. Das and Cliff Roberson, ISBN: 978-1-4200-9978-2

Trends in Corrections: Interviews with Corrections Leaders Around the World
By Jennie K. Singer, Dilip K. Das, and Eileen Ahlin, ISBN: 978-1-4398-3578-4

Trends in Policing: Interviews with Police Leaders Across the Globe, Volume Three
By Otwin Marenin and Dilip K. Das, ISBN: 978-1-4398-1924-1

Trends in Policing: Interviews with Police Leaders Across the Globe
By Dilip K. Das and Otwin Marenin, ISBN: 978-1-4200-7520-5

FORTHCOMING

Trends in Policing: Interviews with Police Leaders Across the Globe, Volume Four
By Bruce F. Baker and Dilip K. Das, ISBN: 978-1-4398-8073-9

Trends in Corrections: Interviews with Corrections Leaders Around the World, Volume Two
By Martha Henderson Hurley and Dilip K. Das, ISBN: 978-1-4665-9156-1

Volume One

Trends in the Judiciary

Interviews with Judges Across the Globe

Dilip K. Das, PhD
Founding President, International Police Executive Symposium, IPES
Founding Editor-in-Chief,
Police Practice and Research: An International Journal, PPR

Cliff Roberson, LLM, PhD
Washburn University, Topeka, Kansas

Michael M. Berlin, JD, PhD
Coppin State University, Baltimore, Maryland

International Police Executive Symposium
Co-Publication

CRC Press
Taylor & Francis Group
Boca Raton London New York

CRC Press is an imprint of the
Taylor & Francis Group, an **informa** business

CRC Press
Taylor & Francis Group
6000 Broken Sound Parkway NW, Suite 300
Boca Raton, FL 33487-2742

© 2014 by Taylor & Francis Group, LLC
CRC Press is an imprint of Taylor & Francis Group, an Informa business

Printed on acid-free paper
Version Date: 20131023

International Standard Book Number-13: 978-1-4200-9978-2 (Hardback)

Library of Congress Cataloging-in-Publication Data

Trends in the judiciary : interviews with judges across the globe / editors, Cliff Roberson and Dilip K. Das, with Michael M. Berlin.
    p. cm. -- (Interviews with global leaders in policing, courts, and prisons ; 4)
Includes bibliographical references and index.
ISBN 978-1-4200-9978-2 (hardback)
    1. Justices of the peace. 2. Lay judges. 3. Police magistrates. I. Das, Dilip K., 1941-
editor of compilation. II. Roberson, Cliff, 1937- editor of compilation. III. Berlin, Michael
M., 1954- editor of compilation.

K2150.T74 2013
347'.014--dc23   2013041375

Visit the Taylor & Francis Web site at
http://www.taylorandfrancis.com

and the CRC Press Web site at
http://www.crcpress.com

Trends in the Judiciary: Interviews with Judges Across the Globe *is part of the series, Interviews with Global Leaders in Policing, Courts, and Prisons, which celebrates the personal and professional stories of those who determine the nature and quality of justice. This book is dedicated to the magistrates, judges, and justices who determine the nature and quality of justice. They face the public each day and define the concept and practice of justice within a nation. These individuals are the true justice makers. This book is tribute to these individuals who have given us a better understanding of how they administer justice within their jurisdictions.*

Contents

Section VII
UNITED STATES
MICHAEL M. BERLIN

Series Editor's Preface

The International Police Executive Symposium, in collaboration with CRC Press of the Taylor & Francis Group Publishing, has launched a series entitled, *Interviews with Global Leaders in Policing, Courts, and Corrections.* The objective is to produce high-quality books aimed at bringing the voice of the leading criminal justice practitioners to the forefront of scholarship and research. These books, based on interviews with leaders in Criminal Justice, are intended to present the perspectives of high-ranking officials throughout the world by examining their careers, insights, vision, experiences, challenges, perceived future of the field, and the related issues of interest.

True, the literature is replete with scholarship and research that provide the academic interpretation of the field, its practices, and future. However, these publications are often found in difficult to access journals and are written from the perspective of the academic, with little interpretation or feasible action items for those professionals working in the field. A comprehensive literature discussing the on-the-ground, day-to-day understanding of how police, courts, and prison systems work, do not work, and need to be improved is lacking. This series provides "inside" information about the systems as told to respected scholars and researchers by seasoned professionals. In this series, the dialogue between scholar/researcher and practitioner is opened as a guided, yet candid, discussion between the two professionals, which provides the opportunity for academics to learn from practitioners, while practitioners also learn from an outlet for the expression of their experiences, challenges, skills, and knowledge.

Throughout the world, the criminal justice field is in juxtaposition and the time is ripe for change and improvements. Many countries throughout the world have long-standing policies that have been successful for their culture and political climate, or are in need of serious revamping due to budgetary concerns or corruption. Other countries are at a precipice and are beginning to establish new systems. In all of these situations, the international criminal justice field stands to benefit from an accessible, engaging, and enlightening series of frank discussions of the leaders' personal views and experiences in the field.

The current volume, *Trends in the Judiciary: Interviews with Judges Across the Globe,* sets the stage to enhance readers' understanding of the judiciary and judicial systems throughout the world from an insider's perspective. The judges interviewed in this volume represent a variety of cultures, political environments, and economic systems. Judicial officials from Australia, Austria, Canada, Bosnia-Herzegovina, India, Slovenia, and the United States federal courts (U.S. District Court for Eastern Missouri) and U.S. state courts (Florida, Georgia, Louisiana, and Maryland) are interviewed. The Introduction familiarizes the reader with the judiciary of many nations and judicial issues from the perspective of noted judges. Each chapter is based on an interview of a member of the judiciary conducted by a scholar or researcher. A brief portrait of the national judicial system and court in which each judge serves is provided as well. The Conclusion at the end of the book is a reflection on the interviews and summary of common themes evident throughout the book.

Thus, *Trends in Judiciary: Interviews with Judges Across the Globe* continues the work of the International Police Executive Symposium (IPES) and CRC Press series, *Interviews with Global Leaders in Policing, Courts, and Prisons* by advancing knowledge about the judiciary, examining comparative judicial systems from the perspective of judicial leaders in a variety of countries, and opening a dialogue between scholars/researchers and practitioners. It is anticipated that this addition to the series will facilitate discussions within and between countries' judicial systems to add value to their current operations and future directions. It is hoped that this series also will bridge the gap in knowledge that exists between scholars and researchers in academia and practitioners in the field. I invite judicial scholars, researchers, and practitioners around the world to join in this venture.

Dilip K. Das, PhD
Founding President, International Police Executive Symposium
www.ipes.info

Book Series Editor for

Advances in Police Theory and Practice
CRC Press/Taylor & Francis Group

Interviews with Global Leaders in Criminal Justice
CRC Press/Taylor & Francis Group

PPR Special Issues as Books
Routledge/Taylor & Francis Group

Founding Editor-in-Chief
Police Practice and Research:
An International Journal, PPR
http://www.tandfonline.com/GPPR

Foreword

This is a fascinating set of documents. I am not aware of another book like it. It is the latest in an innovative and highly original series edited by Dr. Dilip Das with a variety of other distinguished academics and practitioners. Each volume has comprised interviews with leaders across the world in the fields of policing and corrections. Now we have this one on judicial and court leaders. The ambitious plan is to produce similar volumes annually.

The interviews in this volume are based on a common questionnaire, though, in reality, there is a certain amount of deviation from the common core, depending on the particular expertise and experience of the interviewee. Topics cover the interviewees' background, education, and career; their judicial role; the major changes and challenges they have experienced; and the relationship between theory and practice. The interviews present us with rich insights into the thinking of, and problems facing, a diverse array of judicial figures who vary in age, ethnicity, education, background, and seniority. They represent a variety of contexts, from cities to rural areas, developed, and developing countries, from emerging democracies to Western jurisdictions. The end product is a set of resources of great value to anyone who is interested in judicial backgrounds, philosophies, and leadership challenges. Students, academics, and policy makers should all find something of interest here.

The methodology used in the book is one way of studying elites—in this case, in the legal world. The study of elites is always difficult. It is all the more difficult when done on an international scale, as with these volumes. Thus, this book, along with the rest in the series, is a major contribution to the study and practice of judging around the world.

We must, however, remember that any one piece of research—or, in the case of this series, any one way of doing research—is limited. Robert Reiner, the eminent criminologist, quoted the British political scientist Professor Ivor Crewe, in his preface to one of the policing volumes in this series:

> Elites need to be interviewed. The best way of finding out about people is by talking to them. It cannot guarantee the truth, especially from people well practiced in the arts of discretion. But, it is superior to any alternative way of discovering what they believe and do.

I am not sure that I agree that interviews are the best way of finding out about people. They are certainly not the best way of finding out about what people do. However, they are one way of finding things out, and, like every other research method, they enable us to discover some things that other methods of investigation fail to discover. As Reiner observes, interviews are unlikely to reveal wrongdoing or errors, but these are notoriously difficult to discover anyway. We simply need to remember that these interviews add to our knowledge and understanding of judicial leaders without being the last word. If we do that, they will help us to interpret and evaluate insights drawn from other methods and help us to build up a fuller picture of the realities of judicial work.

Comparing these interviews (seeing the similarities as well as the differences) is very instructive. Each interview gives insights about different countries that are new to me, at any rate, particularly as the interviewees seem to be very frank. Therefore, there are some surprises. For example, Stephen Limbaugh, a U.S. judge, is critical of drug courts. He says that the cases that go to drug courts are "cherry picked" and are the ones that will usually make it through the system anyway, giving a false impression of their effectiveness. He draws attention to the lack of probation officers, hindering rehabilitation of the more "everyday" offenders with drug and alcohol problems.

Lack of resources is a common theme. Judge Manmohan Singh, of the Delhi High Court, India, says that the greatest problem facing the Indian criminal courts is the plethora of pending cases because there are too few courts and judges. He worries that, with cases pending for years, thousands of innocent people wait behind bars for their cases to be heard.

Perhaps more surprising, for those who think that the worlds of "real" lawyers and academics are far apart, are the views of many judges about the potential role of research. Gregory Benn, a magistrate in Western Australia, for example, talks about a conference where he learned that sex offenders don't necessarily need to take personal responsibility to achieve rehabilitation because sometimes what they have done is too awful for them to face. It doesn't necessarily mean that they cannot engage in counseling to help rehabilitation. Yet, magistrates regularly have presentence reports saying "these persons don't take responsibility for their actions; they minimize their involvement."

The interviewers and editors are to be congratulated for producing this valuable and entertaining volume. I am sure that I am in good company in looking forward to further volumes in the series.

Andrew Sanders
Professor of Criminal Law and Criminology
University of Birmingham, United Kingdom

Acknowledgments

This book would not exist but for the combined efforts of many individuals.

The judges, justices, and magistrates took the time to meet with the interviewers, answer their questions, and share their experiences and insights on the judiciary. These judges, justices, and magistrates are

Judge Robert M. Bell, Chief Judge, Maryland Court of Appeals, State of Maryland, USA

Magistrate Gregory Andrew Benn, Regional Magistrate, Kalgoorlie-Boulder, Western Australia

Chief Magistrate Winston P. Bethel, Retired, DeKalb County, Georgia, USA

Mag. Friedrich Forsthuber, President of the Vienna Criminal Court, Austria

Judge Aleksander Karakaš, Criminal Judiciary Department of Maribor District Court, Slovenia

Stephen N. Limbaugh, Jr., District Judge, United States District Court, Eastern District of Missouri, USA

Senior Judge McEwen, The Youth Court of South Australia

Judge Wally Oppal, Queens Council (Q.C.), Supreme Court of British Columbia and Former Attorney General of British Columbia, Canada

Chief Judge Wilson Rambo, 4th Judicial District, State of Louisiana, USA

Judge Manmohan Singh, Judge, Delhi High Court, India

Judge Eugene C. Turner, Collier County Court, State of Florida, USA

Judge Hilmo Vucinic, State Court Justice for Bosnia and Herzegovina

The interviewers who skillfully elicited responses from these judicial officials included Ann-Claire Larsen; Daniel King, Andrew Day and Paul Delfabbro; Maximilian Edelbacher and Peter Kratcoski; Laurence French and Goran Kovacevi; Gorazd Mesko; Richard Parent; Vidisha Barua Worley; Diana L. Bruns and Jeff W. Bruns; Michael M. Berlin; Robert Hanser; Cloud Miller and Landon Miller; and Catherine A. Jenks. Also, Senator Ralph Hughes, former Chair of the Department of Criminal Justice and Law Enforcement at Coppin State University, Baltimore, who arranged for the interview of Justice Robert Bell. Those who wrote the overviews of national judicial systems represented in this volume: Ann-Claire Larsen, Maximilian Edelbacher and Peter Kratcoski, Laurence French, Gorazd Mesko, Richard Parent, Sankar Sen, and Michael M. Berlin.

Finally, we thank Professor Andrew Sanders, Professor of Criminal Law and Criminology, University of Birmingham, United Kingdom, for his thoughtful Foreword. Carolyn Spence, Senior Acquisition Editor, CRC Press/Taylor & Francis Group, has been the Florence Nightingale of the project, nourishing it tenderly and with great loving care.

The Editors

Dilip K. Das, PhD, has years of experience in police practice, research, writing, and education. After obtaining his master's degree in English literature, Dr. Das joined the Indian Police Service, an elite national service with a glorious tradition. Following 14 years in the service as a police executive (including chief of police) he moved to the United States where he achieved another master's degree in Criminal Justice as well as a doctorate in the same discipline. Dr. Das is a professor of criminal justice, former police chief, and a human rights consultant to the United Nations. He is founding president of International Police Executive Symposium (IPES) where he manages the affairs of the organization in cooperation with an appointed group of police practitioners, academia members, and individuals from around the world. Dr. Das is also the founding editor of *Police Practice and Research: An International Journal.* He has authored, edited, and co-edited more than 30 books and numerous articles. He has received several faculty excellence awards and was a Distinguished Faculty Lecturer at Western Illinois University.

Cliff Roberson, LLM, PhD, is an emeritus professor of Criminal Justice at Washburn University, Topeka, Kansas. Dr. Roberson's nonacademic experience includes U.S. Marine Corps service as an infantry officer, trial and defense counsel and military judge as a marine judge advocate, and director of the Military Law Branch, U.S. Marine Corps. Other legal employment experiences include trial supervisor, Office of State Counsel for Offenders, Texas Board of Criminal Justice and judge pro-tem in the California courts. Educational background includes PhD in Human Behavior, U.S. International University; LLM (Master of Laws), in Criminal Law, Criminology, and Psychiatry, George Washington University; J.D. American University; B.A. in Political Science, University of Missouri; and one year of postgraduate study at the University of Virginia School of Law. He has authored or co-authored over 60 books and texts.

Contributors

Michael M. Berlin, PhD, is director of the Criminal Justice Graduate Program and an assistant professor at Coppin State University in Baltimore, Maryland. Dr. Berlin's areas of specialization include constitutional law and criminal procedure, community policing, criminal justice leadership and management, and terrorism/homeland security. Prior to his appointment at Coppin State University, Dr. Berlin served as a professor of criminal justice at Baltimore City Community College where he directed both on-campus and Baltimore Police Academy Programs for over a decade. He is an attorney with more than 20 years experience in private practice and is a former Baltimore police officer. His recent publications include *Crime Scene Searches and the Fourth Amendment* (ISJ, 2011) and *The Evolution, Decline and Nascent Transformation of Community Policing in the United States 1980–2010* (CRC Press, 2012).

Diana L. Bruns, PhD, is the interim dean of the College of Health and Human Services. the chairperson of the Criminal Justice and Sociology Department, and professor at Southeast Missouri State University in Cape Girardeau, Missouri. Her research interests include issues in policing, assessment, and leadership in higher education and family violence. She has published in areas of criminal justice, sociology, business, management, and higher education. Dr. Bruns teaches in the areas of research methods, statistics, criminology, and drugs and behavior.

Jeff W. Bruns, PhD, is an instructor in criminal justice and sociology in the Department of Criminal Justice and Sociology at Southeast Missouri State University in Cape Girardeau, Missouri. His research interests include issues in policing as well as assessment, management and leadership in organizational development. He has published in areas of management, business, higher education and criminal justice. He has held various leadership positions in business as well as higher education, specializing in management and organizational behavior. He holds a BS, MS, MBA and PhD.

Andrew Day, PhD, is a professor in forensic psychology and director of the Forensic Psychology Centre at Deakin University, Australia. Professor Day is a member of the Australian Psychological Society's Colleges of Clinical and Forensic Psychology. His current research interests center around the development of therapeutic regimes within prison settings, effective practice with offenders from Aboriginal and Torres Strait Islander cultural backgrounds in Australia, and the role that anger plays in aggressive and violent behavior.

Paul Delfabbro, PhD, is associate professor with the School of Psychology at the University of Adelaide, Australia. His current research focuses on foster care and issues such as the predictors of reunification, the effect of placement movements upon well being, the perceived effects of parental contact, and the additional economic costs of placing difficult children into care. He also is interested in understanding gambling and the role of cognitive and behavioral factors in the maintenance of within-session behavior.

Maximilian Edelbacher was born in Vienna, Austria. He served with the police in Austria from 1972 to 2006. His last assignment was as chief of the Major Crime Bureau in Vienna. From 1995 to 2011, he was a lecturer at Vienna University of Economics, Danube University, Krems, Lower Austria, and from 2000 to 2009, a lecturer at Kent State University in Ohio, and Turku University, Finland. From 1995 to 2007, he worked with the International Expert of United Nations Organization, the Organization for Security and Cooperation in Europe (OSCE), and Council of Europe. Since 2007, he has served as a special investigator of AVUS Group. Since 2008, he has served as a member of ACUNS (Academic Council on the United Nations System)–UNO (Advisory Board on the UN System); since 2010, a board member of Austrian Criminal Investigator's Organization; and, since 2011, as the representative of the International Police Executive Symposium (IPES) at the United Nations in Vienna. He has published several books and articles.

Laurence Armand French, PhD, has a BA, MA, and PhD in Sociology (social disorganization/social psychology) from the University of New Hampshire, a PhD in cultural psychology (educational psychology and measurement) from the University of Nebraska-Lincoln, and an MA in school psychology from Western New Mexico University. He pursued post-doctoral studies in "minorities and criminal justice education" at the State University of New York-Albany and completed the postdoctoral prescribing psychology program including the national exam. He is professor emeritus of psychology from Western New Mexico University and is a licensed clinical psychologist (Arizona). He is a Fulbright Scholar (University of Sarajevo, Bosnia-Herzegovina, 2009–2010) and Visiting Endowed Chair of Criminology and Criminal Justice at St. Thomas University, Fredericton, New Brunswick, Canada (fall semester 2010). He has over 280 publications including 15 books. His latest book is *Running the Border Gauntlet: The Mexican Migrant Controversy* (Praeger, 2010). His major areas of research interest include international and comparative social, human, and criminal justice; Native American and minority issues; police and criminal psychology and neuro-, clinical, and forensic psychology.

Robert D. Hanser, PhD, is an associate professor and head of the Department of Criminal Justice at the University of Louisiana at Monroe.

He is the lead facilitator for the 4th Judicial District's Batterer Intervention Program (BIP) and is the Board president and CEO of North Delta Human Services Authority (NDHSA), which is a nonprofit organization that provides contract therapeutic services for the 4th Judicial District Adult Drug Court and DWI Court in Northeast Louisiana. Dr. Hanser is also a police and correctional officer trainer who specializes in legal liabilities for agency staff and administrators.

Catherine A. Jenks, PhD, is an associate professor, Department of Criminology and director, Survey Research Center, College of Social Sciences at the University of West Georgia. She holds a PhD in criminology and criminal justice from Florida State University (2006). She obtained her undergraduate degree in government from the University of Texas at Austin and a master of criminology and criminal justice from the University of Texas at Arlington. Prior to joining the faculty at the University of West Georgia, she was a survey coordinator for the RAND Corporation in Santa Monica, California. Her research interests include civility, law and society, criminal courts, sentencing and punishment, public opinion, and survey research. She co-founded the Survey Research Center at the University of West Georgia in 2006 and has served as its director since 2007. She was the recipient of the College of Arts and Sciences Excellence in Teaching Award in 2008 for integrating survey research scholarship with teaching through innovative course design.

Daniel King, PhD, is a research fellow in the School of Psychology at the University of Adelaide, Australia. He received his doctorate in 2009 from the University of Adelaide and was awarded the Frank Dalziel Prize (2009) for the Best PhD Thesis in Psychology. He is author of over 30 peer-reviewed journal articles. He is currently undertaking his master of psychology (clin.) at Flinders University, as well as conducting research on the psychosocial impact of gaming and gambling technologies on young people.

Goran Kovacevic was born in Sarajevo in the former Yugoslavia in 1982. He attended local schools earning his BS degree from Faculty of Criminal Justice, University of Sarajevo, and MS degree from the Faculty of Law, University of Sarajevo. He is currently completing his doctorate degree and serves on the faculty at University of Sarajevo in Criminology, Criminal Justice, and Security Studies.

Peter C. Kratcoski, PhD, received a bachelor's degree in sociology from King's College, a master's degree in sociology from the University of Notre Dame, and a PhD in sociology from The Pennsylvania State University. He taught at St. Thomas University in St. Paul, Minnesota, and Pennsylvania State University before assuming the position of assistant professor of sociology at Kent State University (Ohio) in 1969. During his years at Kent State University, he held the position of professor of sociology and justice studies and served as the chairman of the Department of Justice Studies until his retirement in

1998. He has continued to teach at Kent State. He currently holds the positions of Emeritus Professor and temporary instructor in sociology and justice studies. Dr. Kratcoski has authored several books, edited books, and authored many book chapters and journal articles. His most recent book is *Juvenile Justice Administration* (CRC Press, 2012). He also was a co-editor and chapter contributor to *Financial Crimes: A Threat to Global Security* (CRC Press, 2012). His areas of specialization include juvenile justice, corrections, crime prevention, and international policing.

Ann-Claire Larsen, PhD, is a legal sociologist who teaches international human rights and professional ethics for the School of Law and Justice, Edith Cowan University, Western Australia. Her research is associated with the Centre for Innovative Practice also at Edith Cowan University. Areas of research interests include judicial decision making, policing, technologies, sex workers, and health services.

Gorazd Meško, PhD, is a professor of criminology and dean at the Faculty of Criminal Justice and Security, University of Maribor, Slovenia. He conducted a postdoctoral research (OSI-HESP) on crime prevention at the Institute of Criminology, University of Cambridge, United Kingdom, in 2001. Currently, he is heading a national basic research project entitled "Crimes Against the Environment—Criminological, Victimological, Crime-Prevention, Psychological and Legal Aspects" (2009–2012). In addition, Gorazd Meško is a member of the scientific board of the international PhD in criminology at the Catholic University in Milan, Italy. He also serves as the editor in chief of the *Journal of Criminal Investigation and Criminology* (orig. *Revija za kriminalistiko in kriminologijo*) and a member of the editorial board of *Policing—An International Journal of Police Strategies and Management*. His research fields are crime prevention and provision of safety/security, policing, fear of crime, and crimes against the environment.

Cloud Miller, PhD, started his criminal justice career in the area of corrections in 1964, after graduating from Florida State University. He worked with the Florida Parole Commission for 10 years and then was appointed to a position with the Florida governor's office in the development of research and development of criminal justice (CJ) projects to improve the state criminal justice system. Thereafter, he worked as a Florida parole hearing officer interviewing State of Florida prisoners for purposes of parole consideration. Subsequently, he was employed as a federal parole examiner for 10 years and had an opportunity to interview federal prisoners for parole consideration. He completed his PhD in criminology at FSU, and received a law degree from Atlanta Law School in 1990. He has been a practicing criminal defense attorney for the past 20 years, specializing in the area of postconviction. He is admitted to the Georgia Bar, all federal courts of appeal, the United States Supreme Court, numerous state and federal district trial courts. He is currently a full-time graduate studies professor at Kaplan University, serving as chair of the master's degree thesis development classes.

Landon Miller, JD, is a criminal defense lawyer with Mangone and Miller Law Office, in Naples, Florida. He graduated from Florida State University with a BS in criminology, and received a Juris Doctorate from St Thomas University, School of Law in 1994. Previously Landon worked for the Florida Department of Corrections as a probation and parole officer, interned in the Florida State Attorney's Office, 11th Judicial Circuit in Dade County, Florida, and has been a practicing criminal defense lawyer since 1994. He is admitted to the U.S. Supreme Court, Courts of Appeal in the 3rd and 11th Circuit, U.S. District Courts, Southern, Middle, and Northern Districts of Florida, Wisconsin, and Michigan. He is a member of the American Bar Association, Federal Bar Association, National Association of Criminal Defense Lawyers, and the Florida Association of Criminal Defense Lawyers.

Rick Parent, PhD, is an assistant professor at Simon Fraser University, School of Criminology–Police Studies (Vancouver, BC). Dr. Parent recently completed 30 years of service as a police officer in the Vancouver area. He is also a former police recruit instructor and a crisis negotiator, assigned to a regional Emergency Response Team. His area of research includes police ethics and accountability, crisis negotiations, police recruiting and training, and the police use of deadly force. He frequently provides expert opinion reports regarding police shootings and the police use of force. Dr. Parent is also a co-author of the text *Community-Based Strategic Policing in Canada* (Nelson Education, Ltd., 2013), which is widely utilized by both police agencies and academic institutions.

Sankar Sen served as an officer of the Indian Police Service in many significant assignments both at the state level and in the Government of India. He was the Additional-Director General of the Border Security Force and the Director of the prestigious National Police Academy at Hyderabad where he was instrumental in bringing about innovative changes in training and research studies on police issues and problems. On completion of his tenure in the academy, Mr. Sen was appointed Director General of the National Human Rights Commission (NHRC) and served from 1994 to 1998. He was specially assigned to custodial justice programs by the Commission and in that capacity visited prisons and rescue homes in different countries of the world. Mr. Sen joined the Institute of Social Sciences as a Senior Fellow in 1999 and is heading its Human Rights Wing. He has made immense and valuable contribution to bringing about improvement in the functioning of the police forces in the country during the last 12 years. A prolific writer, Sankar Sen has published numerous articles on subjects on trafficking, law enforcement, human rights, criminal justice administration, and other topics. He is the author of eleven books including *Trafficking in Women and*

Children: Myths and Reality, Crisis in Law Enforcement, Community Policing and Enforcing Police Accountability through Civilian Oversight.

Vidisha Barua Worley, PhD, is an assistant professor of criminal justice, University of North Texas at Dallas; contributing editor and columnist for the *Criminal Law Bulletin*; founding member of the Institute for Legal Studies in Criminal Justice, Sam Houston State University; and a licensed attorney in New York. She presented a paper on intellectual disability and the death penalty at the Oxford Round Table, Oxford University, United Kingdom, in March 2010. Dr. Worley's research areas include police and prison officers' liabilities for the use of Tasers˙ and stun guns, death penalty law, prison rape, correctional officer deviance, inappropriate relationships between inmates and correctional officers, ethical issues in criminal justice, crime and media, and terrorism. Her published books include *Press and Media Law Manual* (Universal Book Trading, Co., 2002) and *Terrorism in India* (Sam Houston State University, 2006).

Interviewees

Judge Robert M. Bell is the Chief Judge of the Maryland Court of Appeals, Maryland's highest court. Judge Bell's judicial career spans nearly 40 years and includes service on all four tiers of the Maryland state court system. Judge Bell graduated in 1966 from Morgan State College (now Morgan State University), a historically black college in Baltimore, Maryland. He entered Harvard Law School later that same year. After graduating in 1969, Judge Bell returned to Baltimore, where he became an associate at Piper and Marbury, a prominent law firm. Judge Bell remained at Piper until January 1975, when he was appointed as a judge of the District Court of Maryland for Baltimore City. He served on the District Court bench for five years until his appointment to the Supreme Bench of Baltimore (now the Circuit Court for Baltimore City) on January 22, 1980. He ran for office in the next election and served on the Supreme Bench until his appointment in 1984 to the Maryland Court of Special Appeals. In 1991, Governor William Donald Schaefer appointed Judge Bell to the Maryland Court of Appeals. He was named Chief Judge of the Court of Appeals by Governor Parris Glendening on October 23, 1996. He retired at 70 on July 6, 2013.

Magistrate Gregory Andrew Benn, a regional magistrate in Kalgoorlie–Boulder, Western Australia, works in the city of Kalgoorlie–Boulder, a gold mining town 596 kilometers northeast of Perth. Magistrate Benn has represented Aboriginal people most of his working life. He spent the first couple of years following his admission to practice in a private law firm before taking a job with Legal Aid in Port Hedland, 1647 kilometers north of Perth. For 18 years, he worked for the Aboriginal Legal Service (ALS) in Western Australia (WA). Eleven of those years were spent travelling around WA doing Native Title work and managing the ALS Land and Heritage Unit. During the remaining seven years, he focused on criminal law while managing the Criminal Unit within the ALS. Following that, Magistrate Benn spent 12 months in the Solomon Islands working for their Legal Aid equivalent and representing people in what were essentially war crimes trials. He applied for the Kalgoorlie magistrate's job largely because it involved an innovative pilot project, the Kalgoorlie–Boulder Community Court, which is an Aboriginal sentencing court where the magistrate sits with two respected members of the Aboriginal community. He assumed his current position in Kalgoorlie in November 2007. As well as sitting in the Kalgoorlie Boulder

Community Court, Magistrate Benn is responsible for conducting work in both the criminal and civil jurisdictions of the Children's and Magistrates' Courts, work in the Warden's Court (which deals with mining matters), the Family Court, and as a coroner. He is based in Kalgoorlie with two other full-time magistrates who travel throughout the goldfields and Western Desert regions on a circuit as far south as Esperance on the southern coast and east to Warakurna near the South Australian border.

Judge Winston P. Bethel is a retired Chief Magistrate Judge of DeKalb County, Georgia, where he served as a judge for 25 years. Judge Bethel holds a bachelor of applied studies from Mercer University in Georgia, a master of arts in sociology from the University of West Georgia, a juris doctor from the John Marshall Law School, and a master of laws from the Woodrow Wilson College of Law. During his tenure on the bench, he was instrumental in the development and implementation of several innovative initiatives that were grounded in the philosophy of therapeutic jurisprudence. He has given over 20 professional presentations directly related to this judicial philosophy and served as a grant peer reviewer for several Substance Abuse and Mental Health Services Administration (SAMHSA) grant applications on jail diversion and reentry.

Friedrich Forsthuber, president of the Criminal Court in Vienna, studied law between 1981 and 1985 at the Vienna University, Faculty of Law. In 1986, he served a year at the court (*Gerichtsjahr,* in German) and became an aspirant for the position of judge (*Richteramtsanwärter*) between 1987 and 1990. After passing the selection process, he became a judge at a civil district court at the District Court Döbling. He worked there from March 1990 to April 1991. On May 1, 1991, he became a judge at the Criminal Court in Vienna, where he was a judge from May 1, 1991 until August 31, 2005. He held different positions as an investigative judge, a judge in the presidential administration of the criminal court, a judge of the press agency of the criminal court, and a full-trial judge, responsible for general cases and media cases. From September 1, 2005 to December 31, 2009, he worked in the Upper Court, being responsible for internal revisions and he also worked in the Senate of Appeal. On January 1, 2010, he became president of the Criminal Court in Vienna.

Judge Aleksander Karakaš is a lawyer with a master of law degree. He completed primary and secondary school education in his hometown, Maribor, Slovenia, and, after military service in 1985, he continued studying at the Law Faculty, Ljubljana University. In 1990, he started work as an intern at the Maribor Higher Court. He passed the exam in May 1992 and was reemployed in the Maribor Higher Court. He continued working as a legal assistant in the Civil Judiciary Department. His primary tasks consisted of preparing reports for meetings of the Appeal Chambers, and writing drafts of court decisions. He was appointed a judge in the Criminal Court Department of the Local Court in Maribor. In 2003, he was appointed as a judge to the Criminal Judiciary Department of Maribor District Court, until 2005, when he was appointed as a judge in the Criminal Judiciary Department in the Maribor Higher Court, where he still works today.

Stephen N. Limbaugh, Jr. is a U.S. district judge working in the Eastern District of Missouri. His primary responsibility is to hear criminal and civil cases that fall under the jurisdiction of the U.S. federal government. Judge Limbaugh started his law career working in private practice, but shortly thereafter was elected as a State Prosecuting Attorney of Cape Girardeau County in Missouri. After serving his four-year term, he returned to private practice for the next four and one half years. He was then appointed as a Circuit Judge in the 32nd Circuit of Missouri. He served in that capacity until he was appointed to the Missouri State Supreme Court five years later. He served 16 years on the Supreme Court of Missouri (including serving a two-year term as the Chief Justice) before he was appointed to U.S. District Court–Eastern District of Missouri. Judge Limbaugh was sworn in as a federal judge on August 1, 2008 (and occupied that position at the time of this interview). He earned an undergraduate degree in history and a Juris Doctorate, both from Southern Methodist University, Texas. In addition, he also earned a master of laws degree in judicial process from the University of Virginia.

Senior Judge Stephen McEwen practiced as a solicitor in Adelaide, Clare, and Port Pirie, Australia, from 1980 to 1988. He was a senior prosecutor at the Director of Public Prosecutions from 1988 to 2001, and was a barrister at the private bar from 2001 to 2005. Judge McEwen was appointed QC (Queens Council) in 2006. He also was appointed judge of the District Court and senior judge of the Youth Court the same year.

Senior Judge McEwen's extracurricular legal activities have included numerous presentations to training programs and community groups, training workshops for police and forensic scientists, presentations for universities and law society, advocacy training for law students, and moot judging. He also has chaired a number of Commonwealth Games and Olympic Games Selection Appeals.

Judge Wally Oppal attended the University of British Columbia Law School in the 1960s, graduating with a law degree. For over 12 years, he practiced law in the Vancouver area. Then, in the 1970s, he became a member of Crown Counsel, prosecuting cases for the government before being appointed to the Bench. In 1981, Wally Oppal was appointed to the County Court of Vancouver and, later, to the Supreme Court of British Columbia in 1985. In 2003, he was appointed to the British Columbia Court of Appeal where he served until he resigned to seek election to the provincial government legislature. He is the second Indo-Canadian in the province to have held the title of Attorney General (AG) of British Columbia. Oppal served in the provincial cabinet as Attorney General of British Columbia and minister responsible for multiculturalism. Shortly after the initial interview was conducted, Wally Oppal vacated his seat in government as a result of losing an election. He was soon appointed to head a public inquiry into a controversial and horrific serial killing spree that occurred in Vancouver between January 23, 1997, and February 5, 2002.

Judge Wilson Rambo currently serves as Chief Judge of the 4th Judicial District Court for Morehouse and Ouachita Parishes. He earned his BA in political science from Louisiana State University in 1979 and his Juris Doctor from the LSU–Paul M. Hébert Law Center in 1982. While working on his bachelor and juris doctor degrees, Rambo served on the staff with the state legislature. He also worked as staff with the Louisiana 2nd Circuit Court of Appeal as well as an assistant district attorney for the 4th Judicial District in that same state. While in private practice, Rambo served as in-house counsel for the City of Monroe's Marshal's Office and as local counsel for the Southern States Police Benevolent Association. He likewise worked as a public defender with the 4th Judicial District and served as a past president and founding member of the Louisiana Public Defender Association. Judge Rambo presently serves as a hearing officer for the Judiciary Commission, which deals with ethical violations relative to the conduct of judges and justices of the peace. He also delivers continuing education instruction regularly on behalf of the Louisiana State Bar Association and other professional organizations on a variety of topics including ethics and professionalism for both lawyers and judges. Among his community service activities are participation in the American Inns of Court as a past president and master of the Fred Fudicar local chapter, his service on the Access to Justice Committee of the Louisiana State Bar Association, his membership on the steering committee of the Family Justice Center, his work as a trustee for Our House, his service as a CASA advocate, as well as his membership in various Chambers of Commerce in his jurisdiction.

Judge Manmohan Singh, Delhi High Court, India, lost his father when he was only one year old. His mother brought him up and it was her dream that he join the legal profession and, perhaps, one day become a judge. His maternal uncle, an intellectual property rights lawyer, had practiced in Peshawar, Pakistan, since 1940. He was Singh's role model and guided him to become a trademark and patent lawyer. He started his career in 1980 under his uncle's guidance in the High Court of Delhi. He practiced independently for 28 years in Delhi, Bombay (Mumbai), Calcutta (Kolkata), and Madras (Chennai), specializing in trademarks, copyrights, and patents. On April 11, 2008, he became a judge of the Delhi High Court.

Judge Eugene C. Turner graduated from the University of South Florida, attended law school at Stetson University and received his JD from the University of Baltimore in 1974. Judge Turner served as Assistant State Attorney in the 12th Judicial Circuit from 1974 to 1977. He then entered private general practice and, in 1983, was appointed to the Collier County Court in Florida. Judge Turner has been a county court judge for 29 years and is highly respected by the community and the legal profession as a fair, dignified, and open-minded.

Judge Hilmo Vucinic, State Court Justice for Bosnia and Herzegovina, was born in Gorazde in Bosnia in 1963, where he grew up and attended public school, completing both elementary and high school. He later attended the University of Sarajevo where he graduated with a degree from the Law Faculty. After graduation, he started working in his hometown, Gorazde. For a while, he worked in administrative agencies, then in the economic sector, mainly in the private sector, where he was head of legal services. He spent the war years in Gorazde and, in January 1993, he was appointed as a judge of the District Military Court in Gorazde. After the abolition of the military courts, he was appointed as a judge to the Cantonal Court in Gorazde. He was appointed as a judge of the Cantonal Court in Sarajevo in 2003 and he performed these duties until March, 2005, when he was appointed as a judge of the Court of Bosnia-Herzegovina. Currently, he is a judge of the Appellate Panel and performs the function of the president of Appellate Division of the Court.

Introduction

Trend in Judiciary: Interviews with Judges Across the Globe is an eclectic collection of judicial interviews from around the world. Experienced magistrates, justices, and judges offer their unique perspectives on their own most significant legal developments and issues in criminal and procedural law facing their respective nations. They also share key aspects of their professional development, which offer a glimpse into their personal lives and provide a context for understanding their experiences and views. The interviews also provide insight into career development in the legal profession and judiciary as well. Interview subjects are drawn from a diverse array of nations and cultures ranging from Canada and the United States in North America to Austria, Bosnia-Herzegovina and Slovenia on the European Continent, to India in South Asia, and Australia. Judges and justices interviewed serve on trial and appellate courts at local, provincial, state, and federal levels.

The interviewers are scholars and legal professionals who possess the experience and expertise to elicit critical information. Interviews are grouped by nation and region. A brief overview of each judge's national judicial and legal system is provided to facilitate an understanding of the milieu in which they operate. The interviewers and judicial officials interviewed are:

- Michael Berlin interviewed Judge Robert Bell of the Maryland Court of Appeals (State Supreme Court), and captured the essence of the civil rights revolution. Judge Bell went from being a defendant in a trespass case arising out of a lunch counter desegregation sit-in to Chief Judge of the Maryland Court of Appeals, the state's highest court, in a career that spans over 40 years.
- Diana Bruns and Jeff Bruns interviewed Stephen N. Limbaugh, Jr., District Judge, U.S. District Court, Eastern District of Missouri. Prior to appointment to the judiciary, Judge Limbaugh worked in private practice and served as an elected county prosecutor. Judge Limbaugh began his judicial career as a trial judge in the State of Missouri and later served on the Missouri State Supreme Court. He was appointed to the U.S. District Court of the Eastern District of Missouri in 2008.
- Maximilian Edelbacher, with the editorial assistance of Peter Kratcoski, interviewed Mag. Friedrich Forsthuber, president of the

Vienna Criminal Court. While Austria's legal and judicial system predates those of neighboring Bosnia-Herzegovina and Slovenia, it has undergone significant changes in recent years, particularly relating to Austria's admission to the European Union in 1995.

- Laurence French and Goran Kovacevic interviewed Judge Hilmo Vucinic, State Court Justice for Bosnia and Herzegovina. Their interview provides insight into the judicial system of Bosnia-Herzegovina, as well as the role of the judiciary in a newly established postconflict democracy arising out of the former Yugoslav Republic. It addresses issues concerning the judiciary and war crimes.
- Meško Gorazd interviewed Judge Aleksander Karakaš, Criminal Judiciary Department of Maribor District Court, Slovenia. This interview provides insight into the legal and judicial system of Slovenia, another newly established democracy arising from the former Yugoslav Republic.
- Robert Hanser interviewed Chief Judge Wilson Rambo, 4th Judicial Circuit, State of Louisiana. Judge Rambo's legal career spans 30 years and includes service as an assistant district attorney (prosecutor), city attorney, public defender, and local counsel for a regional police benevolent association. The 4th Judicial Circuit in northeast Louisiana is a trial court that incorporates two parishes, Ouachita and Morehouse, Louisiana. Judge Rambo leads the 10 other judges of the District. Louisiana is the only U.S. state that follows the Napoleonic Code, which derives from a different legal and cultural system than that of the other 49 states.
- Catherine A. Jenks interviewed Judge Winston P. Bethel, Retired, Chief Magistrate Judge, DeKalb County, Georgia. Judge Bethel served as magistrate for over 25 years and was instrumental in the development and implementation of several therapeutic justice initiatives, including accountability courts, behavior modification and diversion.
- Daniel King, Andrew Day, and Paul Delfabbro interviewed Senior Judge Stephen McEwen of The Youth Court of South Australia. The Youth Court is responsible for juvenile justice and child protection matters in South Australia.
- Ann-Claire Larsen interviewed Magistrate Gregory Andrew Benn, Regional Magistrate, Kalgoorlie-Boulder, Western Australia. Kalgoorlie-Boulder is a gold mining town northeast of Perth, Western Australia. Magistrate Benn deals regularly with Aboriginal people, overrepresented in Australia's criminal justice system.
- Cloud Miller and Landon Miller interviewed Judge Eugene C. Turner, Collier County Court, State of Florida. Judge Turner serves as a county court judge in Collier County, Florida, one of Florida's

wealthiest counties. He has a passion for individualized justice and traces changes in the Florida judicial system during his 20 years on the Florida bench.

- Richard Parent interviewed Judge Wally Oppal, Queens Council (Q.C), Supreme Court of British Columbia, Canada. In addition to his tenure as a trial, provincial supreme court, and court of appeals judge, Oppal was elected and served as Attorney General of British Columbia, Canada. He has an understanding of the Canadian criminal justice system from multiple perspectives and offers particular insight with regard to the Royal Canadian Mounted Police and a variety of policing issues.
- Vidisha Barua Worley interviewed Judge Manmohan Singh, Delhi High Court, India. As a judge of the Delhi High Court, located in the capital of India, Judge Singh has played a role in deciding major constitutional and public interest litigation of profound significance.

The general goal of the interviews is to present the justices' views and interpretations of legal developments and current issues in the criminal law and procedures in their respective nations, for example, what they see happening in the legal profession and criminal courts of their countries and how they evaluate or interpret developments.

The interviewers typically began by asking the judges about their career, legal education, occupational history, areas of specialization, factors that influenced their career decisions, and professional development. The interviewers inquired into any surprises that may have occurred during the course of the judges' career development and whether their work proved as interesting or rewarding as they thought it would. The interview then turned to changes experienced during the course of the judge's career. What do they see as the most important changes that have happened in their nations' criminal justice system over the course of their career? Next they explored changes in philosophical approaches, organizational arrangements, policies and programs, technology, personnel issues, and other areas. The interviewees were asked to examine environmental changes, community support, judicial relations with minority communities, political influences, changes in legal powers, and resource provision. Then they were asked whether the overall quality of the criminal justice system had improved or declined.

The inquiry then focused on the judges' personal judicial philosophy. What they think should be the role of the judiciary in society. What should be the job, functions, and roles of the judiciary? What should be left to other branches of government and institutions? What organizational arrangements work and which do not? What policies and practices work well to facilitate improved community and political support and contribute to better relationships with other criminal justice organizations? What hampers cooperation with other agencies and groups? The interviewees were asked their preferred priorities and strategies, the proper balance between hard-edged crime control strategies and prevention- and treatment-based approaches, order maintenance, and social service approaches. And, what mix works best for which types of problems?

Judges discuss the problems and successes they have experienced, what policies or programs have worked well and which have not, and the reasons. What they consider to be the greatest problem facing the criminal courts in their respective nations at the present time. What problems in courts they find the most difficult to deal with. What would be easy to change. We explored internal problems, such as organizational culture, managerial deficiencies, allegations of corruption, and gender-related problems, as well as, externally generated problems, such as resources and community support.

The interviews then explored the relationship between theory and practice, what practitioners can learn from theory, and what theory builders can learn from practitioners. What is the relationship at the present time, does it exist, does it work? What impedes collaboration or interactions between researchers and practitioners? Judges were asked what kind of research, in what form, on what questions would be most useful for practice and what theory builders could do to make their products more useful to you. They also were asked where they find theory-based information—where they look, what journals, books, publications, reports they rely upon, and whether and on what types of issues the judiciary does research on its own outside of research dealing with pending cases.

The impact of transnational relations was considered, how courts and judges have been affected by developments outside their country, such as human rights demands, universal codes of ethics, practical interactions with judges or justices from other countries, personal experiences outside the country, new crime threats and other factors. We asked whether and how these influences have been beneficial or harmful and whether and how have developments post 9/11 affected their work.

We conclude with a general assessment: Is the judge basically satisfied or dissatisfied with developments in criminal law and criminal procedure in his system? What are the most likely developments you see happening and which would you like to see happening? What is most needed now to improve the system?

The interviewers and researchers who contributed to this volume went far beyond simple questions and answers. They asked thought-provoking questions designed to facilitate analysis and reflection. They sought to capture the views of the judicial officials and organized them in such a way as to make meaningful contributions to our understanding of criminal law and contemporary procedural problems.

Michael M. Berlin, JD, PhD
Dilip K. Das, PhD

Australia

I

ANN-CLAIRE LARSEN

A Brief Overview of the Australian Legal System

Australia boasts a well developed and trustworthy common law judicial system that was instituted by British colonizers 200 years ago. Australia's Commonwealth Constitution of 1901 is its founding legal document, though Australian states also have written Constitutions. Australia is a democratic federation of six states, three mainland territories, and seven off shore territories. All state and two mainland territories have state parliaments that pass laws related to any matter not controlled by the Commonwealth under Section 51 of the Australian Constitution. The Constitution requires Commonwealth law to be followed should disagreements arise between state and Commonwealth laws. Australia's court system comprises courts with varying functions at federal, state, and territory levels. Australia's legal attachment to Britain remained until the Australia Acts of 1986 (Cth (Commonwealth) and United Kingdom) granted Australia legal independence. Consequently, the High Court of Australia replaced the Privy Council in London as Australia's final court of appeal.

Australia's judicial system is adversarial. Judges rely on legal precedents established in case law and statutes when making decisions. Prime protections include the presumption of innocence, equality before the law, and procedural fairness. Further, the separation of powers doctrine requires the executive, legislature, and judiciary to function impartially at state, territory, and federal levels. Judges have many sentencing options to choose from to punish perpetrators of crime. Options range from incarceration, community-based orders, and suspended sentences. Certain crimes attract mandatory prison sentences. In 1973, the death penalty was abolished. Victims of civil wrongs may receive compensation.

The summary of legal principles and practices outlined above belies the history of Australia's legal system that is riddled with conflict and controversy beginning when British colonists dispossessed Aboriginal peoples of their lands. Aboriginal customary law and culture, in general, were largely unrecognized. Some British settlers who colonized Australia following the first landing in Sydney in 1788 advocated that British laws apply in full to Aboriginal people, whereas others preferred a more gradual approach (Hunter, 2012, p. 130). Aboriginal testimony was debarred, however, and worse still the history of Australia's legal system toward Aboriginal people is one of prejudice (McRae, Nettheim, Beacroft, & McNamara, 2003, p. 26). Numerous historical examples of violence toward Aboriginal people and discriminatory policies have prompted various law reform commissions and royal commissions that have recommended changes to laws, policies, and practices at various times.

Struggles and conflict over Aboriginal sovereignty to land and land rights continue. It wasn't until the *Mabo* case of 1992, a landmark decision, that land rights for Indigenous people were legally recognized. Since then, some Aboriginal people have received compensation under Native Title provisions.

Australia is the only Western democracy without a Bill of Rights (Byrnes, Charlesworth, & McKinnon, 2009, p. 139). Some have argued that Australia's Constitution provides adequate protection. Others disagree. The State of Victoria has enacted the Charter of Human Rights and Responsibilities Act of 2006 (Vic) and the Australian Capital Territory Human Rights Act of 2004 (ACT). Some other states have been debating about how best to further their population's human rights as Australia's International Human Rights obligations need statutory backing.

Australia's judicial system has undergone recent reforms requiring shifts in the role of the judiciary, shifts not accepted by all. Responses to such problems as the overrepresentation of Aboriginal women, men, and youths in the criminal justice system have been to develop specialist or problem-solving courts, e.g., the Koori Court and the Children's Koori Court in Victoria. All states and territories have specialized children's or youth courts. These modified courts have "enlarged powers to deal with matters summarily" (Australian Institute of Criminology, 2009). Other specialist courts open to all in multicultural Australia include drug courts, mental health courts, and family violence courts, some of which institute therapeutic jurisprudence and restorative justice principles (Roach Anleu, 2010, pp. 176–177). Additional reforms include alternative dispute resolution methods, mediation, Juvenile Justice Liaison, Mental Health Court Liaison Services, and Aboriginal Liaison Officer Programs.

References

Australian Institute of Criminology (2009). "Juvenile Court System" Australian Government. Retrieved from http://www.aic.gov.au/criminal_justice_system/courts/juvenile.html (December 19, 2012).

Byrnes, A., Charlesworth, H., & McKinnon, G. (2009). *Bills of rights in Australia history, politics and law.* Sydney: UNSW Press.

Hunter, A. (2012). *A different kind of 'subject.' Colonial law in Aboriginal-European relations in nineteenth century Western Australia 1829–61.* Melbourne: Australian Scholarly.

McRae, H., Nettheim, G., Beacroft, L., & McNamara, L. (2003). *Indigenous legal issues commentary and materials,* 3rd ed. Sydney: Thomson Lawbook Co. Casebook.

Roach Anleu, S. L. (2010). *Law and social change,* 2nd ed. London: Sage.

Interview of Magistrate Gregory Andrew Benn, Regional Magistrate, Kalgoorlie–Boulder

1

ANN-CLAIRE LARSEN

Contents

Introduction

Gregory Benn is a regional magistrate and works in the city of Kalgoorlie-Boulder, a gold mining town 596 kilometers northeast of Perth, Western Australia. Kalgoorlie is famous for its "golden mile," which is one of the world's richest gold deposits, its red dust and sparsely vegetated plains, its history of water scarcity, its early riots over jobs involving southern European migrants and Anglo-Australians, and, not least, its Hay Street brothels. Located also on Hay Street were the courthouse, police station, primary school, and Catholic church until a section of Hay Street, excluding the brothels, was renamed Brookman Street. The town is prospering. Kalgoorlie is replacing its image of male toughness with a family friendly face. Most of my fellow passengers, though, on the one-hour flight from Perth to Kalgoorlie I took to do the interveiw were dressed in mining company overalls.

I sought to interview a regional magistrate who deals regularly with Aboriginal people as they are overrepresented in Australia's criminal justice system. Magistrate Benn responded right away to my email to the Kalgoorlie courthouse requesting an interview. By chance, Magistrate Benn was hearing a sentencing matter on the morning of the interview. That matter was the last of four that Magistrate Benn had heard over the death of Mr. Ward, an Aboriginal leader and Elder who had spoken nationally and internationally on behalf of his people. Following a driving offense in January 2008, Mr. Ward was taken into custody in Laverton, WA, and later transported in the back of a prison van 400 kilometers in sweltering heat to Kalgoorlie. At no time during the trip did the two custodial officers assess Mr. Ward's welfare. They were unaware that the air conditioning unit had failed in the van's pod where Ward was locked. The air temperature inside the pod reached over 47°C (116°F); metal surfaces were 56°C (132°F). Mr. Ward died of heat stroke in Kalgoorlie hospital shortly after being admitted. He also had suffered burns to his abdomen from contact with the metal surface. WorkSafe Western Australia, a state government agency, prosecuted the Western Australian state government (fined A\$285,000), G4S the privately owned prison transport company (fined A\$285,000), and the two custodial officers: Graham Powell (fined A\$9,000) and Nina Stokoe (fined A\$11,000). All parties had eventually pleaded guilty over Mr. Ward's preventable death.

Magistrate Benn invited me to attend the sentencing court for Stokoe over which he presided. Most compelling were Magistrate Benn's insights and frankness about the offender's violation of the duty of care. Once the final decision was handed down, Stokoe apologized via the media to Mr. Ward's family. Mr. Ward's widow had received A\$3.2 million compensation. This case received national and international coverage.

Australia's Legal System

Aboriginal People's Contact with the Criminal Justice System

The following statistics appear in a Senate Select Committee report (2010). They illustrate the plight of Indigenous adults who are almost 14 times more likely to be imprisoned than non-Indigenous people. Aboriginal people comprise approximately 3 percent of Australia's population. Yet:

> Indigenous adults are imprisoned at a rate of 2,308 per 100,000; 25 percent of prisoners in Australia are Indigenous (Aboriginal and Torres Strait Islanders). Nationally, 1 in 15 Indigenous men aged between 25 and 29 are in jail. The most common offence by Indigenous prisoners is acts intended to cause injury (32 percent). On average, Indigenous prisoners receive shorter sentences than non-Indigenous prisoners for the same crime. (Committee Secretariat, 2010, p. i)

Indigenous juveniles are also overrepresented, but at an even higher rate than Indigenous adults:

> Indigenous juveniles are detained at a rate of 397 per 100,000, which is 28 times higher than the rate for non-Indigenous juveniles. In 2007, Indigenous juve-

niles accounted for 59 percent of the total juvenile detention population. (Committee Secretariat, 2010, p. i)

Recidivism among Aboriginal offenders is rife:

Indigenous people are more likely to re-offend following release from prison, with one study finding that 55 percent of prisoners returned to prison within two years. 75 percent of Indigenous prisoners have served a prior prison sentence, suggesting a pattern of repeat offending. (Committee Secretariat, 2010, p. i)

Though statistics are useful in pointing to serious problems with Aboriginal offending, they do not capture the full effects of offending and incarceration on Aboriginal offenders, victims, and communities as a whole. As most offenders are males, Aboriginal women and children are left unsupported (see Bedells, 2010). Multiple explanations for Aboriginal offending abound including colonization that devastated Aboriginal culture (McRae et al. 2003, Ch. 1); destructive colonial law, policy, and practices (Cunneen, 2005, p. 59); and discriminatory policing practices (McRae et al., 2003, pp. 499–513).

The Interview

After a short break following the hearing, I interviewed Magistrate Benn in his office at the Kalgoorlie courthouse. The interview lasted approximately 50 minutes. I began the interview by asking Magistrate Benn about his career. He related the following milestones.

Magistrate Benn has represented Aboriginal people most of his working life. He spent the first couple of years following his admission to practice in a private law firm before taking a job with Legal Aid in Port Hedland, 1,647 kilometers north of Perth. For 18 years, he worked for the Aboriginal Legal Service (ALS) in Western Australia (WA). Eleven of those years were spent traveling around WA doing Native Title work and managing the ALS Land and Heritage Unit. During the remaining seven years, he focused on criminal law while managing the Criminal Unit within the ALS. Following that, Magistrate Benn spent 12 months in the Solomon Islands working for its Legal Aid equivalent and representing people in what were essentially war crimes trials. He applied for the Kalgoorlie magistrate's job largely because it involved the Kalgoorlie–Boulder Community Court, which is an Aboriginal sentencing court where the magistrate sits with two respected members of the Aboriginal community. He assumed his current position in Kalgoorlie in November 2007. As well as sitting in the Kalgoorlie–Boulder Community Court, Magistrate Benn is responsible for conducting work in both the criminal and civil jurisdictions of the Children's and Magistrates' Courts, work in the Warden's Court (which deals with mining matters), the Family Court, and as a coroner. He is based in Kalgoorlie with two other full-time magistrates who travel throughout the goldfields and western desert regions on circuit as far south as Esperance on the south coast and east to Warakurna near the South Australian border.

I then asked Magistrate Benn **whether any career developments had surprised him**.

I didn't think I would ever be a magistrate. My partner nudged me in that direction. I don't know whether my hesitation to do so was a confidence issue or thinking I would not enjoy the job. I did like working at the Aboriginal Legal Service (ALS). It was very satisfying on a number of levels. As it turns out, I thoroughly enjoy working as a magistrate, particularly in a regional area.

How has your job been rewarding?

I think working as a magistrate is a very rewarding and thoroughly enjoyable job. It's an extremely challenging and stimulating work environment on both an intellectual and emotional level, in which no two days are ever the same. There's the social justice dimension (the application of the law and interests of justice permitting), something that I've always believed matters. What's been a primary motivating factor for me in whatever work I do is wanting to make a difference in the world in whatever small way I can, to improve things. So, I'm not saying I've achieved that goal, but that's what drives me and, to a small extent, I did achieve that at times at the ALS, although the work was also often very frustrating. You'd represent someone, you'd spend a lot of time with them, and they would get a result. Then they would be back again. It wasn't often, but occasionally you'd see someone step out of that pattern and change their lives for the better. I feel in this job I have got more capacity to influence positive change or change in people than I did as a lawyer in ALS. I think there is more respect and authority in this job than I had as a lawyer. There is the same degree of frustration as there's only ever been a small proportion of people you might have made a difference to. I am more optimistic that I can make a difference even if it's not necessarily with the offender I am dealing with. If it's a positive impact on the complainant or the victim or the victim's family or a perception of something in the community, I have got greater ability to achieve that result from time to time in this job in the magistrates' court than I did as a lawyer.

What do you do to change the life of an offender?

Well, I'm a novice in this. I haven't had any specific training other than some gained in conferences and reading—motivational interviewing techniques—that help someone identify and for me to identify where they are at and helping to see that they do have choices, however difficult it might be for them to engage in those choices. Those choices will lead to different lives in the future for some people.

I ask them questions to get them to see what's going on. What they need to do differently and what they would get out of doing things differently. And what they can look forward to. If they keep doing the same thing in terms of their lives, what that leads to.

We can use presentence orders where the court manages someone. You get them back before the court every month or so. If I don't put them on a presentence order, I put them on bail conditions that require them to do certain things and then come back with a report to see how they're doing. They have pleaded guilty and are facing the very real likelihood of a jail sentence. I say, "I am going to give you a chance to show you can change." It is often quite onerous. They have to do counseling and urinalyses, have got to stay out of trouble, stay off alcohol and drugs, and if they do all of that then you won't impose a prison term. You impose a fine or suspended sentence or further community supervision and counseling, if they require it.

How does retribution fit with that approach?

It still fits with that approach because at the end of the day there has to be a punishment. An important part of any sentencing is rehabilitation and the protection of the community. But, often, the two go hand in hand. The best long-term protection for the community is not necessarily to send someone to jail. That's short-term protection. The best long-term community protection is for them to bring about their own rehabilitation in the community via counseling and other support. Yes, there is always a victim. It is striking a careful balance in leaving the victim feeling like they have been heard. There has been a punishment. Victims and the community knowing that their interests have been taken seriously and also showing that what might be better in the long term for the victim and the community. Is this person showing some glimmer of hope by making some changes in their lives? It is not an easy way out. These orders are onerous. They require a lot of work and a lot of energy and a lot of vigilance from offenders. It's not as if they are getting off lightly with that penalty and, hopefully, the victim and the community gets to see that as well.

In addition to time factors, are there any differences in how you approach matters in the courthouse and the community court?

The law that's applied is exactly the same, but you have more time to spend with people in the community court. The Elders are actively involved in talking to offenders and giving them feedback. Usually it's a combination of positive encouragement and some growling or telling off. The other difference is the offender gets a chance to talk rather than stand or sit there mute and have the lawyer do the talking. They are actively encouraged to participate in the community court.

What changes have there been over the course of your working life?

The community court has been a major change. But, the biggest change probably I have seen has been in Native Title. When I started at the ALS, there was no Native Title. There was no recognition that Aboriginal people had any interest or claim to traditional land. What followed was the decision in *Mabo* and then the Native Title Act and, finally, mining companies sitting down with Aboriginal groups at the negotiation table and actually entering into the negotiation process. When I first started at the ALS, negotiation was unheard of. Now it happens as a matter of course. That's been one huge change.

In terms of criminal justice, I think one huge change has been the development of Therapeutic Jurisprudence and its increasing appreciation and understanding and application of principles that the court can make a positive difference—a therapeutic difference rather than a nontherapeutic difference. Not just with the offender, but with the victims and everyone else involved in the criminal justice system. If you apply the principles of Therapeutic Jurisprudence successfully, and I am not saying that is easy and that I get it and apply it successfully all or part of the time, but I think the ultimate aim is that everyone involved walks away feeling they have played a valued role and been heard and participated, and feeling that from their point of view justice has been done.

What is your philosophy?

My philosophy, as I said, is that in whatever I do I aim to achieve the best result possible, to try to make a positive difference and that doesn't necessarily mean not sending someone to jail. It may be that the positive difference is in recognizing what someone has done that needs to be dealt with severely and have the community and victims understand they are protected and their views have been considered.

I have a passion for social justice and to bring about social justice as far as I can in this job and bearing in mind what I am required to do is apply the law and to the best of my ability in applying the law that justice is done. If I can achieve those objectives and in doing so bring a dimension of broader social justice, then that's a real bonus! I have a huge passion or philosophy around education and ongoing learning for judicial officers. One of the things I am involved in with other magistrates is the ongoing creation of an online Bench Book for magistrates. That's a passion of mine, helping to create a useful resource that's available to all magistrates.

Is there a place for academic research in your work that would help you?

Yes, absolutely. It would be wonderful if we had a researcher attached to the magistrates' court. They could look at all sorts of things. Because as magistrates, between sitting in court, preparing for matters, writing judgments, considering matters, you don't get a lot of time to engage in research that is not particularly related to a matter you are engaged in. Recently at a conference, the relations between rehabilitation and the need to take personal responsibility for what you've done were discussed and I know there is some research around that with sex offenders. What research indicates is that, no, the sex offender doesn't necessarily need to take personal responsibility to achieve rehabilitation because sometimes it might be what they have done is too horrendous at a particular time for them to face. It doesn't necessarily mean that they cannot engage in counseling that could lead to their rehabilitation. That is a powerful concept because we regularly have a presentence report telling us, "This person doesn't take responsibility for their actions; they minimize their involvement." And that can translate into a harsher penalty in terms of the need for personal deterrence. Some research directed into areas like that is something that would never happen directly within the magistrates' court, but it would be such a luxury and that's just one example. There would be very strong value in having a researcher attached to the magistrates' court for a range of issues.

Can I also say something else that I think is incredibly important to do this job properly? It's to focus on your own self care. Leading a life outside work that is satisfying, happy, balanced, and involves a good diet, good exercise, and some other hobby or outlet or interest is essential because if you are not leading a healthy, balanced life, I think it is very difficult to do this job properly and all that this position requires of you. You need to have that objectivity, that degree of calmness and clarity of thought to be able to deal properly with a lot of matters that come before the court. Some matters, like this case I dealt with this morning, are quite horrendous and distressing in the circumstances they present.

For me, in terms of having a balanced life, being in a loving, happy, and supportive relationship and being able to bounce thoughts, ideas, issues, and concerns off my partner is, I find, a big advantage in this job. My partner's background and expertise is in nursing, midwifery, industrial occupational health and safety, and education. When we met, at a weekend yoga retreat, she was working two weeks on and two off on an oil rig off the northwest coast, running her own contract/employment service for OH&S [Occupational Health and Safety] nurses and running a health and beauty therapy business. That didn't leave a lot of time for someone like me, but thankfully I somehow managed to worm my way into her life. From time to time, she'll come and sit in court and not only is it great knowing she's there, but she often has valuable feedback she's able to give me about how I do my job.

Do you have time to read journals?

Yes, I do have time. You sort of make time in your own personal time, really. The job does require a certain amount of reading. It's part and parcel of what you've got to do. Plus, I still get time to read for my own enjoyment.

Are we as a society becoming more punitive?

I disagree. I think there's an increasing move not just in magistrates' courts, but in all jurisdictions toward appreciating that a jail term, although necessary in certain cases, isn't necessarily going to solve anything. Probably it's going to create more harm than good in the long term for the community as well as for the perpetrator. There is an increasing interest in Therapeutic Jurisprudence and in looking for penalties that would bring about the greatest good in terms of rehabilitation and protection of the community. So, there's the use of pre-sentence orders in our court as an alternative to an immediate term of imprisonment. In the District Court and Supreme Court, there is also the option of conditional suspended imprisonment orders that combine suspending a term of imprisonment with counseling and support within the community.

How have the events of September 11, 2001 affected your work?

I think it changed all of us in terms of it being such a horrendous event flowing from an act of terrorism. I could not identify a change that flowed from September 11 in terms of my work as a magistrate.

Would you like to comment about theory and practice?

Therapeutic Jurisprudence effectively came from overseas and the 50 United States, largely, and interest is increasing. A greater interest is being taken by judicial officers about what practices are being taken up in other parts of the world. What works and what doesn't work particularly in respect of community courts, neighborhood courts, drug courts, and domestic violence courts. I think the exchange of ideas and experiences around the world between judicial officers is becoming more and more important. A number of judicial officers are part of a Therapeutic Jurisprudence network where judicial officers from around the world share views, experiences, and discoveries about their areas of work with everyone else. All very important.

How will the problem of Aboriginal offending be solved?

Not by the courts. We can do a certain amount in terms of things like community courts, presentence orders, and apply the principles of Therapeutic Jurisprudence, but that's never going to solve the roots of these problems. No. It's not a problem the court can solve. It is a problem that has its roots in people's lives long before they come to court and depends on programs being developed that tackle issues like poverty, alcoholism, domestic violence, and lack of education from a much earlier stage in people's lives. The Aboriginal community suffers very much as a result of all those kinds of social issues as well as other issues including the background history of dispossession from land and culture that have an ongoing effect. I think it's not easy to solve that. I do think programs can be developed that turn people's lives around. But they need to be programs that are developed locally in the context of a particular community that work for that community and over time bring about changes. Programs need to clearly involve the Aboriginal community in their development and delivery. I recently attended a half day, cross cultural training workshop in which it was suggested that there is a strong link between the lack of development of a person's positive core values and offending within the Aboriginal community—particularly for those Aboriginal members of the stolen generation. If that is the case, then developing a person's core values as an adult is a huge task and one that is likely to take more than a generation to address.

There are three magistrates here in Kalgoorlie, which is great for us because we have got that camaraderie and collegiate support that magistrates based by themselves in the country don't have. They are still only a phone call away to talk about a matter, but that's nowhere as easy as me being able to go into the office next door and being able to sound out a colleague about an issue. So, it's a real luxury here in Kalgoorlie having that collegiate support.

Are there specific groups of people who trouble you?

Within the criminal justice system, the degree of domestic violence against women within the Aboriginal community is a problem. There isn't a week in which multiple cases of such matters come before the court here in Kalgoorlie and I don't think there is any segment of our community more abused physically and emotionally than Aboriginal women. I think this court has an important role to play in sentencing Aboriginal perpetrators of domestic violence, in trying to turn that violent behavior around and making it clear that that kind of behavior will not tolerated, that the victims of such violence will be taken seriously and be listened to when they are prepared to take the risk of reporting such violence to police.

The fact that children come before the court is also a very troubling issue. Here in Kalgoorlie, I have the role of sitting in both the children's court and the magistrates' court. If I was in Perth, I'd generally only do one or the other.

The children's court has a very important role to play with those who come before the court and their families. Usually more time is spent by the court with juvenile offenders and endeavoring to engage in therapeutic practices to try and turn their lives and the lives of their families around. In that respect, I think being a parent myself generally makes me a better person and a better magistrate in dealing with a whole range of people who come before me in terms of my own experience and challenges raising a child. That's certainly not to say that magistrates who aren't parents aren't good magistrates, or that necessarily being a parent makes you a better person and judicial officer. My own experience, though, as a parent is that it brought about a fundamental shift in my view of the world and of myself, removing a focus I'd previously had on myself and placing that focus on my child who instantly became the most important thing in my world and who now has an influence on everything I do or say and think. Although in hindsight, taking my child, who had not yet turned one, to the Solomon Islands to live for a year in the course of which my family and I had to be evacuated by RAAF Hercules after full-scale rioting broke out in Honiara following their first elections after a major period of civil conflict may not have been the best idea I ever had.

Conclusion

A magistrate's working life in the WA goldfields is extremely demanding, responsible, and influential. Magistrate Benn is committed to social justice, to improving the plight of Aboriginal people who are the most disadvantaged and disaffected social group in Australia. His quest for fairness to the victim's family and community balanced with fairness to the accused was demonstrated in his decisions in the Ward case. For him, Native Title claims and Therapeutic Jurisprudence reforms have been two major favorable changes in criminal justice concerns. A researcher attached to the magistrates' court would be a welcomed "luxury." Though recidivism is rife and cases distressing, Magistrate Benn seeks to contribute to improving the lives of all people who have contact with Kalgoorlie–Boulder's magistrates' court. An aspect of his commitment was his willingness to spend valuable time being interviewed.

References

Bedells, S. (2010). Incarcerating Indigenous people of the Wongathalands in the eastern goldfields of Western Australia: Indigenous leaders' perspectives. Master of Criminal Justice thesis. Retrieved from http://ro.ecu.edu.au/theses/137/

Committee Secretariat. (2010, March). The Senate Select Committee on Regional and Remote Indigenous Communities: Indigenous Australians, incarceration, and remote Indigenous communities. Discussion paper. Retrieved from http://www.aph.gov.au/senate/committee/indig_ctte/Final_RRIC.pdf

Cunneen, C. (2005). Colonialism and historical injustice: Reparations for Indigenous peoples. *Social Semiotics* 15 (1), 59–80.

McRae, H., Nettheim, G., Beacroft, L., & McNamara, L. (2003). *Indigenous legal issues commentary and materials,* 3rd ed. Sydney: Lawbook Co. Casebook Thomson.

Interview with Senior Judge Stephen McEwen, The Youth Court of South Australia

2

DANIEL KING
ANDREW DAY
PAUL DELFABBRO

Contents

Introduction

There are few areas of practice in the criminal justice arena quite so contentious as how to respond to young people who commit serious and/or repeated offenses. Our views about what should be considered as appropriate responses (both in terms of the type of sentence that should be handed down by the courts and the programs that should be offered) are determined by our beliefs about the degree of responsibility that young people should take for their actions. There are those, for example, who regard young offenders as vulnerable young people who are "at risk" of encountering a wide range of problems across different domains of life. It follows that young offenders, particularly the younger age group, should be offered compassion and support, and that programs should be made available that address a broad range of social and emotional needs. Others, however, regard the offense that the young person has committed as a more appropriate focus, and are mindful of issues of due process and the need to both punish those who break societal rules and deter others from behaving in similar ways. It follows that interventions for young offenders should seek to reduce the harm caused by the young person to the community through intervening in ways that reduce the risk of further offending taking place.

These themes arise repeatedly in this interview with Senior Judge Stephen McEwen, who has worked in the court system for over 30 years and is firmly committed to providing a timely, efficient, and welfare-oriented service to the State of South Australia. Senior Judge McEwen received his law degree from Adelaide University in 1978, and his graduate diploma in Legal Practice in 1980 before practicing as a solicitor in Adelaide, Clare, and Port Pirie from 1980 to 1988. He was a senior prosecutor at the Director of Public Prosecutions from 1988 to 2001, and a barrister at the private bar from 2001 to 2005. McEwen was appointed QC (Queens Council) in 2006, appointed judge of the District Court in 2006, and the senior judge of the Youth Court in August 2006.

Judge McEwen has, over many years, demonstrated an overarching concern for the welfare of young people through his public service activities on Law Society of South Australia (SA) subcommittees, as well as training workshops he provides to criminal justice professionals and students, and through his long-standing engagement with various sporting organizations, including participation in the sports of judo, squash, distance running, and equestrian eventing. He also has chaired a number of Commonwealth games and Olympic Games Selection Appeals.

In this interview, the senior judge was asked about the strengths and challenges of the South Australian Youth Court, including those related to the Youth Courts' basic aims and philosophy, current procedure and operation, guiding legislation, and overall effectiveness as a system of justice. The interview was conducted in person by the authors, and followed a semi-structured format containing 20 open-ended questions with added flexibility to accommodate the interviewee's specialized knowledge and particular interests. The interview took approximately 60 minutes and was digitally recorded and then transcribed. Before describing the interview, however, it is first important to briefly describe the current structure and functioning of the South Australian juvenile justice system.

Overview of the Jurisdiction

The Youth Court of South Australia is an independent and autonomous court authority, which, in its current form, is guided by three specific pieces of legislation, the Youth Court Act of 1993, the Young Offenders Act of 1993 (for juvenile justice matters), and the Children's Protection Act of 1993 (for child protection matters). The court hears criminal trials and pleas for youths aged 10 to 17 years, as well as child protection applications and applications for the adoption of children.

The court is comprised of two District Court judges, one of whom is designated by proclamation as the senior judge of the Youth Court, plus two specialist magistrates. Structurally, the Youth Court comprises the court, a family conference team, and a care and protection unit. While all three branches of the Youth Court of South Australia usually act independently of each other, criminal files may be referred from court to a family conference, and from a family conference to court. For administrative purposes, the Youth Court registry, the family conference team, and the care and protection unit are managed by the court registrar, the senior youth justice coordinator, and the senior care and protection coordinator, respectively. Each of the Youth Court judicial members are supported by a private secretary or clerk. Clerical and administrative support in the Youth Court registry, the family conference team, and the care and protection unit is provided by Courts Administration Authority clerical officers. Youth Court hearings, family conferences, and family care meetings are conducted in both metropolitan and regional areas of South Australia.

South Australia's youth justice system can be broadly characterized as "welfare"-oriented because of the strong emphasis that is placed on diversion (Noetic Solutions, 2010). The Young Offenders Act of 1993 introduced a multitiered system of precourt diversion designed to deal with minor offenses (Moore & Wilkinson, 1994). This system applies to youths who at the time of the alleged offense are aged 10 to 17 years inclusive, and provides four processing options: (a) informal caution, (b) formal police caution, (c) family conferencing, and (d) a court appearance. The decision regarding the type of action taken against a youth (i.e., whether he or she will receive a caution or a family conference, or be directed to the Youth Court) rests primarily with the police and with specialist Community Programs Unit managers. Recent statistics suggest that, each year, approximately 33% of police apprehensions result in a referral to a formal police caution, 20% are referred to a family conference, and almost half of all apprehensions are referred to the Youth Court (Office of Crime Statistics and Research, 2010). However, it should be noted that the type of action taken depends largely on the characteristics of the offender and the type of offense committed.

Offenses that are considered too serious for a caution may be referred to a family conference if the young person admits to the commission of the offense (Wundersitz, 1996). If a young person commits a serious offense, is a repeat offender, or fails to comply with a family conference undertaking, then he or she may be formally charged and sent to the Youth Court. The court can remand a young person in custody or sentence him or her to detention, requiring residence in a secure young offender training unit for a specified period of time, if no other order is appropriate. As an alternative to detention, the Young Offenders Act of 1993 allows the court to order a period of home detention, to be served either as a stand-alone option or as a joint secure care/home detention order. Notably, the court is obliged to carefully consider the effect that any proposed sanction will have on the individual child. Given that detention is not typically regarded as in the interests of many young people, it is typically used as a sentencing option of last resort. There is, however, some concern about this principle being eroded in the Statutes Amendment (Young Offenders) Bill of 2007 that, in line with legislation introduced in other jurisdictions around the world, requires community safety to be taken into consideration (e.g., declare a young person a "recidivist young offender" and an "appreciable risk to the community" and imposing a different set of rules for conditional release through the proposed Youth Parole Board).

Career

Stephen Kevin McEwen was born in Millicent, SA, where he attended Reedy Creek Primary School and Kangaroo Inn Area School, then boarding school for his senior schooling. McEwen received his law degree from Adelaide University in 1978, and his graduate diploma in Legal Practice in 1980.

McEwen practiced as a solicitor in Adelaide, Clare, and Port Pirie from 1980 to 1988. He was a senior prosecutor at the Director of Public Prosecutions from 1988 to 2001, and a barrister at the private bar from 2001 to 2005. He was appointed QC in 2006, was appointed judge of the District Court in 2006, and the senior judge of the Youth Court in August 2006.

Senior Judge McEwen has extensive experience serving on committees for both professional and community groups, including various Law Society of SA subcommittees, Magill Primary School Governing Council, Horse SA, Pony Club president, and representative at Zone and Executive; Equestrian S.A. Eventing Committee, and Equestrian S.A. Board. Judge McEwen has participated over many years in sports including judo, squash, distance running, and equestrian eventing.

Senior Judge McEwen's extracurricular legal activities have included numerous presentations to training programs and community groups; training workshops for police; forensic scientists; presentations for universities and Law Society; advocacy training for law students; and moot judging. He has also chaired a number of Commonwealth Games and Olympic Games selection appeals.

The Interview

Personal Judicial Philosophy

When asked about what he sees as the key purpose, main aims, and underlying philosophy of the Youth Court, Senior Judge McEwen pointed to the guiding legislation, highlighting the importance of the focus in the Young Offenders Act of 1993 on individual rather than general deterrence. This is significant insofar as the Court in South Australia is obliged to consider the effects of any disposal on the individual defendant, rather than the wider community. It thus provides the court with some discretion as to how cases are managed. Generally, the senior judge saw the guiding legislation as appropriate.

> Well, I suppose to implement the provisions of the Children's Protection Act and the Young Offenders Act, respectively, in terms of child protection and criminal law. That's a fairly legalistic answer, but it's a fairly broad question.
>
> I think it's commonly not appreciated that it's not our role to generally deter youths from offending, so if there is a spike in youth offending, well, it would be a bit illogical to look to this court, to attribute responsibility when it's statutorily not our role to do that.
>
> By and large, the Acts are sound. I think they allow for more flexibility and innovation than people realize if they really wanted to. Particularly the criminal [legislation], the Young Offenders Act.

Problems and Successes

The need to balance the provision of welfare with the administration of punishment was highlighted as a key challenge for the court. Senior Judge McEwen acknowledged that for many young people their offending behavior will not be addressed by punishment alone and, therefore, a more sympathetic approach is necessary—especially for first-time or less-serious offenders. The Youth Court, in this sense, was viewed as serving a significant welfare role in the lives of many young offenders in much the same way as it did at the time of its inception over 100 years ago. Senior Judge McEwen reflected on the historical practice in Australia of detaining children who had committed a crime or who were subject to neglect or abuse within a single, all-purpose facility. In the past, little or no distinction between juvenile justice and child protection responses was made, as all children entering the system were viewed, fundamentally, as being in need of state care. This contrasts with the contemporary Youth Court system that makes a clear distinction between youth justice and child protection matters. As Senior Judge McEwen explained, one of the guiding principles for the court is to provide an individualized service, tailored to the needs of each young person.

My understanding is we run in this state a mixed welfare and justice model. I think having a balance of the two is the appropriate way to go … Because of the focus in the Act, we're running a much more intensive aim at the particular individual.

We've got a wide scope to fashion individual sentencing packages. They can involve a whole lot of different components. Diversion, fines, community service, detention, suspended, home detention, blended orders, some in, some suspended, and then, of course, Obligations. Then under Obligations, a whole range of orders we can put them on. Attend programs, not drink, be under a curfew. There's an enormous range of the things that we can choose from to bring to bear on a particular kid.

Generally, the senior judge expressed cautious confidence that the court was offering an appropriate and responsive service, particularly in regard to juvenile justice matters. This is despite the highly politicized context in which the work of the court occurs, and local media scrutiny and commentary on youth justice matters. If anything, the senior judge felt that there was a need to more confidently publicize the positive work of the court.

I think juvenile justice is working quite well, notwithstanding the media [criticism] from time to time suggesting it's not, or assessments coming out saying there's a crisis. That's all rubbish. And, if I didn't think that, I'd say so. If I thought we were doing a terrible job, I'd say so.

Now I've been here for a while and I'm not just saying this because of my particular role, but I actually think that it's running a lot better than you would think from the amount of scrutiny, reports, reviews, media criticism, beat ups, that it gets. I know we've made some entrenched criticisms of care and protection jurisdiction, but, even then, it's not a complete disaster. And, in the criminal jurisdiction, I think it's running as well as you could expect.

There's a disconnect between what's served up to the public and what's actually going on. We need someone within the court area that becomes our spokesperson to nip in the bud these misconceptions and so forth and to engage with the media. To get on the front foot and say this is what we do, this is what we're doing well.

A significant strength of the Youth Court was seen as its ability to respond to young offending within a relatively rapid turnover and resolution of cases. A rapid response was regarded as fundamental in dealing effectively with young offenders, and perhaps even more important than the nature of the response. This, he felt, was because young people often experience difficulties in relating their behavior to the consequences of that behavior and, as such, any delay in responding (irrespective of the actual response) has the potential to increase the risk of that response being ineffectual. It was further noted that the need to act quickly was compounded by the fact that some young people commit offenses in close succession to each other.

I've got an absolute obsession about how quickly we turn things over. I'd be surprised if there was a jurisdiction [in Australia] that would be up with us in that regard.

I've been associated with courts now for 30 years or something, and I really have come to the conclusion that turning matters over rapidly is not strictly a matter of how many matters you need to do, even over, say, a time frame of a year or something. It's not as simple as that, actually. It's not simply a matter of how serious or how resourced you are, it's actually more a matter of culture. If everyone's determined to turn things over rapidly, they'll find a way. If they're not, they won't.

Indigenous justice is an area of some concern in youth justice across Australian jurisdictions. In the Youth Court, a disproportionate number of Aboriginal and Torres Strait Islander youths are apprehended by police, and about 1 in 4 court appearances involve an Aboriginal youth (Office of Crime and Statistics Research, 2010). Such figures highlight the need for the Youth Court to respond effectively to Aboriginal offenders. Senior Judge McEwen acknowledged the emergence and development of specialist courts intended for Indigenous peoples, but expressed some reservations concerning their purpose in the wider context of youth justice. It was thought, for example, that the establishment of additional specialist courts could compromise the Youth Court's primary objective of serving justice to all young people.

I'm sure you'll go around the place and everyone will say what a wonderful job they're doing with their Indigenous (or Nunga) courts. Look, it's great and it's well-intentioned, but I actually think it's misguided. It should be under the banner of the Youth Court making sure that they get individual attention that's fashioned for that particular kid and that particular circumstance. It shouldn't be any different because they're Nunga or because they're Sudanese or because they're Australian.

At this point in the interview, we received some further comments and clarifying remarks from another Youth Court judicial officer who was also present at the interview. He drew attention to the high number of arrests among Indigenous youth, and their underrepresentation in the Youth Court diversion program. Current figures suggest that 6 in 10 Aboriginal apprehensions (57.6%) are directed to court compared with less than half (41.9%) of non-Aboriginal apprehensions. Additionally, Indigenous offenders are overrepresented in regard to lack of compliance with family conference undertakings (18.9% vs. 11.2%) and often fail to attend a family conference. According to the judicial officer, some Indigenous offenders do not cooperate with police (a requirement for diversion), which subsequently leaves the court officers with little choice but to require the offender make a formal court appearance.

We actually get a lot of matters that are not diverted where there is power to divert by the police at the earliest instance, but we do not get them diverted earlier. They're coming into court and I'm speaking particularly with the young Aboriginal offenders, because of a policy that's perpetrated by the Aboriginal Legal Rights Movement (ALRM) not to have their clients involved in interviews with police. So, the standard arrangement with ALRM is to advise the police that clients will not speak to them and that's left the police with an arrest. No discussion. No discretion, and those matters come into court. So, the answer to your question is [that] we do more than would otherwise occur if that policy was not in place and then which the diversion arrangements worked as some might think the parliament has intended.

Child removal poses ongoing dilemmas for the care and protection jurisdiction. It was noted that in recent times there has been an increase in long-term orders for removal, which places a growing burden on the out-of-home care system to locate suitable arrangements. In some cases, such living arrangements are less than ideal, or are inappropriate for a child's needs. While Senior Judge McEwen viewed child removal as a justifiable measure in some extreme circumstances of abuse and/or neglect, he lamented the court's and the broader system's lack of other available welfare-oriented options for addressing complex issues of neglect, abuse, and disadvantage among vulnerable youth and their families. Whether some children's life situation was markedly improved following child removal was questionable.

The longer I'm here, the more I think that we're doing exactly what was done a decade ago. And largely what was done a century ago. Probably exactly what will be done in another decade and probably in another century. … It's a jurisdiction I don't get a lot of satisfaction out of. The ones that do get through and we signed off on the orders, I still don't walk out with a warm glowing feeling that I've solved that kid's problems. I got to tell you.

This idea of getting a guardianship is some kind of panacea, I think, is quite illusory. Quite a number of kids under guardianship are … I suppose, they are marginally better off, but they're nowhere near as better off as the department seems to believe. They seem to believe that as quickly as possible any kid in dysfunctional circumstances should become the subject of a guardianship order, then they can sit back and be happy that they've successfully intervened.

Now, I'm not suggesting it's an easy jurisdiction or an easy area of work, it's not. You won't ever solve the problem of kids living in dysfunctional circumstances. I do really think there's an overemphasis on guardianship orders as distinct from other more imaginative, innovative, and earlier interventions.

Theory and Practice

Diversion is a significant component of the work of the Youth Court of South Australia and provides the theoretical underpinning of much of the work that is done. Upon recommendation by the Parliamentary Select Committee, a family conferencing system (modeled on the New Zealand Youth Court family conference system) was introduced in 1993. The SA Youth Court conference system diverts over a thousand youths from undertaking formal court proceedings each year (Office of Crime and Statistics Research, 2010), and it is regarded positively by a wide range of local stakeholders (King, Day, & Delfabbro, 2011).

Senior Judge McEwen noted that the family conferencing system was regarded as a highly effective diversionary system, which had garnered positive feedback from offenders, victims, and the prosecution. This point is supported by recent positive family conference statistics (Office of Crime Statistics and Research, 2010), which reveal that in approximately 90% of family conferences an agreement is successfully reached (with the majority of these agreements complied with by the youth). However, it should be highlighted that rates of victim participation in family conference are typically quite low. In 2007, as in previous years, victims were present in only 30% of cases. Therefore, reported "high" levels of victim satisfaction with the family conference process may not necessarily be representative of all cases.

The senior judge felt that although the Youth Court is currently well served by the family conference system and other diversionary services, the range of available options outside the metropolitan area is often limited. Additionally, Senior Judge McEwen felt that it was difficult to maintain up-to-date knowledge of which programs are available, particularly when some programs were only offered temporarily due to a lack of continued funding. In general, regional areas offered fewer rehabilitative options, and rural areas were extremely limited in terms of youth training and community services. Senior Judge McEwen noted, however, that barriers to effective diversion were not simply resource-related. There is also an issue of offender nonparticipation in family conferences and diversionary programs, particularly among Indigenous[*] and recidivist offenders. Reasons for an offender failing to attend a conference include indifference or resistance to the conference process, or lack of understanding or appreciation of how to comply with the conference requirements, and/or limited support or assistance from family or case workers to attend.

> The difficulty, I find, is knowing what kinds of programs are out there and the programs change all the time. … So it's hard to keep on top of it and the lack of continuity. They come and go like fashion. So, I'm not saying that it's perfect;

---

[*] In Australia, the term *Indigenous* is used to refer to both Aboriginal and Torres Strait Island peoples. Although Indigenous people make up around 2% of the general population, they are massively overrepresented across all areas of the criminal justice system (see Day, Nakata, & Howells, 2008).

I'm saying that criticism there aren't enough programs that's easily made and is often a bit hollow.

And it is frustrating when some worthwhile programs get wound up when you just think "well, it's taken you three years to get that program up to speed and it seems to be working really well and you've suddenly turned it." … That's really frustrating and that's almost the nature of the beast with programs. The short lifespan. The particular funding that dries up. That is very frustrating.

Obviously, you need a lot of programs for kids, but a lot of kids who are recidivist offenders, it's not for the absence of programs. It's for the absence of the kid being at the program that they were supposed to be at. So, it's much more complex than just saying there aren't enough programs.

A lot of emphasis is placed on the preparation of detailed social background reports and associated expert evidence. Such material was regarded as highly important in assisting judicial officers to reach decisions in regard to dealing with young people, particularly when recommending rehabilitation options for young offenders. For Senior Judge McEwen, expert testimony offers an opportunity for theory to inform practice. Generally, expert testimony was regarded as being of a high standard, although at times the volume of evidence received was regarded as excessive and concern was expressed about the independence of some opinions and the tendency to, at times, offer opinions that protect the expert rather than perhaps represent the best interests of the child. In particular, in child protection matters, there was some concern that the psychological reports prepared by psychologists at the government department responsible for Care and Protection matters may, at times, reflect or be unduly influenced by departmental policy. Many such reports would recommend long-term orders to place at-risk children under the care of the guardianship of the Minister for Education and Child Development in South Australia.

As a generalization, we're well served with expert material and lots of it. It's just that we get overwhelmed by it, and that's counterproductive. The psychological services work for the department. So, that's an issue, but it would take major reform to do otherwise. Also, they have recourse to experts more often than they need to at times.

Shorter reports …we're addressing it, but we're still getting it. Shorter reports.

In this jurisdiction, and all the other jurisdictions, I bet you find that a lot of the motivation, whether it's admitted or not, is risk management or risk aversion of the workers. … I think, unfortunately, a lot of practice is dictated by the looking over the shoulder, rather than just grappling with the issue.

Senior Judge McEwen was asked to give his feedback on some recent suggestions that the Youth Court should consider alternative approaches to dealing with vulnerable children in care and protection matters (e.g., case-conferencing approaches). He acknowledged that the child welfare system was in need of some innovation to address its growing difficulties in accommodating an increasing number of removed children with limited foster care and other arrangements. It was highlighted, in particular, that significant time and resources are invested each year in providing out-of-home care arrangements and that this emphasis on child removal may not be tenable indefinitely. Alternative court responses should be explored in collaboration with other relevant stakeholders and agencies. For instance, an expansion of the availability of adoption orders was raised as a possible, albeit limited, alternative to long-term care orders in some cases.

> I suspect that if you had practitioners from [the government department] sitting around a table without us present, I suspect that they'd advocate strongly that the best intervention is an early order of guardianship until the child turns 18. Now, maybe they're right and I'm wrong, but from where I sit, I just don't see that. What you really need to scrutinize is: "Do you mean in terms of you being protected, so that you won't get hauled over the coals in the witness box or best for the child?" From where we sit, especially as we go from one jurisdiction to another, we see the very same kids. As soon as we've signed off on a guardianship order, then they're criminally offending.
>
> It seems to me, looking from afar, that if you took all those kids on whom there's guardianship orders and they're either in residential care or they're sitting in houses specially set up for them with 24-hour nanny careers … if you'd adopted all those kids and then all that money … well, all the remaining kids who perhaps you don't have to get a guardianship order over, do other interventions. You'd have bucket loads of money to spend. It just seems to me absurd that there's all these removals and there's all these kids, either in residential care or worse, or various houses dotted all over the place with several shifts of workers, sometimes for one child in the house. There's got to be a better way to spend that money. Whoever runs [agency names] and all those contractual organizations must be thinking this is an absolute monster of a problem.

General Assessment

For Senior Judge McEwen, the Youth Court's ability to operate effectively is affected in no small part by its architecture and physical makeup. Overall, the metropolitan Youth Court building was felt to be adequate for its intended purpose, but had some limitations. While the Youth Court's positioning as a court that combines two jurisdictions was felt to increase efficiency of processing, particularly for complex matters involving both jurisdictions, it was felt that having all parties from both jurisdictions congregate together posed some challenges and operational difficulties. For example, the shared waiting area could be quite (understandably) emotionally charged due to the stress associated with court decisions, particularly in regard to court-ordered child removal. As a practical suggestion, some additional space or separate waiting areas in each jurisdiction was thought to be beneficial in reducing the burden sometimes placed on young people, families, and court staff.

> We've got two courtrooms that are shockingly small. I think kids need more space. The staff need more space. Two particular courtrooms are woefully inadequate for a modern court structure. We need to be able to deal with people in a relatively flexible environment.
>
> The most glaring issue, if you compared us, say, to [another Australian jurisdiction], they've got a clear physical delineation between criminal and care and protection. Which there really should be. And then, within that, they've got room to move. We've got no delineation or room to move. So, if we have a removal here at court, it is either a tug of war out on the street or a tug of war in the limited reception area we've got with other parents and children from both jurisdictions sitting around and that's just not good. Not only should there be delineation, but the space should be designed in a thoughtful, architectural way to facilitate the sort of things that are going to happen here. The things that are going to happen here are going to be highly charged, traumatic, emotional situations. This building gives no thought to that at all. I don't want to overdramatize this; we deal with it.

The senior judge was then asked to reflect on possible ways to measure the effectiveness of the work performed by the Youth Court. He referred to recidivism rates as a potentially useful indicator of court processes addressing offending. However, it was cautioned that prima facie recidivism statistics may not always convey accurately the complexity of the young people that enter the juvenile justice system, nor properly acknowledge that the court deals with complex offenders in myriad ways. Additionally, it was argued that a selective treatment of the figures could potentially yield different statistical profiles of the court's overall effectiveness.

> It's not easy, is it? Because, even on the recidivism rate, you'd have to be a little bit careful on ... if you just get some knee-jerk comparison about how many recidivists there were or something, I don't think that would really get you anywhere. I think, I'm suggesting it's something more subtle than that because the fact is we are going to get before us a spectrum of offenders—in any Children's Court—from kids who just come from good, supervised homes and occasionally do something because they're kids, right through to kids who do it fairly constantly through to kids who graduate to fairly serious offending.
>
> The trouble is I'm a bit suspicious of all the stats I've seen. It depends whether you're measuring time from, say, arrest to when you finalize the charge, time that the person first appears in court, or finalize the charge, whether you're measuring per charge or per defendant or all sorts of other things. ...

Discussion

Specialist courts to deal with young offenders are not universally regarded as providing the most appropriate service. As Feld (1998) argues, despite their humanitarian ideals, children's courts have been transformed from their "original model as a social service agency into a deficient second-rate criminal court that provides people with neither positive treatment nor criminal procedural justice" (p. 90). The rationale for specialist children's courts is that most juveniles are less responsible for their actions than adults and, therefore, should be treated differently from adults who commit the same criminal offenses (see Casey, 2011). Scott and Grisso (1998) have further argued that there are substantial differences between children and adults in moral, cognitive, and social development (e.g., higher levels of grandiosity and impulsivity may lead to greater risk taking in children, young children may have a limited ability to think about long-term consequences of actions, and often children are highly susceptible to peer influences) that require special consideration. However, Scott and Grisso also argue that these differences are more subtle by midadolescence and provide an insufficient basis for public policy (although they feel there may be a case for discounted sentences). Morse (1998) similarly suggests that it is often difficult to distinguish between the moral responsibility of children from young adults ("poor judgment is not a moral excuse") and concludes, somewhat provocatively, that the idea of a court that attempts to combine criminal social control with social welfare is doomed to fail.

This interview with a senior judicial officer in an Australian jurisdiction presents a somewhat different perspective. Senior Judge Stephen McEwen argues that the Youth Court of South Australia is, on the whole, able to provide a more timely, more efficient, more responsive, and ultimately more effective response than if matters were heard in the adult courts. He argued that a specialist court was necessary to consider the individual circumstances in which offending takes place, and to finalize matters in a timely fashion. Of particular interest were the comments that sufficient programs are available, and it is the consistency and reliability of program delivery that creates problems for the court.

The fundamental difference between the South Australian Youth Court and the North American Children's Courts critiqued by Feld (1998) and Scott and Grisso (1998) is the development of a system that is welfare-oriented and places great emphasis on diverting matters before they are heard in court. In many respects, this is a distinctive feature of the juvenile justice system in South Australia, and one that differentiates the work of this jurisdiction from others. It is in this context that the Youth Court in South Australia is able to function reasonably smoothly.

References

Casey, S. (2011). Psychological maturity and antisocial behavior. *Open Criminology*, 4, 32–39.

Day, A., Nakata, M., & Howells, K. (eds.) (2008). *Anger and indigenous men*. Annandale NSW: Federation Press.

Feld, B. C. (1998). Abolish the juvenile court: Youthfulness, criminal responsibility, and sentencing policy. *The Journal of Criminal Law and Criminology*, 88, 68–137.

King, D. L., Day, A., & Delfabbro, P. (2011). The emergence and development of specialist courts: Lessons for juvenile justice from the history of the Children's Court in South Australia? *Open Criminology*, 4, 40–47.

Moore, T., & Wilkinson, T. (1994). *Youth Court: A guide to the law and practice*. London: Longman Publishing.

Morse, S. J. (1997). *Immaturity and irresponsibility. Journal of Criminal Law and Criminology*, 88, 15–68.

Noetic Solutions Pty. (2010). *Review of effective practice in juvenile justice*. Report for the Minister for Juvenile Justice. Melbourne, Australia.

Office of Crime Statistics and Research. (2010). Crime and justice in South Australia; juvenile justice. Report prepared for the South Australian Attorney-General's Department.

Scott, E. S., & Grisso, T. (1998). The evolution of adolescence: A developmental perspective on juvenile justice reform. *The Journal of Criminal Law and Criminology*, 88, 137–174.

Wundersitz, J. (1996). *The South Australian Juvenile Justice System: A review of its operation*. Office of Crime Statistics, SA Attorney-General's Department, Adelaide.

Austria

II

MAXIMILIAN EDELBACHER

Introduction

Austria is a small state in Central Europe. The territory of 32,377 square miles (83.856 square kilometers) has a population of about 8.4 million people. Nearly 1.6 million of these have origins in countries other than German-speaking countries. Small communities of ethnic Magyars and Croats have settled in Burgenland, and the Slovenes, who have immigrated to Austria, live in southern Carinthia. The characteristics of the population of Austria have changed rather drastically since the 1970s for several reasons. After the fall of the "Iron Curtain" in 1989, and later in 1994, when Austria became a member of the European Union, foreigners immigrated to Austria to improve their economic and/or political situation. The economic crisis, starting in 2008, resulted in a large influx of Germans, especially from former East Germany, who were looking for jobs and, hopefully, a higher standard of living.

The higher standard of living found in Austria, as well as the political stability of the government, can be partially attributed to the efforts of the United Nations and the United States. At the end of the World War II in 1945, Austria was occupied by other countries and its economy was depressed. With the help of the Marshall Plan, which provided food, supplies, equipment, and financial aid, Austria recovered economically and, in May 1955, the country again became a free nation. When the pre-World War II period is compared with post-World War II, including the present time, we see that many changes were made in the Austrian legal system. These changes will be considered in the section below.

Overview of Austrian Legal and Court System

On the first of October in 1920, a constitutional convention adopted a new Federal Constitution (*Bundes-Verfassungsgesetz*, B-VG) for Austria. The Federal Constitution was amended in 1925 to implement the separation of powers between the federation and the nine provinces (*Länder*). It was amended again in 1929 to strengthen the presidential powers pertaining to the government of Austria. Essentially, this constitution was readopted in 1945, beginning with the Second Republic. The Austrian Constitution is based on several principles:[1]

- Democratic Principle
- The Republican Principle
- The Federal Principle
- Separation of Powers
- The Liberal Principle
- Rule of Law

Democratic Principle

According to Article 1 of the Constitution, Austria is a democratic republic, whose law emanates from the people. On this provision rests a system of indirect parliamentary democracy, which is detailed in the Constitution and supported by the Political Parties Act of 1975. The plurality of political parties is an essential component of the Austrian political system. Currently, five political parties are represented in the Austrian parliament.

Republican Principle

The Republican principle can be seen as a reaction to the previous political system of the Monarchy. As a consequence of this principle, the Constitution (Article 60(3)) prohibits members of the Habsburg family from running for the office of federal president.

The Federal Principle

Article 2(1) of the Constitution states: Austria is a federal state. The Federation (Bund) is composed of nine autonomous member states (*Länder*)— Burgenland, Carinthia, Lower Austria, Upper Austria, Salzburg, Styria, Tyrol, Vorarlberg, and Vienna. The Länder have limited legislative powers, some executive powers, but no separate court system.

Separation of Powers

This principle is not expressly named in the Constitution, but some of these aspects appear in formulations, such as "judicial and executive power shall be separated on all levels" (Const. Article 94) or "the legislative power of the federation is exercised by the National Council jointly with the Federal Council" (Const. Article 24). However, the Austria Constitution also contains elements of concentration of powers in parliament, to a large extent subordinating the executive branch to the legislative. A system of checks and balances encompasses parliamentary control of the executive, the right of administrative authorizes to pass regulations, and a special system of judicial review of administrative acts.

The Liberal Principle

This principle finds expression in a series of fundamental rights and freedoms developed under the influence of political liberalism and designed to protect the individual against unwarranted state influence.

Rule of Law

The notion of a state under the rule of law finds formal expression in the legality principle of Article 18(1) of the Constitution, and in the competencies of the Constitutional Court and the Administrative Court to supervise the constitutionality and legality of all actions. It also is reflected in the existence of independent courts adjudicating civil and criminal matters.

Sources of Austrian Law[2]

The Austrian law system generally is based on the Roman law, the German Tribe law, and can be understood as an outcome of the continental law development. Austrian law is primarily statutory law. There is very little room for customary law. Judge-made law is not recognized as formal precedent. Nevertheless, the jurisprudence of the Supreme Courts provides important guidelines for law application. Legal science has a significant indirect influence on lawmaking and implementation.

Austrian legal theory distinguishes between general norms containing more or less abstract rules that are directed at groups (e.g., constitutional law, statutes, regulations), and individual norms containing specific (concrete) rulings addressed to individuals (e.g., judgments of courts,

Table 3.1   Organizational Structure of the Austrian Court System: Criminal Procedure

OGH (Supreme Court)			
OLG 3 judges (*volle Berufung*–full appeal)	OLG (Appeals Court) 3 judges (*Berufung*–appeal)	OLG (Court of Appeal) panels of 3 judges (*Berufung*–appeal)	
(The Austrian Court System contains 20 *Landesgerichte*:- LG = Trial Courts) *Nichtigkeitsbeschwerde*–nullity appeal			
20 LG	LG	LG	LG
3 judges	single judge (punishment 1–5 years)	(as *Schöffengericht*) 1 judge, 2 assessors punishment above	(as *Geschworenengericht*) (3 judges, 8 jurors punishment 10–20 Maximum 5 years) (*volle Berufung*- full appeal)
100 BG (single judge) Punishment up to one year			

Note: Panels of five judges (The Austrian Court System consists of one Supreme Court and four Appeal Courts).

administrative rulings). The eminent constitutional law scholars Adolf Merkel (1890–1970) and Hans Kelsen (1881–1973) developed a "hierarchy of norms" (*Stufenbau der Rechtsordnung*), at the top of which is constitutional law (*Verfassungsrecht*), which determines the scope of "ordinary" legislation (*einfaches Gesetzesrecht*, statutory law). Statutes may be specified in more details by administrative regulations (*Verordnungen*), and ultimately applied to individual cases by administrative rulings (*Verwaltungsbescheide*) or court judgments (*Gerichtsurteile*). A legal norm may only be abrogated by norms of equal or higher rank in this hierarchy. However, a lower norm that contradicts a higher norm will generally be applied until it is nullified by the Constitutional Court. As far as norms of the same level are concerned, a more recent norm overrides an existing enactment (*lex posterior derogate priori*), and a special provision abrogates the general (*lex specialis derogate generali*). Table 3.1 outlines the structure of the Austrian Court System.

Explanation of Court System

The Oberster Gerichtshof (OGH) is the Supreme Court and highest court in Austria. The OLG (*Oberlandesgericht*) is an appeals court. There are four *Oberlandesgerichtes* in Austria (The OLG in Vienna has jurisdiction and hears cases for Vienna, Burgenland, and Lower Austria; the court in Graz is competent to rule on cases for Styria and Carintia; the Linz appeals court rules on cases for Upper Austria and Salzburg; and the Innsbruck court hears cases from Tyrol and Vorarlberg).

There are 20 *Landesgericht* (courts competent for all offenses) courts in Austria. These Landerichtes in the whole are competent to rule on civil and criminal law matters.

The LGs are composed of one or three judges and in certain instances two assessors qualified to assist the court—depending on the severity of the possible punishment.

The *Bezirksgerichte* (BG) (district) courts are competent to decide cases involving petty offenses. There are approximately 100 district courts located within the various regional areas of Austria.

The *Volle Berufung* is a full appeals court and can hear cases pertaining to guilt of an offense, punishment, and grounds for nullifying a decision. The *Berufung* (appeals) court has competency in deciding punishment and grounds for nullity and the *Nichtigkeitsbeschwerde* (nullity appeal) court has grounds relating to nullity, incorrect legal evaluation, or serious procedural error.

References

1. Hausmaninger, H. (1998). *The Austrian Legal System*. Vienna: Manzsche Verlags und Universitätsbuchhandlung, Kluwer Law International, The Hague, pp. 7–11.
2. Ibid., pp. 20–27.

Interview with Magistrate Friedrich Forsthuber, President of the Vienna Criminal Court

3

MAXIMILIAN EDELBACHER
PETER KRATCOSKI

Contents

The Interview

How does the Vienna Criminal Court fit within the Austrian Court system?

The Vienna Criminal Court is one of 20 regional courts, but specialized only for criminal cases. Today 71 judges are employed in this court. These judges act as single judges, *Schöffengericht* (1 judge and 2 assessors) and as jury (3 professional judges and 8 jurors). The prosecutor's service is located in the same building as the Vienna Criminal Court and the 93 prosecutors cooperate with the judges of the Vienna Criminal Court on criminal cases.

Please describe the Criminal Court in Vienna?

The Criminal Court in Vienna, Austria, is the largest court in Austria. The Criminal Court building was built between 1831 and 1839 during the Austrian Monarchy. At the present time, 71 permanent judges work in the Criminal Court in Vienna and there are about 1,200 offenders in the prison (jail). These prisoners are arrested and held in jail (criminal court prison), in some cases, for a very short and, in other cases, for longer periods, depending on the time it takes to complete the formal judicial process. If they are sentenced, the prisoners are moved to different penal institutions. In Austria, with a population of about 8.4 million people, about 8,000 are in Austrian prisons.

Tell us briefly about the history of the Criminal Justice System in Austria and the Criminal Court?

Several steps of historical development of the criminal justice system happened in Austria since the Middle Ages:

1. In the 14th century, the Criminal Court in Vienna was housed in a building named *Schranne*. This building existed until 1839.
2. In May 1839, the new court building was opened.
3. On July 1, 1850, a complete new criminal justice organization of the court system was implemented. Basically, it is the system currently in operation. The *inquisitor system* was abolished, duties of judges and prosecutor's service were separated and fundamental procedural rules, such as public and oral principles, came into force.
4. In 1873, the *Jury system* was started in the new court building. A large Jury Trial Room was specially built.
5. In 1918, the procedural code in Austria was changed again and the outcome of this change was that only one professional judge makes the decision in most of the criminal matters as defined by the criminal procedural code.
6. In 1920, the so-called *Schöffengericht* court was established by combining one professional judge and two assessors to decide on cases involving special criminal matters.
7. From 1980 to 1996, an additional building was erected and this building became the home of new trial rooms and the new court prison.
8. In 2003, the former Juvenile Court in Vienna was closed and the Vienna Criminal Court became competent for these criminal cases.

An exhibition about the history of the criminal court was shown from June to November 2012 in Vienna. The exhibition concentrated on the history of the court, the history of the prosecutor's service in Austria, the history of the lay justice system, the dilemma with death penalty, the Nazi crimes, and examples of spectacular cases. The exhibition was held in the Vienna Court building, which is called *Graues Haus*. This is the nickname given to the building by the people of Vienna. Just now, this exhibition remains in the Court House and is not shown anywhere else.

Career of Mag. Friedrich Forsthuber

Friedrich Forsthuber studied law between 1981 and 1985 at the Vienna University, faculty of law. In 1986, he absolved a year at the court (*Gerichtsjahr*) and became an aspirant for the position of a judge (*Richteramtsanwärter*) between 1987 and 1990. After passing the selection process, he was named judge of District Court Döbling, a civil district court. He worked there from March 1, 1990, to April 30, 1991. On May 1, 1991, he became judge at the Criminal Court in Vienna. This tenure lasted from May 1, 1991, until August 31, 2005. He held different positions as investigative judge, judge in the presidential administration of the criminal court, judge of the press agency of the criminal court, and full trial judge, responsible for general and media cases. From September 1, 2005 to December 31, 2009, he worked in the Upper Court, being responsible for internal revisions and he also worked in the Senate of Appeal. On January 1, 2010, he became president of the Criminal Court in Vienna.

The selection process to become president of the largest court in Austria is a complicated one. In that three judges were running for the presidential position, the first step was a hearing of all interested candidates in the Upper Criminal Court. After the hearing, one candidate was eliminated and the two remaining candidates were interviewed by the Minister of Justice. Each of the candidates had to present their plans and projects for the future of the court, along with their work.

Continuing Questions

Was there anything that surprised you about how your career developed?

The first surprise was to start as a judge, not in the province Burgenland, Court of Eisenstadt, the provincial capital, as was originally planned for me, but to start in Vienna, at the District Court Döbling. There I was responsible for civil cases. When I started there, I felt very comfortable, because the working climate was excellent. There were eight or nine judges who worked at the court and some of the younger ones, like me, later became very prominent in their personal careers.

The second surprise was while I started in the field of civil law, being responsible for family matters, rent and chartering cases, and, as a district judge in criminal matters, I was invited to change my position to the criminal court. This turn I never expected when I was a young judge. I discussed this move with my father, who was at that time the First Leader of the Upper Prosecutor's service in Austria, and he convinced me to make the move.

Did your work prove as interesting or rewarding as you thought it would?

Yes, I always was and continue to be completely satisfied with my work as judge and currently as president of the Criminal Court in Vienna. Every day brings in new challenges, opportunities, and interesting views on the topic of criminal justice. Being a judge is a challenging job. A day should have 48 hours because there are so many interesting duties and challenges that should be handled.

Changes Experienced

What do you see as the most important changes that have happened in criminal justice over the course of your career (philosophies, organizational arrangements, specializations, policies and programs, equipments, personnel, or diversity, for example)?

The most important changes in criminal justice that happened in Austria include:

- 1991 implementation of Measures of Diversion
- 1997 liquidation of Criminal District Courts and reduction of the area of competence of the Criminal Court of Vienna
- 2003 liquidation of the Juvenile Court in Vienna
- 2005 liquidation of the gendarmerie in Austria (only police)
- 2008 new procedural code of Austria
- The consequences of the new procedural code were new role definitions of what prosecutors, judges, and police have to do. The prosecutor is the leader in the criminal procedure, the police have to fulfill the advice the judge decides. The duties of the judges have expanded and there are smaller numbers of judges to do the work. For example, in 1991 there were about 93 judges and 50 prosecutors working in the Criminal Court and Prosecutor's service in Vienna. In 2010, there were about 68 judges and 93 prosecutors working in the Criminal Court and Prosecutor's service in Vienna.

Another change I have noticed is in the gender and personalities of judges. The job is very attractive for young men and women. It is interesting to know that in 1991 about one third of the judges at the criminal court were women and, in 2012, about two thirds of the judges were women. This can be recognized as a dramatic change.

Please discuss in more detail the consequences of the 2008 reform of the Procedural Code in Austria.

By reforming of the Procedural Code in Austria, the understanding of the roles of police, prosecutor, and judge was changed dramatically. Under the new Procedural Code, the process consists of the following:

1. The prosecutor leads the pretrial examinations.
2. The prosecutor formulates the different coercive measures, but often needs the permission and authorization by the judge, who is the only one who can give orders restricting the fundamental human rights of the individual.
3. If one of the individuals appearing before the court feels restricted by such a coercive measure of police or prosecutor within the pretrial procedure, the judge decides about the protest.

4. The Reform of 2008 strengthened the rights of the victims. For example, if the case was dropped by the prosecutor's service, the victim can ask the court/judge to decide about continuing the procedure (*Fortführungsantrag,* Continuation Appeal).

What do you mean by changes in the personality of judges?

We have experienced over the last two decades or so more women finishing their law studies. Perhaps they have helped in the change toward making the job of a judge more "family friendly" than the job of a lawyer. In our country, discrimination of women is discussed very much. To fulfill the so-called "quota of women," it is a fact that women work very hard to be included in the quota of 40% of women to be employed by the justice system, including the courts. Applications of qualified women, therefore, have to be given some preference and, as a result, the number of women in the justice system has increased dramatically.

What changes in external conditions (support from communities, legal powers, judicial relations, relations with minority communities, resource provision, political influence, or other matters have had a significant impact on criminal justice?

On the one hand, legal powers have increased because of terrorism and because of the European Union and international responsibilities. More laws have been enacted to deal with these issues. On the other hand, even though there are many more laws relating to security and other international matters, this development had been checked and balanced by a number of measures providing more protection for victims. Victims' rights have improved very much because of the new criminal procedural law. The duties and rights of community and minority groups are primarily regulated by the Austrian Constitution and have not changed dramatically. Generally the parliamentarian rights have improved.

Can you elaborate a little bit more on changes in external conditions?

Although, globalization is always a challenge for the legal system of the judiciary of a country, it is a fact that there is more cooperation in fighting crime organizations because of the existence of the European Union. For example, EUROJUST, the organization of European Prosecutor's service was implemented to reduce formal procedures and to bring in more efficiency and effectiveness in processing international criminal cases. The directives of the European Union and decisions of the European Court have had a great influence on the law development in the member states.

Overall, has the quality of criminal justice system improved or declined?

This is difficult to say. The general impression is that frame conditions have improved, but the judicial system is hit very hard by financial restriction measures and the administration and judges are overworked. When Austria became a member of the European Union, the budget criteria became very strict. The general reaction was to reduce the number of public servants in all categories. These measures included the justice system, although they were at their limit. Cutting the budget presents a real danger for the quality of the overall justice system, a system that is well respected and noted for its quality. Generally, the Austrian justice system offered high quality and rather fast, excellent decisions. That can change if the tendency of cutting down the budget continues.

What do you mean by frame conditions?

In my understanding, frame conditions mean better education, better training, better selection process of personnel, opportunities for personnel to continue in their education in order to provide high-quality service and the implementation of IT—infrastructure supporting the daily work of judges.

What do you mean by administration–executive powers?

Generally, it is recognized that judges and their assisting administration bodies (secretaries, office servants) are completely overworked. There is a similar tendency that can be seen in the law enforcement agencies using their executive powers. Since 2000, the government has tried to reduce costs of public employees by reducing their number.

In general, is it more or less difficult to be a judge or justice now than in the past?

Generally, I think it is more difficult. Today a judge is under enormous pressure, because so much more work has to be completed. The system has reached the maximum of permissible case and work load. Complex and complicated economic cases are enormous challenges. Especially in the last decade, Austrian judges have been confronted with many white collar crime trials that have national and international dimensions. Another issue is the tsunami of reforms. Judges are confronted with many changes of the system itself that make them feel insecure and asking for some form of stability in the future.

Personal Judicial Philosophy

What do you think should be the role of the judiciary in society?

Judiciary is one of the three powers in a democracy. In our legal educational understanding, legislation, administration, and the judiciary are the important backbones of a democratic society's constitution and legal understanding. It is very important to have an independent justice system. The judiciary always has to check and balance powers. The judiciary is the bulwark of control. It is very important that our constitution states that understanding of splitting powers of legislation and executive judiciary shall not be influenced by politics. Therefore, in a correct understanding, judges should not be active in politics. The judiciary should be free of any political influence. A judge should have no special affinities to any party. Of course, a judge shall be and can be a political thinking human being, but not while performing the job. Politics should only take place in his or her private life.

What should be their job, functions, and roles?

As mentioned earlier, the role of judges in the society should be arbitrary. That is, he or she should be as objective as possible, not being influenced by any political party, and following the rule of law and human understanding when performing official duties as judge. In Austria, we're lucky to have professional judges who are educated and trained by universities, and who receive practical and theoretical training at the courts. The selection process is a difficult one, and only a small number of interested academics are able to reach the position of a judge. The main duty of a judge and the justice system is the control function. This control function is very much connected with the public trust of the judiciary system. If judges fail, the confidence and trust of the people will suffer. At the present time, people have a high regard for judges because they are not corrupt, are not influenced, and act correctly and independently.

What do you mean by arbitrary?

In my understanding, arbitrary means the role understanding of a judge. He has to act neutral, to follow the constitution and the law as a professional, and not prefer any of the parties.

What activities should be left to others?

Political influence, as it already was mentioned, should not play a part. Investigation and prosecution shall be done by the prosecutor's service and police. Judges shall control, watch human rights issues, and follow the rule of law.

What organizational arrangements work and which do not?

Austrian law education, especially in the justice system has reached a very high level, and it is very professional and selective. It can be understood as very efficient and it works. Today there is very much discussion about how much lay involvement in justice should be changed. In the constitutional understanding, *jury justice* was seen as an important element of democracy.

In our modern understanding, *jury justice* in an anachronism that influences the quality of law and justice and sometimes hinders the quality of justice.

Can you be a little more specific about legal education?

In Austria, we have professional judges. You can become a judge after passing the study at the universities. Following the European study model, you can reach degrees of bachelor, master, or doctor (PhD). Having passed a practical training in the justice system, at the courts, one can apply to become a judge, but has to complete and pass a four-year training program. In addition, the applicant has to work at a court for three months. There are so-called education and training courts where the new applicants become familiar with all of the facets of the work of a judge. In addition to the practical training, there are also theoretical modules the trainee must complete. At the end of the education period, an applicant for judge has to pass final exams.

What policies on relations with the community, with political groups, with other criminal justice organizations work well? What hampers cooperation with other agencies and groups?

In Austria, we have professional judges. They are not elected by people or a political party, they are selected by the judiciary system. It is very important that judges act independently of parties in their own organization. Because they do media work and give critical statements about legal actions of the parliament, they have a high reputation with the people.

Organization and Implementation of Austrian Legal System

Mag. Friedrich Forsthuber acted as chair of an expert group of criminal judges. In this function, he and the experts had to handle many special problems, including implementation of measures against mentally ill prisoners and representing the judiciary to the public. Judges build their own expert groups in all matters of law, are invited to the parliament or the ministry of justice, and are in a strong position to have their opinions heard.

Justice administrators have to be free in their actions to keep their colleagues' "heads free" for their work. Just now, the problem is that all of the reforms in the judiciary and the police system are still not free of conflict. Time was needed to handle the police reforms of 2005 and the justice reforms of 2008.

How should the criminal legal system in Austria be organized and implemented? What should be the preferred priorities and strategies? Should the greatest emphasis be placed on hard-edged crime control, prevention, services, or public order work? What mix of strategies should be used for specific types of problems?

The Austrian judiciary system has always been well known as a sophisticated system of checks and balances to handle criminal justice in a correct way and to handle all issues of repression, prevention, therapy, and punishment. Therefore, people have a high opinion of the judiciary and justice system. They accept and recognize the independent work of judges very much. Judges are ranked very highly in public opinion.

Problems and Successes Experienced

In your experience, what policies or programs have worked well and which have not? Can you speculate about the reasons for their success or failure?

Programs influenced by rather modern views of criminology and sociology programs had a better chance to succeed. For example, such influences on juvenile justice in the fields of diversion measures, rehabilitation measures were very fruitful.

What would you consider to be the greatest problem facing the criminal courts at this time?

Challenges of international crime cases, white collar crime in connection with organized crime, and financial crimes are creating enormous problems for the criminal courts.

What problems in courts do you find are the most difficult to deal with?

When I became president of the criminal court in Vienna, I had to deliver a lot of very practical-oriented solutions dealing with problems of the criminal court. The main problems included:

- General security issues
- Entrance security control
- Organizational issues (splitting prosecutor's service and judge's facilities)
- Modernizing the building
- Implementation of a Service Center
- Secretaries and centers for writing
- Modernization of computer use
- Implementation of a new procedural code in the Austrian law system

What would be more easy to change, internal problems (culture of the organization, managerial deficiencies, allegations of corruption, or gender related problems), or externally generated problems (resources, community support)? Is there a need to improve relations with the community? Is anything easy?

The Ministry of Justice, judges, and prosecutors experience a rather high reputation in Austria. People trust judges and the justice system. This happens by the daily work of judges, but although by the professional public relation work of the Ministry of Justice with the communities. There exist regular contact and communication between journalists, judges, administrative authorities of the Ministry of Justice, representatives of the society. An excellent example was the exhibition about "The History of the Criminal Court," the prosecutor's services, the Austrian system of the lawyers, the crime of the Nazis, and the history of death penalty. When this exhibition was shown (June to December 2012 in Vienna at the Criminal Court in Vienna), two important historical trials were reconstructed and performed in the big jury hall of the court. Many people listened and reports were launched in the Austrian print media and television channels.

A very important fundament of public trust into the justice system is the fact that all trials are open to the public. Basically, we have a system that can be shown internationally and we do not need to hide it.

What shall be changed? First of all, the lay law system is anachronistic. It is an international standard that sentencing is based on reasons and these reasons have to be elaborated. Secondly, the main trial has to be reformed completely. We are used to our legal understanding that a judge still is a driving part in the main trial. But, his or her role shall not remind us of behaving like an investigative judge. We have to find a new definition of the role of a judge, between just deciding in a fair trial and finding the material truth. What is missing is:

- Better transparency
- More use of experts
- Reduction of formalism
- Motivation
- Communication is not optimal

Can you say a little bit more about some of the practically oriented problems and solutions, so-called "bulleted points?"

For example, just now a new security concept is planned. This concept starts with simple housekeeping issues. Recently, a new "Housekeeping Order" was instituted and it brought many technical changes, the modernizing of the Central Security Station and upgrading many other features of house security. Another example of a need for change is the daily arrangement of secretaries. There are only 15 secretaries working in the Vienna Criminal Court and they serve about 50 judges who negotiate about 400 times in open court sessions each month. This is an enormous problem for the president of the Criminal Court, in that these cases have to be solved each month. Very often law students, serving their law practicum, have to support secretaries and judges. In some cases, audio and video devices are used as substitutes for the secretaries during some proceedings and these devices support the negotiating judges, but, of course, all of these protocols will eventually have to be transcripted on paper by the secretaries.

To elaborate a little bit more, I have to speak about the Amendment of the Procedural Code in Austria, which came into power with January 1, 2008. This Amendment resulted in an enormous change in the justice and court system because completely new definitions were given for the roles of judges, prosecutors, and police. The so-called investigative judge was abolished. Basically, all investigations of the police and other law enforcement bodies are controlled by prosecutors. As leaders of all investigations, prosecutors have to fulfill a complete new role. They have to give orders, have to control the flow of the investigation, and have to be outside on the crime scene, if necessary. Because of this new role of prosecutors, there has been an enormous fluctuation of prosecutors. Ninety prosecutors started work at the prosecutor's service in Vienna in the last three years. There was considerable confusion among the prosecutors regarding their role and a lot of changes needed to be made to achieve the goals of the new legal situation. The quality of investigations suffered very much in the beginning and judges came under pressure by this development.

Can you say a little bit more about better transparency and the use of experts?

The idea is to bring in more transparency into the field of administration of the court system. The court system, especially administration, suffers from a lack of resources, different forms of influence on the work of judges, and from problems created by the insufficient number of assisting secretaries and office administration personnel. But, these are not the only problems. There is a need of more rooms, more technical equipment, more Internet technical support, more computers, and special software to handle all the administrative matters that need to be completed if the court system is to be efficient and complete its tasks in a timely manner. In addition, there is a need to bring in experts for certain cases. Practitioners, like judges or prosecutors, should be important partners and should be heard when changing the organization of courts or planning legal reforms. Generally, experts should be used much more as support especially dealing with complicated commercial crime cases. Just now, they are only used in the special unit called: Prosecutors Service on Economic and Corruption Crime (*Wirtschafts- und Antikorruptions-Staatsanwaltschaft(WKStA)*). This unit includes such experts as accounting and tax advisors. If outside experts have to be engaged, that is much more costly for the court system and the cases take much longer to be finished.

Theory and Practice

What should be the relationship between theory and practice? What can practitioners learn from theory, and what theory can be built on the experiences of practitioners?

A relationship between theory and practice is necessary. Both can learn from each other. In the field of justice, there exists a long tradition of relationship between practitioners and researchers. The discussion is often very controversial. Sometimes it takes a long time to develop solutions that university research and practical decisions of the highest court find together.

What is the relationship right now? Does it exist? Does it work? What interferes with the collaboration and interaction of the academics/ researchers and practitioners?

The relationship exists. For example, private interdisciplinary seminars were started dealing with the question: How to translate correctly? Together with the institute of languages, body language, cultural background, and diversity were compared and studied. For example, it was discussed how a witness with an African community background react to authorities.

What kind of research, in what form, on what questions would you find most useful for practice? If not very useful, what could or should theory builders do to make their products more useful to you?

There are relations with Austrian universities. A special research institute is run by the Ministry of Justice, that is the Institute for Law and Criminal Sociology (*Institut für Rechts- und Kriminalsoziologie*). It covers studies of special interests. Beside this, a new institute was founded in 2011 in connection with the Vienna University faculty of law, the Austrian Law Enforcement Institute, ALES, which cooperates with the Ministry of Justice and the Ministry of Interior. Basically, it is difficult to bridge ideas of researchers and practitioners, but it works.

Where do you find theory-based information? Where do you look? What journals, books, publications, or reports do you use?

I use all kinds of information facilities: internal and external ones. The Austrian judiciary system is very much linked with universities and research institutions.

Does the judiciary do research on its own, outside of research dealing with pending cases? On what types of issues or questions is the research conducted?

Yes, I mentioned some of this research in an earlier question.

Transnational Relations

Have you been affected in the work of your organization by developments outside the country (human rights demands, universal codes of ethics, practical interactions with judges or justices from other countries, personal experiences outside the country, or new crime threats)? If so, what has occurred?

In the European Union, *EUROJUST* was founded. This is an international organization of prosecutors who cooperate in criminal matters. International cooperation becomes more and more necessary. The European Court on Human Rights is an institution dealing with all human rights issues and influences the European law decisions very strongly. The International Criminal Court was very important in the Balkan war genocides.

Have those interactions been beneficial or harmful? What kind of external international influences are beneficial and which ones are less so?

There is intense contact between justice representatives. Colleagues from foreign countries are visiting Austria and the opposite also occurs. The tendency to become international is a beneficial one. The development of law in the European Union plays an important role.

How have developments post-September 11 affected your work?

In Austria, 9/11 has not had so much influence directly, but, of course, because of the international relationship, the fight against terrorism became a priority.

General Assessments

Are you basically satisfied or dissatisfied with developments in criminal law and criminal procedure in your system?

Basically, it is a satisfying relationship working in the field of criminal justice and influencing the development in criminal law and criminal procedural law in the legal system of Austria.

What are the most likely developments you see happening and which would you like to see happen? What is most needed now to improve the system?

Austria has been a member of the European Union since 1995. The international development working together, and the work and influence of the European Court are changing the Austrian system, step by step. What has to be improved and what is needed now is the employment of more judges and experts to handle the increasing quality crisis of judiciary work and challenges in Austria.

Bosnia–Herzogovina

LAURENCE FRENCH

Overview of the Bosnia-Herzegovina Legal System

The judicial system in Bosnia–Herzegovina (BiH) is unique, even among the new states carved out of the former Yugoslavia in that it was an outgrowth of the 1995 Dayton Peach Agreement that settled the 1991 to 1995 component of the Third Balkan Wars (1991–2002). Even then, the Socialist Federal Republic of Yugoslavia (SFRY) was unique among the European Communist nations in that it was the only country to have a system of constitutional courts. Under the leadership of Marshall Tito, the SFRY had a Constitutional Court at the federal level as early as 1963 also allowing for Constitutional Courts for the six component "republics" (Slovenia, Croatia, Bosnia–Herzegovina, Serbia, Montenegro, and Macedonia) as well for the two "autonomous provinces" carved out of Serbia—Kosovo and Vojvodina. The SFRY Constitutional Court for Bosnia–Herzegovina was established in February 1964 and confirmed by the Constitution of 1974. The 1963 Constitution of Yugoslavia articulates the conditions for the "Republic Constitutions" under Articles 145-159. Article 150 noted:

> Constitutional courts shall decide on the conformity of law with the constitution and the conformity of other regulations and general acts with the constitution and law. The constitutional courts, pursuant to law, shall also safeguard the rights of self-government and other basic freedoms and rights established by the constitution whenever these freedoms and rights have been violated by any decisions or action and court protection has not been provided.

The ensuing war of 1991–1995 led to the November 1995 Dayton Peace Agreement that settled this phase of the Third Balkan Wars that was waged between Croatia, Bosnia–Herzegovina, and the Federal Republic of Yugoslavia (Serbia and Montenegro). The Dayton Peace Accord was unique in that it was written in American English and not in the Slavic language common to the former Yugoslavia. The new constitution was a major component of the Dayton Peace Agreement, designed to accommodate the complex dimension of the newly created state of BiH with its three autonomous entities: Federation of Bosnia–Herzegovina (FBiH), the Republic of Srpska (RS), and the protected enclave, the Brcko District (BD); as well as the three major sectarian groups within BiH: Muslim Bosniaks, Catholic Bosnian-Croats, and Orthodox Bosnian-Serbs. Annex 4 of the new Constitution stipulates that:

- Bosnia–Herzegovina will continue as a sovereign state within its present internationally recognized borders. It will consist of two (major) entities—FBiH and RS.
- The FBiH will comprise of about 51% of BiH with the majority being Bosniak and Catholic Croats, and the RS making up the remaining 49% with a majority of Bosnian Serbs.
- The Constitution provides for the protection of Human Rights and the free movement of people, goods, capital, and services throughout BiH.
- The Central Government will have a presidency, a two-chamber legislature, and a *constitutional court*. Direct elections will be held for the presidency and one of the legislative chambers.
- No person who is serving a sentence imposed by the International Tribunal (ICTY), and no person who is under indictment by the Tribunal and who has failed to comply with an order to appear before the Tribunal, may stand as a candidate or hold any appointive, elective, or other public office in the territory of Bosnia–Herzegovina.

Thus, while the new BiH Constitution allowed for strong entity governments in addition to the statewide government, where members of the three major sectarian/ethnic groups were enfranchised, other minorities were listed in the new Constitution as "*others*" and, consequently, disenfranchised relevant to elective positions. Suits by a Bosnian Roma (gypsy origin) and a Bosnian Jew were filed before the European Court of Human Rights in 2006. The cases were consolidated as presented as *The Case of Sejdic and Finci v. BiH*. The case against BiH was presented to the European Court of Human Rights in July and August 2006 under Article 34 of the Convention and Fundamental Freedoms ("the Convention"). Here, the applicants complained of their ineligibility to stand for election to the House of Peoples and the Presidency of Bosnia and Herzegovina on the ground of their Roma and/or Jewish origin. BiH was a party to the European Court of Human Rights by virtue of its 2002 membership in the Council of Europe, making it eligible for review by the European Commission for Democracy. In this regard, the Parliamentary Assembly of the Council of Europe reminded BiH that it needed to adopt a new constitution ending discrimination against "others."

The European Court of Human Rights ruled in the petitioner's favor in 2009 essentially ordering BiH to revise its Dayton Constitution. In not doing so, the Court's ruling found BiH in violation of its 2008 "Stabilization and Association Agreement" (SAA) with the European Union (EU)—a major condition for full recognition in the EU. Toward this end, a SAA requirement is for BiH to amend electoral legislation regarding members of BiH presidency and House of Peoples to ensure full compliance with the European Convention of Human Rights. As of February 2013, these conditions have not been met and are unlikely to be met given the complex system of government currently in BiH.

Interview of Judge Hilmo Vucinic, State Court Justice for Bosnia and Herzegovina

4

LAURENCE FRENCH
GORAN KOVACEVIC

Contents

The Interview

Could we start by getting some background information, such as where you grew up, where you were educated and what motivated you to go into the legal profession? Did your family support and encourage you in doing this? Do they still support you today?

My name is Hilmo Vucinic. I was born in Gorazde in 1963 where I grew up and attended public school, completing both elementary and high school. I later attended the University of Sarajevo where I graduated with a degree from the Law Faculty. After graduation, I started working in my hometown, Gorazde. Initially, my legal work was not in the judiciary. For a while I worked in administrative agencies, then in the economic sector, mainly in the private sector, where I was head of legal services. I came into contact with the judiciary when I was legal council for private agencies with business before the court. These activities were before the court in Gorazde and dealt with debts and unpaid utility services that the users were required to pay to the housing and other agencies. After that, I worked for a while as legal representative for the utility company. I spent the war years in Gorazde and, in January 1993, I was appointed judge of the District Military Court in Gorazde. So, my direct involvement in the courts dates from this period. Before this, I had some experience as an *ex officio* counsel in cases that were prosecuted before the military court in Gorazde. After the abolition of the military courts, I was appointed as a judge to the Cantonal Court in Gorazde and I performed those duties up to December 2003. By the decision of the High Prosecutorial Council, I was appointed judge of the Cantonal Court in Sarajevo in 2003 and I performed these duties until March 2005 when I was appointed a judge of the Court of Bosnia–Herzegovina. I have remained in this position and have been performing these duties ever since. Currently, I am a judge of the Appellate Panel and perform the function of the president of Appellate Division of the court.

Where did you get your legal training? Did you clerk for another judge or work in other judicial environments prior to your current position?

It was my personal desire to get involved in legal studies. While I was not persuaded by my family per se, they, nonetheless, never were opposed to my career choice. So, I can say that it was a personal choice that I got into this line of work. I have always had the support of my relatives, especially my wife, who provides me with strong support in my profession. I think this is a very responsible job and, for a judge to be able to perform well on the job, he must be satisfied with his family and have a harmonious family life. To a large extent, this harmonious family life gives the judge the ability to perform this complex job.

Has your job turned out to be as interesting and satisfying as you thought it would be?

Believe me, I was not an idealist—thinking that by doing this kind of work I would be changing the world. But, I realized that this is a responsible job and that it requires devotion. Our work is unique, complex, and requires a lot of time and effort. People who observe our work think that the job just comes down to what we do in the courtroom. But, I must say that the judge's job is not done only in the courtroom. A judge must be well prepared for trial, must study the laws, and research each case. It often happens that judges, even when we leave the courtroom, when we visit at your house, we bring homework with us, reading case law and court decisions. You cannot stop thinking about your work. Sometimes, I joke and say that I go to bed thinking about my work, I wake up with the same thoughts, so essentially judicial work is 24/7. We even joke with each other, talking about how we dream about the cases we are working on. I'm not sure that a person can perform well as a judge if they are not totally dedicated to their work. In each case, the judge must strive to be objective and free of any outside influence in making decisions and rulings. This is important because the decision has to be based upon established facts resulting from evidentiary proceedings. So, decisions must be totally objective. When I say this, I emphasize that the judge must take this into account when it comes to his social life, so as not to cause doubts about the objectivity of his decisions. Thus, the judge must take this into account when choosing the places he visits and people he or she socializes with. Our public image is very important.

In your opinion, what is the ideal role of the judiciary, in society in general, as well as its role in regards to other public policy agencies, such as law enforcement, corrections, the legislature?

Usually it is said that the judge, or the court, is the mouth of the law. The court is the agency responsible for implementing the laws. We all know that the laws are made by the legislature; however, it is the role of the courts to see that these laws are implemented as intended. Regarding the court's relations with other authorities, I can say that there exists a separation of powers in these matters. Here the court has the final say, taking into account the input from all parties involved in the judicial proceeding—in our case, criminal proceeding. In this process, we have to work closely with the police and prosecutors. In this relationship, the police are the first to come into contact with criminal activity. The police are under the authority of the prosecution, so now it is the prosecutor who leads the investigative process. The prosecution must evaluate the evidence they receive from the police and, once this assessment is done, bring the case before the court. Thus, the court is the agency that monitors the quality of law enforcement, that is, it is the control mechanism seeing that police practices are fair and legal. In this regards, the court, through the implementation of its decisions, ensures the protection of human rights, particularly in determining the legality of evidence obtained and investigations conducted.

How has the judiciary, as you understand it, changed since the end of the conflict and the Dayton Peace Accord? How do you compare the two systems?

Overall, I can say that most professionals see that the judicial reforms in Bosnia–Herzegovina that took place since the end of the war, as being very positive. You have to keep in mind that the international community invested heavily in the reforms instituted following the war. This resulted in about a third of the judges being replaced. A lot of courts that existed under the previous system no longer exist. These changes were the result of legislation resulting in a new Code of Criminal Procedure. In general, there is a positive assessment associated with these changes. Unfortunately, ordinary citizens have not yet come to fully appreciate the magnitude of these changes—with many of them still thinking that the courts are the same as they were before the war. One major change was removing the political element from the judiciary. Now the only political contact with the courts is through the budget. We are still tied to the state budget of Bosnia and Herzegovina with its complex processes. Otherwise, there is complete separation of the courts from the executive and legislative political influence. This separation of influence is overseen by the High Judicial and Prosecutorial Council, which is responsible for reforms within the judiciary.

Can you tell us something about the history, structure, and organization of the court?

The Court of Bosnia–Herzegovina is a relatively new court, with the new structure of the judiciary in B-H going back to demands stipulated in the Dayton Accord. Initially, these changes were imposed by the High Representative in B-H and were later adopted by the Parliamentary Assembly along with changes over time. The court, created specifically to prosecute war crimes, organized crime, corruption, and election complaints, was first established in 2002. This was a time of many electoral complaints, and the court was formed with that intention of settling these issues. Over time, the court underwent organizational changes and now has special divisions: criminal, administrative, and appellate.

What is the jurisdiction of the State Court regarding the components of the criminal justice system within Bosnia and Herzegovina, especially in terms of the penal code of Bosnia and Herzegovina and how it relates to the three subcomponents of B-H: the penal code of Federation of Bosnia and Herzegovina (FBiH); the penal code of Republika Srpska (RS); and the penal code of the Brcko District (BD)?

This is a very interesting question since the amendments to the law on the court in 2003 determined that it is the role of the court to resolve disputes between the entities and the district as well as the B-H institutions with public authority mandates. Essentially, the court has primary jurisdiction over crimes defined in the Criminal Code of Bosnia and Herzegovina as well as all civil and administrative laws, including laws that specifically fall under the jurisdiction of FBiH, RS, and BD, when it is deemed that these crimes may endanger the sovereignty and territorial integrity, political independence and national security, and international reputation of Bosnia and Herzegovina, or if these actions can have harmful consequences for the economy of B-H and any other legal matter that may have consequences beyond the territory of the entity or district level. These conditions, as stipulated in Article 7, paragraph 2, of the B-H law places the prosecution of these criminal offenses within the jurisdiction of the State Courts over that of the entities of the Brcko District, especially in cases involving political and judicial abuses at these levels.

Has the legislature, or any other public institution, set sentencing guidelines for specific convictions? If so, what are they?

There are no specific sentencing instructions. However, the court is bound by the criminal laws of B-H that dictates general rules prescribing procedures for the court. Of course, the court always acts on legal principles because, for the court to act professionally, it has to follow legal dictates.

Does your Court have the jurisdiction/authority to sentence someone to death?

No. In the current system, there is no death penalty. The maximum sentence now is a sentence of 45 years.

Was there a death penalty under the former Yugoslavia legal system?

Yes. Under the SFRY [Socialists Federal Republic of Yugoslavia], there was a death sentence that was used for the most serious crimes, such as murder and war crimes. However, this punishment was an exceptional punishment and [not] used in all cases. It was left to the disposition of the court to impose an alternative sentence of 20 years in prison in lieu of the death penalty.

Can your court transfer/refer a case, like that involving terrorism or war crimes, to another jurisdiction outside B-H and vice versa?

Cases can be referred to us from the ICTY [International Criminal Tribunal–Yugoslavia]. To date we have had seven such cases referred to us from ICTY. It is also possible for our court to cede some cases to a lower court according to Article 27 of the CPC B-H, but there are no provisions for transferring jurisdiction to another court of equal status. We can, however, cooperate with other out-of-country courts if the suspect is not available to be tried before our court. We subscribe to the principle of territorial jurisdiction.

Are you aware of any cases where a person was arrested in the territory of B-H for a crime committed in another country? If so, would B-H extradite the person even if it is likely that he/she would receive the death penalty in that country if convicted?

There are special protocols, regulated by international conventions, that dictate the rules for referrals of criminal cases outside our jurisdiction. Two conditions come into play here, one that this is not a political prisoner and, two, that it is not a capital offense case where the person is likely to be executed.

As I understand it, under the new system the prosecutor is responsible for bringing cases before the court and replacing the old system with an investigating judge.

Yes. This is true. Since the changes brought about in 2003, the investigating judge has been replaced with an independent prosecution. Now responsibility for any investigation is given to the prosecution. Of course, this does not mean that there is no judicial influence by the court in the investigation. While the prosecutor is the one who heads the investigation, judges can be involved in the preliminary proceedings, influencing the role of the prosecutor in the investigative stage. The prosecution needs to gain the court's approval to proceed with an investigation.

What is the adequacy of defense lawyers in these cases? What are their qualifications in criminal law and is there a separate public defender program for those who cannot afford their own lawyer?

When it comes to defense counsel, there are special rules and procedure for them. In Sections 1 and 2 of the War Crimes and Organized Crime regulations, accused persons can request a defense counsel to represent them in their case. The Registry Office of the Judiciary has a Division of Criminal Defense whose task it is to prepare lawyers appearing before the court of B-H. Now lawyers are well prepared to provide representation and defense for their clients at the state level. This especially applies to those lawyers who are doing these jobs *ex officio*. All those lawyers who are on the list must pass the training, which in some way provides a guarantee of greater professionalism and legal protection for the accused in these cases. Plus, there is the special public defender's office. The Criminal Procedure Code describes the conditions under which a public defender is mandated. One condition is when the suspected cannot afford his own defense counsel. This is known as the poor law condition.

What are the qualifications for the public defenders and what is the procedure of his appointment?

There is a list of qualified lawyers created by the Criminal Defense Department. This list is provided to each defendant or suspect, depending on the stage of the proceedings, so that he has an opportunity to select an attorney. This is his law-given right under the revised judicial system.

What if the person does not want to choose a lawyer, then what?

Then the court has an obligation to assign him a lawyer from the list. In these cases, care is taken relevant to the workload of lawyers. We try to avoid situations where some lawyers have too many cases and others too few. Once assigned by the court, these lawyers must comply with their assignments. They are paid for their services by the state.

Can you tell me something about the previous criminal justice system in the former Yugoslavia, such as the role of judges, prosecutors, defense lawyers, police, and corrections?

I can only speak from my position as a judge. We already stated that major reforms of the law in Bosnia–Herzegovina were made in 2003. These changes greatly affected the role of judges. In the former system, the court led the entire process, from investigation to sentencing. The judge was *dominus lidis* throughout this procedure. The legislative reform reduced the role judges played in the adjudication process. Our new system is based upon the Anglo-Saxon model where the defense and prosecution are separate elements of the adjudication process. We now adhere to the adversarial judicial process based upon legal criminal procedures. Even then, the judge has the right to active participation in the implementation of the evidentiary process, especially in the stage of direct and cross examinations. When you compare this role now with the authority judges had in the former justice system of Yugoslavia, it is much smaller, and the judge has much less authority in respect of the evidentiary proceedings. However, the essence of sentencing and the decision making remains the same, because the court is required in both systems, on the basis of established facts, to make a lawful decision.

Overall, in your estimation, has the quality of criminal justice system improved or declined under the new system? If so, how?

This is a difficult question. I can say from the perspective of the judge that the role of the judge is slightly easier regarding his/her involvement in the process of conducting evidentiary procedure and argumentation of evidence. From the judicial side, the job is somewhat easier because the parties in the proceeding, both the defense and the prosecutor, have more obligations regarding the rules of evidence, and persuading the court of the veracity of their claims. However, some argue that the system of fair sentencing has deteriorated somewhat bearing in mind the fact that in the former system, the court had a greater role in the investigative stage of proceedings and the protection of human rights. So, this is really a complex issue and deserves a detailed analysis. There is already a strong opinion that our system is becoming similar to the American legal system, where, again according to some perceptions, the person being judged, if not in a position to hire a good lawyer, he/she cannot prove his/her innocence. I think this is a good lesson for us to remember given all of these reforms. We do not yet know if our new system provided easy access to the courts for all those who may feel that their rights may have been violated like the old system did.

Speaking about undue influences, are there mechanisms for controlling the actions by defense lawyers in relation to their clients' right to plea bargaining? Can defense lawyers deliberately avoid using it because they stand to get significantly more money if they take the case to trial instead of copping a plea for their client?

Unfortunately, the court is not able to control this process. Now, it is something that falls under the privileged agreements made by the accused and his counsel, hence it is difficult to monitor this process. I've noticed in my practice a couple of cases where the attorneys, while representing the interests of their clients, represent their own interests more than that of their client. There have been cases where lawyers were more interested in taking their cases to the end even when their client could have received a lesser sentence through a plea agreement. Perhaps a bigger paycheck is a motive for some lawyers at the expense of both their client and society, which has to pay them for their delay tactics. However, the regulation on fees for lawyers adjudicated before the court of B&H and other courts would eventually see these patterns of misbehavior and would respond to them. When this does happen, it also enters into the realm of legal ethics, and this is something that the Bar Association needs to monitor as well.

Do you feel that the loss of the judge's absolute control over the judicial procedures has resulted in a decline in the protection of human rights?

I would not say that this is a negative thing. It is true that the investigative judge previously conducted the entire investigation representing the interests of both sides. Now that the prosecutor conducts an investigation based upon the Criminal Procedure Code, he does the same, because the prosecutor is obliged to, when conducting the investigation and collecting evidence, collect evidence in favor of the accused as well as against him. If the prosecutor in the investigation came up with some evidence that may be in favor of the defense, he is obliged to submit that evidence to defense. On the other hand, there is also the possibility that the judge can get involved in the investigation. Also, in the course of the proceedings, the court has an obligation to make certain that everyone does things according to the law in order to guarantee a fair trial, as defined in Article 6 of the European Convention on Human Rights, which is a guideline for all judges in the area. This document has supremacy over all laws in B-H. If the judges are in doubt about an article of the law that directly touches the problem of a fair trial, or any other right guaranteed by the European Convention, it is required to apply the provisions of the European Convention directly.

What are the most dramatic and significant changes that you have experienced in criminal justice over the course of your career (philosophies, organizational arrangements, specializations, policies and programs, technology, personnel, diversity etc.)?

Well, I must admit there have been dramatic changes in the organization of courts and the role of judges at all levels in Bosnia–Herzegovina. Despite considerable criticism, especially from politicians, I think that these reforms have had a positive effect, especially in the formation of the High Prosecutorial Council. That is, perhaps, the most notable of all the reforms within the judiciary. This is particularly evident in the realm of appointing judges. Today we are in a position to appoint judges for life or until 70 years of age. In the past, judges did not have any real job security in that he or she was constantly subjected to political oversight. Under the previous system, judges were reviewed every four years by the legislature. Today, this is no longer the case. But, this does not mean that judges have no obligation to maintain a high quality of professional performance on the bench. On the other hand, the appointment of judges is now conducted by an independent team of qualified professionals, thus eliminating the interference by the executive and the legislative branches of government, as was the case in the past. Today, they have no influence in the appointment of judges. Of course, there is a disciplinary prosecutor who looks into judicial misconduct cases including corruption and conflict of interest. Today, we have the means to objectively review any judicial or prosecutory misdeeds. There have been cases where charges have been leveled against judges or prosecutors and they have lost their job, and, in some cases, faced charges of corruption.

Is this process different from that under the former system, where a judge was evaluated every four years?

No, the major difference here is that there is no political influence in the appointment and mandate of the judges.

In general, do you feel that the process for becoming a judge in B-H is more or less difficult than in the past?

The conditions are the same except that, under the earlier system, a person could immediately be appointed to a judge position as soon as they passed the bar exam. Today, a person needs at least three years experience in the legal field in order to be appointed to the position of judge or prosecutor. Also, bear in mind that there are now educational requirements as well. So, maybe, in today's system with these requirements, the procedure for appointing judges is clearly more complex. Nonetheless, in both systems there was a requirement that anyone appointed to the level of a judge must be a qualified professional individual.

Is it true that a major change is that you needed to be a member of the Communist Party during SFRY, while now it is other way around?

Yes, political influence is now avoided. There is a requirement that there is to be no political influence or involvement by those working in the office of judges or prosecutors.

So, this means we have gone from one extreme to another?

Yes.

Can you compare differences in the workload and responsibilities between then and now?

I think basically the responsibilities are the same because we are essentially doing the same job and that is decision making. The major difference is that now the judge is not involved in the investigative stage. So, we can say that judicial work is a bit easier in relation to the role of judges in the previous system. However, the new system requires the prosecution of some cases and some applications that were not specific in the previous legal system, so that each time brings its challenges.

What changes in external conditions (support from communities, legal powers, judicial relations, relations with minority communities, resource provision, political influence, etc.) have had a significant impact on criminal justice in B-H?

We have already spoken about the system and changes of election of judges to life function, etc. These are all things that affect the quality of performing. On the other hand, the democratization of society bears some of the new forms of expression of public awareness. We have many nongovernmental organizations [NGOs] with a mandate designed for the protection of specific human rights and they appear as a control mechanism on the objectivity of both the prosecution and the judiciary. Also, the public is now much more focused on the courts. Whether this is due to specific cases, the sensitivity of the matter, or because it is about people who are attractive to media when they appear as an accused party in the proceedings. So, from that perspective, we see a much higher degree of public interest in the judicial process. This is good for the court because now the court must take into account the international laws relevant to human rights. We are aware that our work is much more subject to public scrutiny, not only the public, which is reflected in the media, but also of the NGOs where work people who [have a] very good knowledge of legal matters, and often specialize in issues of human rights, and even from this aspect can make the assessment of judges.

Which agencies provide the most support for the judiciary today: local or international?

Both local and international influences are important in the proper functioning of the court system in B-H. Regarding local interest, the State Court has a special relationship with the local community. The court has a special department designed for public relations. Part of the role of this department is to work cooperatively with nongovernmental organizations that provide support to the court. It has already become the practice of the judiciary to hold periodic meetings with nongovernmental organizations in certain areas, particularly when it comes to war crimes cases. Here the court is trying to reach out to the local community, to point out all issues and complexity of these cases, and also for members of the local community to learn about these issues and with cases, and especially for local communities to be aware of all the things that have happened in the area of that community. And, this is all done in order to determine the truth and achieve reconciliation among people who live in the community. On the other hand, there is good support from the international community as well. We have good communication with other courts and often go to visit courts in other states. We have good communication with colleagues and we are able to compare experiences, in order to improve our work.

According to your knowledge, are there any obstacles that generally hamper cooperation with other agencies or groups?

Not to my knowledge. Perhaps the biggest problem is sufficient money to adequately cover all the cases we have before us. There are plenty of good ideas being put forth, but often we lack the money to implement them within either the court or at the community level. Just as important is a high level of cooperation among all the parties involved.

If it were up to you, how would you organize a perfect criminal justice system in B–H?

That is a tough question. When this is viewed from a professional point of view, a need for the existence of the Supreme Court is obvious. I think this is the main drawback of the entire judicial reform in B&H. Unfortunately, this reform is the result of some political compromise and a reflection of the political situation in B&H. Under the current B–H Constitution there is no provision for such court. This court would allow uniform judicial practice in the entire territory of B–H. It would also further contribute to the protection of human rights.

What do you see as being the preferred priorities and strategies: hard-edged crime control, prevention, services, order work, what mix for which types of problems, etc.?

As I have already said, certain procedural steps of the court were transferred to the prosecution and now there exists the need to work on establishing better links between police and prosecutors. In addition, it is necessary to implement a permanent training program of police in the areas of contemporary trends in crime because criminals are often one step ahead of us. So, this would be an important aspect of future strategy.

In your experience as a judge, what policies or programs have worked well and which have not? Why?

Sometimes it seems that in the criminal law there are certain principles that are outdated, for example, sovereignty, as understood by 19th century theorists, is an outdated category. Essentially, we have to be able to adapt to the emergence of new crime networks. This trend then should be followed by the entities and they should work to establish better cooperation that will result in faster response to the challenges that crime represents.

What would you consider to be the single greatest problem facing the criminal courts in Bosnia–Herzegovina at this time?

Well it seems to me that the workload has increased and it is not accompanied by adequate staffing of the courts. Obviously, a shortage of staff impacts upon the productivity of the courts. Eventually, a specialization of courts and judges needs to be implemented, so we could have specialists for organized crime, and terrorism, etc.

What would be easier to change—internal problems (culture of the organization, managerial deficiencies, allegations of corruption or gender related problems, etc.) or externally generated problems (resources, community support, etc.)? Is any of this feasible?

First, there is the problem of the independence of the courts. The courts are independent when it comes to the merits of their work. On the other hand, there is the dependence of the courts when it comes to financing their work, since the legislature can indirectly put pressure on the courts through the budget. This can cause problems in the efficient functioning and independence of the courts. Of course, the judges, as holders of judicial authorities, must be aware of the gravity of work they do. The High Judicial and Prosecutorial Council must take into account, when appointing judges, candidates that have high personal and moral standards, so that we do not come into a situation that the person appointed as a judge uses his or her position for some improper purpose and thereby damage the public reputation of the court. It is in all of our best interest that corrupt individuals are dealt with appropriately, so that the public will not judge the entire judicial apparatus on the behavior of these individuals. So, given this scenario, I think that it is easier to deal with internal problems than with those that are generated from outside.

When someone is being considered for an appointment to the court are they submitted to testing by any standardized test like MMPI? [Minnesota Multiphasic Personality Inventory]

Not to my knowledge, but a general criterion of the High Judicial and Prosecutorial Council, in appointing judges, is to assess the competence and moral standards of the candidates. It depends on the council as to how far it will go while performing these checks. I remember the review process when it was carried out for the renewal of judges in 2003 and this process included looking at the social network surrounding judge's everyday lives. They even went to the pubs judges visited after work.

What do you see as the pragmatic relationship between theory and practice? What can practitioners learn from theory, and what theory builders from practitioners?

Well, you know the best combination would be that the person is the practitioner and theorist. Unfortunately, most judges are practitioners, and they rarely pursue theoretical studies mainly due to their workloads.

What is the relationship between those two categories right now? Does it exist? Does it work? What holds collaboration or interactions back?

There is no relationship between theory and practice. Those are two parallel units that exist separately. Perhaps we should try to find some common ground where a connection could be made. As for cooperation, it probably depends on the traditional understanding of the separate role of education. For example, while I was studying, we had an opportunity to visit the court and to us it was like a practicum. While I was in America [United States], I had the opportunity to see how theory and practice are interrelated. While visiting one law school, we witnessed an exercise where students conducted a mock trial. To me this was a very good example of integrating theory and practice within the judiciary.

What type of research would you find most useful for practice?

We encounter situations before the courts in B–H that are new—for the first time. In these situations, it might be well to handle the matter from the theoretical aspect, to analyze the practice of other courts that have dealt with similar situations and had their outcomes published. As it stands now, we have little access to manuals and case material that would be helpful for us when we find ourselves in situations where no other precedence exists.

What could or should legal theorists do to make their products more useful to you?

They should present their research in the form of textbooks or manuals, with analysis of specific problems and offer solutions to these problems. That would be a great help.

Where do you find theory-based information?

The structure of the court is specific and we have a legal department where our assistants work, so they can research certain legal documents for us. And we can do it ourselves as well. For example, we are able to follow the work of the Supreme Courts of Serbia and Croatia, and the Court of Human Rights in Strasbourg, on the Internet. In this way, we are able to find some procedures that are applicable to cases in which we work.

What resources are currently available to you in your work?

We, at the court, have a very good library and we are also able to recommend the purchase of books for which we feel we could use in our work. Additionally, we have access to the works of the ICTY [International Criminal Tribunal for the former Yugoslavia] in both electronic and printed format. We have the ability to search online for court decisions in neighboring countries. We have Internet access to documents of the court in Strasbourg. We have a legal department with young people working that are fluent in English and French. It is very important to be able to carry out analysis of materials that are available in English and French.

What case law resources are currently available to you in your work? What is the quality of case material available to you in rendering a judgment?

We often follow the practice of other courts in reaching a legal position, especially the judgments of the ICTY, and even the practice of the U.S. Supreme Court and other courts, when we want to provide a theoretical basis for our decisions. If it is a good legal argument, we use it as our legal argument as well. This is not a reference to judicial practice in terms of precedent; we do not have to act in the same fashion as other court in reaching our judgments. However, in terms of case law, we are obliged to use the European Court of Human Rights because they represent a direct interpretation of the European Convention on Human Rights that are part of a convention. On the basis of Article 2 of the Constitution, we know that this convention has supremacy over all legal documents in Bosnia–Herzegovina, which means that we still have our jurisprudence as a source of law.

Do you have sufficiently qualified court clerks to assist you in your legal research?

Yes, I really have to commend our young colleagues who work in the legal department of the court. The working requirements are that they completed law school and [have] passed [the] Bar Exam as well as demonstrate knowledge of English or French. Some of our people hold Master's of Science degrees. Our assistants are highly qualified to perform complex legal analysis, especially in cases that are interesting for us. Unfortunately, such a service exists only in the Court of B–H, while other courts do not have this service. Of course, the lower courts can address the Court of B-H for legal expertise, but so far we have not had such requests from the courts in B&H. All materials, our judgments, are available on our Web site so they can be accessed. We add to these materials certain theoretical interpretations and practices of the courts of other states on these issues so that our lower courts in B–H can become familiar with this practice.

How large is your law library and what major journals, books, publications, reports does it have in its holding?

I think we have over 1,000 titles in our library. It is a remarkable number of resources, given that it is a professional library, and that the court is a young institution. In our library, we have titles, not only in B&H, but also from neighboring states and foreign literature in English. We also have various magazines that deal with legal matters available to us.

What type of expert assistance do you have, especially from the UN, EU, or USA? Specifically, how has the U.S. Office of Overseas Prosecutorial Development, Assistance and Training (OPDAT) influenced the current judiciary in B-H?

Regarding OPDAT, they directly cooperate with the prosecution and indirectly with the court in terms of education. When we have a need for a specific training, we coordinate with them on that front. Through them, we have had the opportunity to visit the USA and to observe their legal system and what [we] saw influenced our operations in B&H.

What is the role and impact of foreign judges, not only those from the United States, but also from other states, in the criminal justice system in B–H?

I must say that their role is very important because the new criminal legislation in Bosnia is a compilation of continental and Anglo-Saxon law. When you observe our Code of Criminal Procedure, it leads to [the] conclusion that it is neither a continental or Anglo-Saxon legal system, but a mixture of both. In such situations, some shortcomings always arise. That is when the prominent role of foreign judges, especially those from the USA, is obvious, especially when legal institutes that we have built into our Code of Criminal Procedure are applied, which originate from the USA legal system.

In September 2013, when Judge Vucinic was asked to assess the role and influence of the foreign judges with the revamped judicial system in Bosnia-Herzegovina, he said, "In my opinion their [foreign judges] presence helped domestic judges start thinking out-of-the-box, and they helped a lot in expanding our laws to accommodate our new Constitution. Foreign judges acted as an instrument of education for domestic judges providing us with the opportunity to expand our practice of law under their supervision."

Are there differences between domestic and foreign judges regarding legal matters, since they come from various law traditions?

I would not say that there are disagreements per se, but more a difference of opinion. In the final analysis, each judge is independent in making his/her decisions. But these differences are sometimes good because this dialogue and discussion can result in better decision making.

What is your professional relationship with these people [foreign judges]?

Very good, you always have the opportunity to learn from them, and I noticed that they are very good practitioners, and have a good ability to separate the important from the unimportant in terms of facts. They have, so to say, applicative knowledge.

For what period of time do you think they will continue to be here?

The deadline was December 2012, and the foreign judges left.

In your opinion, is their leaving positive or negative?

They have been here since the beginning of 2003 and have left a deep imprint in the work of the court. I would also like to think that they learned something from us as well. On the other hand, we have also learned a lot from them given that it was an interactive process. These years of tutelage has helped local personnel to better assume the burden of work regarding these complex cases. I think that we are now trained, through previous work, to deal with the most complex cases in the Court of B&H. So, I think that this period, until 2012, is quite sufficient and that the judges of the Court B&H can independently perform these tasks after that date.

Was there any public disagreement with their presence [foreign judges] in the judicial institutions of Bosnia and Herzegovina?

To my knowledge, there were no objections among the judiciary. On the other hand, all negative comments came from the political realm. It has to do with politics and little to do our professional work, so these disagreements can be ignored.

Have you been affected by, and how, in the work of your organization by developments outside the country (human rights demands, universal

codes of ethics, practical interactions with police from other countries, personal experiences outside the country, new crime threats, etc.)?

I think so. B&H is a country in transition and all of the changes that occur in the immediate and wider environment are also reflected in B&H. So we are in a position to continually meet with new colleagues, to become familiar with their experiences and to apply these experiences in Bosnia. Two years ago, we were in the United States and for the first time we had a chance to see how their parole system works, and there we saw those metal [electronic] bracelets intended to control their movements. In the U.S., we were convinced of the positive sides of this legal institution, and I was glad to see that such provisions should be incorporated in the Law on Execution of Criminal Sanctions in Bosnia, which is in preparation. This practice is especially effective when it comes to short prison sentences where parole is significantly more efficient than serving the sentence.

When we are talking about interactions with international subjects, have those interactions been beneficial or harmful? What kind of external international influences are beneficial and which ones less so?

I would look at that only from the aspect of The Hague Tribunal and we can talk only about the positive aspects. I must emphasize that the Court of B&H was the first court in the region, which had cases transferred to the prosecution by the ICTY. That shows what kind of court it is, and that this court is able to process each case that is put to the prosecution. Positive aspects are reflected in the fact that the court acknowledges the practice and jurisprudence of the ICTY. The argumentation of The Hague Tribunal is also reflected in the judgments of the court. In addition, it is possible for us to use the evidence presented before the ICTY. Another positive aspect of this relationship is that we have been able to maintain informal and personal contacts with the judges of the ICTY, which is very useful for a judge of our court. We are able to readily access their opinions and all this results in better work of the court. Furthermore, we have a good cooperation relationship with the special Court in Serbia. We are able to collaborate with other courts in the neighboring countries and beyond. In criminal law, the necessity of cooperation and joint implementation of some procedural actions is imperative especially in situations where witnesses who are key to one of our cases are on the territory of another country and vice versa. I have to say that there is always good cooperation and I think this relationship will continue to be so in the future.

Have the events after September 11, 2001 impacted your business, precisely whether there has been a shift of focus of interest to the criminal acts of terrorism?

I would not say so, actually I have not noticed that there was a larger inflow of cases. The fact is that the general climate in Bosnia has changed in terms of understanding the threat of terrorism. [The] 9/11 event had the most impact on citizens' awareness about terrorism and not a significant effect on the criminal justice system in B–H. As far as I remember, at that time, we delivered Algerians living in B–H to [the] USA and I think this was it. Social control might have been strengthened. Since the establishment of the court, several cases of terrorism have been prosecuted, but I cannot say that this is a direct product of the events of September 11, 2001.

Basically, are you satisfied with the development of criminal law and procedures in B&H?

In principle, yes, Bosnia–Herzegovina is a country in transition, and much has happened particularly in the organization of the criminal justice system. I am often able to communicate with colleagues from the Serbia, Croatia, Kosovo, etc., and I think that B–H, in the criminal justice system, has gone the furthest of all the countries of the region. I know that there exists great interest from these colleagues about what is happening in Bosnia. They look to us when gathering information on certain legal solutions.

What are the most likely developments you see happening and which would you like to see happening?

It is expected that there will be some evolution, within the court. The court is likely to expand its jurisdiction because eventually war crimes and similar offenses will diminish in frequency. The future of the court is likely to grow in the area of the prosecution of organized crime, corruption-related crimes, cybercrime, and the like.

What is most needed now to improve the system? In the end, what kind of justice system do you envisage for B–H in the future? Will it be a unified system across entities? How will it correspond with the other nations that once comprised Yugoslavia, the European Union, or the United Nation expectations?

Unfortunately the legal system and judicial power is a reflection of the constitutional concept, which currently exists in B–H. That is the way it is, and it is limited by the partition of the country into entities where any constitutional amendment toward unity is slight. However, the biggest need in the near future is the establishment of the Supreme Court. When I say this, I speak from a professional point of view and not from the aspect of politics. The existence of this court is the guarantor of protection of everyone in Bosnia–Herzegovina.

Thank you for your cooperation.

Comments of the Judiciary in Bosnia–Herzegovina

Dictates of the Dayton Peace Accord

The court system in Bosnia–Herzegovina was transformed following the end of the hostilities and the signing of The Dayton Peace Accords: General Framework Agreement for Peace in Bosnia and Herzegovina in November 1995. Article VI of this agreement addresses the creation of the Constitutional Court.

1. Composition. The Constitutional Court of Bosnia and Herzegovina shall have nine members.
   (a) Four members shall be selected by the House of Representatives of the Federation, and two members by the Assembly of the Republika Srpska. The remaining three members shall be selected by the President of the European Court of Human Rights after consultation with the Presidency.
   (b) Judges shall be distinguished jurists of high moral standing. Any eligible voter so qualified may serve as a judge of the Constitutional Court. The judges selected by the President of the European Court of Human Rights shall not be citizens of Bosnia and Herzegovina or of any neighboring state.
   (c) The term of judges initially appointed shall be five years, unless they resign or are removed for cause by consensus of the other judges. Judges initially appointed shall not be eligible for reappointment. Judges subsequently appointed shall serve until age 70, unless they resign or are removed for cause by consensus of the other judges.
   (d) For appointments made more than five years after the initial appointment of judges, the Parliamentary Assembly may provide by law for a different met of selection of the three judges selected by the President of the European Court of Human Rights.
2. Procedures
   (a) A majority of all members of the Court shall constitute a quorum.
   (b) The Court shall adopt its own rules of court by a majority of all members. It shall hold public proceedings and shall issue reasons for its decisions, which shall be published.
3. Jurisdiction. The Constitutional Court shall uphold this Constitution.
   (a) The Constitutional Court shall have exclusive jurisdiction to decide any dispute that arises under this Constitution between the Entities or between Bosnia and Herzegovina and an Entity or Entities, or between institutions of Bosnia and Herzegovina, including but not limited to:

- Whether an Entity's decision to establish a special parallel relationship with neighboring state is consistent with this Constitution, including provisions concerning the sovereignty and territorial integrity of Bosnia and Herzegovina.
- Whether any provision of an Entity's constitution or law is consistent with this Constitution.
- Disputes may be referred only by a member of the Presidency, by the Chair of the Council of Ministers, by the Chair or a Deputy Chair of either chamber of the Parliamentary Assembly, by one-fourth of the members of either chamber of the Parliamentary Assembly, or by one-fourth of either chamber a legislature of an Entity.

(b) The Constitutional Court shall also have appellate jurisdiction over issues under this Constitution arising out of a judgment of any other court in Bosnia and Herzegovina.

(c) The Constitutional Court shall have jurisdiction over issues referred by any court in Bosnia and Herzegovina concerning whether a law, on whose validity its decision depends, is compatible with this Constitution, with the European Convention for Human Rights and Fundamental Freedoms and its Protocols, or with the laws of Bosnia and Herzegovina; or concerning the existence of or the scope of a general rule of public international law pertinent to the court's decision.

4. Decisions. Decisions of the Constitutional Court shall be final and binding.

ICTY and the Balkan War Crimes Court

The International Criminal Tribunal or the Former Yugoslavia's (ICTY) War Crimes Chamber (WCC) of the Court of Bosnia and Herzegovina is the first permanent domestic court established to prosecute those people accountable for the human rights violations that occurred during the Bosnian phase (1992–1995) of the Balkan Wars of 1991–2002. The WCC is a joint endeavor between the ICTY and the UN Office of High Representative (OHR). The UN Security Council established the ICTY to prosecute four types of crimes:

1. Grave breaches of the 1949 Geneva conventions.
2. Violations of the laws of customs of war.
3. Genocide.
4. Crimes against humanity.

Although the changes relevant to the reconstruction of the courts in Bosnia–Herzegovina began in 2003, the WCC, itself, began operations in

Sarajevo on March 9, 2005. The WCC is unique in that it is designed to be part of the domestic legal system of the countries in which it operates—Bosnia–Herzegovina, Serbia, Croatia, etc. The WCC consists of five panels of two international judges and one national judge, with the latter presiding. This format is designed to transition to panels comprised of two national and one international judge and eventually (2010) to strictly national judges. The Appellate war crimes chamber consists of one panel with two international judges and one national judge, again with the national judge presiding (panel president). The WCC operates under the revised Criminal Code of Bosnia and Herzegovina and has original jurisdiction of issues involving international, interentity crimes, notably genocide, crimes against humanity, war crimes, and violations of laws of war. The WCC can initiate its own proceedings as well as hear cases referred to it by any court of Bosnia's two entities or the Brcko District.

Republic of Slovenia IV

MEŠKO GORAZD

Overview of the Slovenian Legal System

Republic of Slovenia is a democratic republic with the parliamentary system of democracy. According to the Constitution, Slovenia has an "incomplete bicameral system," meaning that the upper chamber (in Slovenian case, the National Council) does not have equal competences with the lower chamber (in the Slovenian case, the National Assembly), but it only supervises the work of the lower chamber.

Slovenia is organized in a two-railed system, which means the national level and the local municipal level to which self-government is guaranteed by the Constitution (Art. 9).

The **Slovene legal system** is a part of the continental legal system with the strong influence of German law and legal order. As the territory of today's Slovenia was a part of the Austrian Empire for a long time, the influence has rather historical roots. The law was transformed after the socialist models in the postwar time when the territory joined the Yugoslav republic. The impact of the institutions, such as socialized property, socialistic self-management, protection of workers and lower social class can still be found in the legal system today (such as denationalized procedures that are about to come to an end, a social security system, special arrangements of the labor and social courts, etc.).

After the favorable referendum on accession from Yugoslavia on June 25, 1991, the Slovene Assembly enacted the Basic Constitutional Charter on the Sovereignty and Independence of the Republic of Slovenia, which became the legal basis for its independence. The Constitution was adopted on December 23, 1991, and hereinafter the laws started to pass. Until they were put into force, the old Yugoslav Republic and Federal laws and rules were applicable. In this legislation activity, the legislator followed the German model in a number of the areas.

The legislation is still very prominent in Slovenia, which was especially necessary before joining the European Union (with taking over *aquis
communitaire*). Also the Constitution has been changed several times since
it was first enforced.

The **National Assembly** is composed of 90 deputies, of which two posts
are guaranteed for the representatives of ethnical minorities (Italian and
Hungarian). A deputy's term of office normally lasts four years.

The National Assembly of the Republic of Slovenia is the supreme representative and legislative institution, exercising legislative and electoral
powers as well as control over the Executive and the Judiciary. It also exercises control through parliamentary questions. In addition, the National
Assembly decides on the declaration of war or state emergency, and on the
use of armed forces. The National Assembly confirms the elections of deputies, and decides on the immunity of deputies and judges.

The **government** is a collective body presided by the prime minister.
Other members are the ministers responsible for a certain field of work. The
Government of the Republic of Slovenia is the executive body and, at the
same time, the supreme body of the state administration.

The **National Council** ("the upper chamber") is, in accordance with the
Constitution, the representative of social, economic, professional, and local
interest groups. The 40-member National Council comprises 22 representatives of local interests, 6 representatives of noncommercial activities, 4 representatives of employers and 4 of employees, and 4 representatives of farmers,
crafts, and trades, and independent professionals.

The **President of the Republic** represents the Republic of Slovenia and he
is the commander-in-chief of its defense forces (Art. 102 of the Constitution).
The president is elected by popular vote, in general elections by secret ballot
for a term of five years.

The President of the Republic: (a) calls elections to the National Assembly;
(b) promulgates laws; (c) appoints state officials where provided by law;
(d) appoints and recalls ambassadors and envoys of the Republic, and accepts
the letters of credence of foreign diplomatic representatives; (e) issues instru-
ments of ratification; (f) decides on the granting of clemency; (g) confers
decorations and honorary titles; and (h) performs other duties determined by
this Constitution. Where required by the National Assembly, the President of
the Republic must express his opinion on an individual issue.

Judicial Power

The task of the judiciary is to decide on the rights and duties of citizens, and
charges brought against them. All courts in the Republic of Slovenia are regular courts, and act in accordance with the principles of constitutionality,

independence, and the rule of law. The unified system of courts consists of courts with general and specialized jurisdiction. Courts with general jurisdiction include 44 district, 11 regional, and 4 higher courts, and the Supreme Court, while specialized courts comprise four labor courts and a social court (they rule on labor-related and social insurance disputes), and the Administrative Court, which provides legal protection in administrative affairs and has the status of a higher court.

Judges are independent in the performance of the judicial function (Art. 125 of the Constitution) and their office is permanent (Art. 129 of the Constitution). In Slovenia, there is no institute of a jury that passes verdicts of guilt; all the decisions are brought by the single judge or by the panel.

The Courts Act regulates the jurisdiction and composition of the courts in Slovenia. In general, there are two different kinds of courts of first instance (43 county courts and 11 district courts) and 2 stages of appeal: first one being High courts (4) and the second one the Supreme Court of the Republic of Slovenia. In some cases, the rulings of the later also can be examined by the Constitutional Court. Beside the general civil and criminal courts, there are several different types of specialized courts in Slovenia; their capabilities are defined by special acts and they proceed pursuant to special rules of procedure. Specialized courts (courts of specialized jurisdiction) have the jurisdiction *ratione materiae* and not *ratione personae* (there are no specialized courts for juvenile cases, for example). Specialized courts in the Republic of Slovenia include:

- Labor and social courts with a High Labor–Social Court (appeals court for labor and social courts)
- Administrative Court of the Republic of Slovenia

It is prohibited to establish extraordinary courts, as well as military courts in peacetime (Art. 126 of the Constitution). It is in the domain of the Civil District courts and of the Labor courts to organize the legal aid for the people that cannot afford to pay the costs of the legal procedure and their lawyers. The costs are paid from the budget, but the help is limited to the people who do not exceed the census of the legally determined minimal salary (Legal Aid Act of the Republic of Slovenia).

Courts of General Jurisdiction

Civil courts: The general civil jurisdiction lies on the civil courts. The rules regulating courtroom procedure are governed either by the Civil Procedure Act or Nonlitigious Civil Procedure Act. The courts of first instance are county and district courts. The jurisdiction between them is divided according to the subject of the trial.

Criminal Courts: The criminal procedure in Slovenia is a contradictory one with the strong influence of the "material truth" principle, which gives the judge an active position in the procedure and that is why Slovene criminal procedure is still rather inquisitorial (it has to be noticed, though, that the presumption of innocence is strictly followed). The criminal procedure law (governed by the Criminal Procedure Act) regulates courtroom procedure (together with the composition of the courts) as well as actions of the police and the investigational procedure in front of the court (the prehearing procedure).

Labor and Social Court

Jurisdiction of the labor and social courts is determined by the Labor and Social Courts Act. They have the position of district courts at the first instance and their appeal court is High Labor–Social Court in Ljubljana. Appeals against rulings of the High Labor–Social Court as well as extraordinary appeals are trialed by the Supreme Court of the Republic of Slovenia. Both first instance courts sit on the panels composed of one judge and two lay judges (one of them being elected by the National assembly from among employers/institutions and one of them being elected from among employees/insurants for the fixed period).

Administrative Court

The administrative court ensures, in accordance with the Administrative Dispute Act, judicial protection of rights and legal interest of individuals, legal, and other persons, if they hold rights and responsibilities, against decisions brought by administrative or other state bodies authorized by law. The establishment, organization, and function of the Administrative Court of Republic of Slovenia are governed by the Administrative Dispute Act. The court is situated in Ljubljana and has external departments in Nova Gorica, Celje, and Maribor. In Ljubljana, the workload is divided among five departments: public finances; property relations; protection of Constitutional rights; environment, spatial planning, and construction; and customs and other taxes.

The Supreme Court

The Supreme Court is the highest appellate court in the state. It functions primarily as a court of cassation. It is a court of appellate jurisdiction in criminal and civil cases, in commercial lawsuits, in cases of administrative review, and in labor and social security disputes. It is the court of the third instance in almost all the cases within its jurisdiction. The grounds of appeal to the Supreme Court (defined as extraordinary legal remedies in Slovenian procedural laws) are therefore limited to issues of substantive law and to the most severe breaches of procedure. The Supreme Court also handles the uniform case law. To decide on questions related to the uniform practice of the courts, the court sits on a panel composed of all the judges of the Supreme Court (*obča seja*).

Constitutional Court

In relation to other state bodies, the Constitutional Court is an autonomous and independent state body. It regulates its organization and work by the rules of procedure and other general acts. The existing organization is determined by the Constitutional Court Act, Rules of Procedure of the Constitutional Court and the Rules on the Internal Organization and Office Operations of the Constitutional Court. The Constitutional Court is composed of nine judges, elected on the proposal of the president of the Republic by the National Assembly. The judges are elected for a term of nine years and may not be reelected. The president of the Constitutional Court shall be elected by the judges from among themselves for a term of three years. Most powers of the Constitutional Court are explicitly determined in the Constitution; however, they also may be determined by statute.

Court of Audits

The Court of Audit entered the Slovene legal system with the new Constitution. It is the highest body for supervising state accounts, the state budget, and all public spending (Art. 150 of the Constitution); it may audit any act on past operations as well as the act on the planned operations of public fund users. The Court of Audit cannot be categorized within any of the three branches of power: legislative, executive, or judicial. The court is independent in the performance of its duties and bound by the Constitution and laws. Its functioning is determined in the Court of Audit Act as well as in a number of other laws dealing with functioning of public fund users.

Ombudsman

The institute of the human right ombudsman has been created in Slovenian law according to the Scandinavian model and is part of the new constitution adopted in 1991 (Art. 159 of the Constitution). His/her function is a constitutional category that does not fall under the executive, judicial, or legislative branch of authority; therefore, it is not part of any mechanism of authority, but rather acts as an overseer of authority since as an institution it restricts its capricious encroachment of human rights and fundamental freedoms. In his/her work, the ombudsman is not only limited to handling direct violations defined as human rights and freedoms in the constitution, moreover, he/she may act in any case whatsoever dealing with a violation of any right of an individual arising from a holder of authority. He/she can intervene also in the case of unfair and poor state administration in relation to the individual. The Human Rights Ombudsman is elected by the Parliament upon the nomination made by the president of the Republic for the term of six years. According to the Constitution, special ombudsmen for the rights of citizens also may be established by law for particular fields, but that provision has not been realized in the practice as of yet. The position and functioning of the institute of the ombudsman is regulated by the Human Rights Ombudsman Act.

Reference

Čarni, M., & Košak, S. (2006). A guide to the Republic of Slovenia legal system and legal research. Retrieved from http://www.nyulawglobal.org/globalex/slovenia.htm

Interview of Judge Aleksander Karakaš, Criminal Judiciary Department of Maribor District Court, Slovenia

5

MEŠKO GORAZD

Contents

The Interview

The Interview

Describe some of your background and career.

I am a lawyer with a university degree and 20 years working experience—somewhere in the middle of my career. I completed my primary and secondary school education (*Gimnazija*, grammar school) in my hometown, Maribor, and after military service in 1985, I continued studying at the Law Faculty, Ljubljana University. I had a good quality education, and I will always remember my college days as a curriculum free from ideology, a broad range of knowledge from lecturers, and piles of books I read on their recommendation, and discussions in "closed groups" of students, or wider circles when it was already becoming clear that we were on the brink of great social changes, meaning the end of a certain historical era.

After finishing exams, I chose to study, as my undergraduate thesis, the topic, Subculture in Prisons, because it was first being discovered and widely discussed (theoretically and empirically), especially among American criminologists. This issue also has been acknowledged in other countries, which I covered in my work as well. My thesis was successfully defended in 1990, and that year I started work as an intern at the Maribor Higher Court.

This was a typical professional path then, and considerably less uncertain as compared to today, when Slovenia is faced with a large number of university graduates from three Law Faculties. After completing their studies, the majority of these graduates still do not know where and when they will start an internship.

The internship proceeded according to a predetermined, individual program, and included following the work of practically all, the then, Lower Court departments: public prosecutor and departments for internal affairs (police). As an intern, I also had the option to do one of the tasks independently. Judges (that is, a general mentor and a mentor in an individual department) who evaluated the internship at the end, were responsible for program's completion. A positive evaluation of the internship was a precondition for the bar exam. That is equivalent to today's state judicial examination, which is one of the key tests in a legal career, because it provides the "ticket" for independent work or, in other words, without this exam, every important legal profession for a young professional is literally out of reach.

I passed the exam in May 1992 and was reemployed in the Maribor Higher Court. Due to personnel needs and despite my interest expressed in criminal law, I continued working as a legal assistant in the civil judiciary department under my previous mentor. My primary tasks consisted of preparing reports for meetings of the Appeal Chambers, and writing drafts of court decisions. I carried out both tasks with pleasure as they allowed specialist autonomy, and width and flexibility of civil law disciplines. It also seemed a good foundation for my professional growth. My knowledge and practical experience kept increasing substantially, as did my professional confidence. The latter is one of the key conditions for independent and responsible legal work. Without hesitation, I can say that I felt capable of performing the work of a civil procedure judge.

Due to the planned judicial reform, election to the position of judge was uncertain and, as old love does not die, I was employed at the Law Faculty at Maribor University, in 1994, after being elected as an assistant to the department for criminal law and criminal process law. My tasks were not that different from the tasks of other assistants around the world. Firstly, I was assigned to work with students (carrying out practical lectures and seminars, technical implementation of exams, etc.), but I also had obligations in the department for postgraduate studies from the above mentioned areas, which I had to complete within a set period. There was also my own, growing, research "garden," consisting of a wider range of topics from which I first remember organized criminality. My postgraduate studies and already commenced independent research demanded participation in scientific and professional meetings at home (Rogaška Slatina, Portorož, and Ljubljana) and abroad (Croatia, Austria, and Germany), publishing articles in various publications (*Pravna praksa, Pravnik, Revija za kriminalistiko in kriminologijo, Hrvatski ljetopis za kazneno pravo I praksu, Iudex*, etc.), and guest lectures at foreign universities or institutes.

The last task proved to be of great help in my master's work, titled *Minor (criminal) offense, de minimis lex non curat?* This way I was able to gather all the materials necessary for my assignment at the Law Faculty at Graz University, and at the European Institute in Amsterdam, which were clearly divided according to the main questions and after consulting with the professors from those universities, and then processing the topic from a legal and theoretical point of view.

I primarily relied on the findings of German theorists on the teachings of criminal offense. I was skeptical of the Slovenian legislative regulation, in which minor criminal offenses were listed under reasons to expel illegality, and proposed its allocation under reasons to omit a criminal prosecution, whereby the criminal proceedings should formally end. I defended my work successfully in 1999 and thereby received a master's degree in Criminal Law.

I left the Law Faculty, despite the aforementioned achievement, and was elected to be a judge in the Criminal Court department of the Local Court in Maribor. Here, allow me to roughly explain to the foreign reader that the jurisdiction of Slovenian Criminal Trial Courts is divided between Local Courts and District Courts. The first have jurisdiction over criminal offenses punishable with a fine or a penalty involving deprivation of liberty for up to three years. The second type of courts have jurisdiction over all serious criminal offenses and offenses against reputations and good names, if they were committed by means of public information.

This division between Local Courts and District Courts is reflected in the legal processes, in that Local Courts pass judgments according to the provisions of the shortened criminal procedure, which, by definition, should be simpler and faster; whereas the extended regular procedure is intended for District Courts. Another visible difference is that Local Courts are always presided over by professional judges, and District Courts have senates, usually comprised of professionals as well as lay judges; the number of judges depending on the difficulty of the criminal offense on trial. In the latter example, exceptions, with merely one individual judge, are very rare.

Considering the differences described, it is understandable that judges usually begin their career in Local Courts and then proceed to District Courts. Due to the low interest in the profession of judge, it is possible that attorneys from "outside the courts," with a longer period of employment, can apply for such positions. Trial at the Courts of Appeal is entrusted to Higher Courts, with authorization for annulment and reform, and, at the third stage, we have the Supreme Court, with the same level of authorization, but its scope is somewhat smaller.

Later, I worked as a judge, individually, until 2003, when I was appointed as judge to the criminal judiciary department of Maribor District Court, where I worked until 2005. Then, I was appointed as judge in the criminal judiciary department in the Maribor Higher Court, where I still work today.

My general impression on the time spent working in the trial courts is that the inflow of matters to the Local Courts, of approximately 400 cases per judge, is too large, despite regulations and some new selection mechanisms (deviation from criminal prosecution—diversion). And procedures, though for minor (sometimes trivial) criminal offenses, are normally simplified, they are still complicated and considering the means and quantity of judiciary work invested, they are inefficient.

The inflow of cases to District Courts is considerably lower, but the extent of proceedings is wider by definition and, consequently, also lengthy. This alone would not be wrong if a substantial part of the proceedings was given to organizational and technical questions instead of focusing on the true purpose of criminal proceedings.

As I left for the Courts of Appeal, the situation did not change. On the contrary, I am often faced with questions connected with the completion of applications, costs of criminal proceedings, and other issues, which could hardly be classified under the central questions of these proceedings and which could be resolved at other levels without damage to clients. Impressions, especially from trial courts, are partly confirmed by results of the analysis of the process, and the duration of criminal proceedings, in the Republic of Slovenia (*Analize poteka in trajanja kazenskih postopkov v. Republiki Sloveniji*) for the period between 2002 and 2004, performed by The Institute of Criminology of the Law Faculty in Ljubljana (*Bošnjak M.* (ed.) ur.), *Potek kazenskih postopkov v. Sloveniji-Analiza stanja in predlogi za spremembe*, Pravna praksa, Ljubljana, 2005. Results imply that "fault" for delays in criminal proceedings, and, consequently, their prolongation, is distributed between reasons of a "conceptual nature" when we do not know which of the three historic types of criminal proceedings should be used, and reasons of an organizational and technical nature, which are considerably increased after every legislative change.

Besides my work as a judge and in the organization of the Center for Education, I also participate in various forms of passing on my experience to younger colleagues. These are normally shorter lectures or proceedings of actual questions and practical problems. Lately I have been leading simulations of main trials, where older judges try to prepare new judges or legal associates, in a direct manner, for situations they will surely have to get used to and respond to, in the future. Last year I was finally elected external associate for criminal law and criminal process law and I am, thereby, cooperating on practical lessons at the Law Faculty again. An important difference from before is that I can now also offer students textbook explanations, as well as actual cases from my work, which confirm certain theoretical findings or suggest other solutions, which I then try to identify, together with students, and test the solutions in short discussions. Their response is mutually beneficial. Students get to cooperate in a current issue, and I receive feedback, as a judge, on my decisions, which are not always straightforward.

Are you satisfied with your career development and the responsibility that it entails?

Generally speaking, I am not surprised by my career development. My ambitions have always been aimed at working in a court or in a science department, and I have always felt at home in classrooms among younger judges or students. Other legal environments, such as notaries or insurance companies, seem foreign to me, and I do not know how I would perform that type of work. If I look around, the above-stated legal areas show that, despite my focus on criminal law, I could have worked in the civil law department with the same level of interest if I had not been presented with the opportunity to work at the Faculty in 1994.

In an intellectual sense, my work as a judge is an excellent interplay of four basic contradictions: abstract versus tangible, general versus specific, objective versus subjective, and content versus form. From a methodological point of view, this is a path where thesis and antithesis are tested—with the aim to be regulated in future synthesis—to find resolutions to disputes between clients, or the latent conflict between an individual and society, which arise from a criminal offense. When we combine both, we get the work that faces an individual with many challenges, and work that will undoubtedly provide an individual with inner fulfillment. A judge also has to have a very good education, be generally well-informed, and excel in professionalism—all of which is the aim of the additional education that adds necessary freshness to the profession.

It is typical intellectual work with results that are subject to further testing, either by specialists or the broader public. But, on the other hand, I never imagined that this work would be so demanding from a professional point of view; that it activates the conscience, that it is sometimes accompanied by bitter moments, and that it requires some upsets to your private life, which is very important for me as a father of three.

As it is typical for judges, coming from a mixed type of criminal proceedings, Slovenian judges take responsibility for the correct decision in individual matters, but not merely in a legal manner, but also in the true sense. By becoming involved participants, the influence of clients on the outcome of individual proceedings is limited, their undefined burdens are considerably smaller compared to ours, at least at the legal level. If we add the changing nature of criminal legislation, high standards in decision making set by the Supreme Court and Constitutional Court, and the lack of preparation by participants to cooperate in these proceedings, the work is anything but mundane and routine, and far from being a predictable path toward a peaceful retirement.

What are some of the changes you have witnessed?

The most important changes include the adoption of the Slovenian Constitution in 1991; notification on succession of the recognition of the International Covenant on Civil and Political Rights, in 1992; and the ratification of the European Convention for the Protection of Human Rights and Fundamental Freedoms, in 1994. All three acts, and the later acts based on them, present a new paradigm in processing criminal offenses and their perpetrators. If the understanding of criminal law, in its broader sense, was corrected by individual guaranteed starting points in the past, the situation is now reversed. I can, therefore, consider past changes to the criminal legislation and to the organizational level of authorities processing criminal offenses as merely foreseen, despite their extent and meaning, which had to happen.

The other question arising has to be how consistent and successful we have been in implementing the aforementioned paradigm. The processes of democratization was not performed in a laboratory, but in a society that was also undergoing a change in the economical and ownership structure, was opening up to other markets, and was also faced with occurrences that could not be evaluated, much less provided with a criminal legal definition (for example, during privatization), or in new forms of crime (organized crime, computer-related crime, etc.) where the proceedings required special effort, even in developed democratic countries—sometimes to the cost of human rights.

The constitutional division of authority was the first among the external changes that had an important effect on the work of the criminal judiciary. This does not function according to the expectations of the legislative and executive authority, as these two have to adapt their expectations to court decisions. The latter does not always prove easy in Slovenia. Incomprehension of the constitutional role of courts and an open, not merely verbal, aversion toward the decisions of courts are frequent, and create a mutual lack of respect, despite the mentioned division.

The decisions of the Constitutional Court presents the second important factor. According to the Constitution and the Constitutional Court Act, their subject matter jurisdiction is relatively wide, and, in the event of nullification of legal decisions, individual legal provision, or even a court decision are binding on all courts. This creates a new legal corpus that has a considerable influence on the work of the criminal judiciary, that is, on the legality of its actions.

The third factor is politics, which is rarely derived from specialist platforms in creating strategies on processing crime, and which sometimes cannot hide their ambition toward a ruling in their favor. I do not wish to guess whether this is due to individuals lacking a legal education, a short democratic tradition, a low level of culture, or trivial circumstances, or due to a certain number of politicians and affiliated economists either facing, or convicted of, criminal proceedings.

Bearing in mind the constitutional, compulsory independence of courts, conflict becomes inevitable in any case. Externally, this can be seen by the fact that politics define the material status of judges, using legislative and executive authority, whereby the status of judges is lesser when compared to the status of representatives of both authorities. Slovenian judges have proved this twice before the Constitutional Court. Here, I have to assess, with a bitter aftertaste, that both decisions are yet to be exercised.

Constitutional Court and Criminal Courts must separately ensure a certain level of quality of trials. An increase in quality is always welcome, but a decline in quality can be ruinous. Therefore, the real question is whether, today, the quality of trials is adequate. According to statistics, criminal courts are undoubtedly working, so the answer has to be positive, but it could be considerably better if there was conceptually clear legislation, with a less complicated implementation process, and if we had a standard number of judicial personnel, without the departure of entire generations of excellent lawyers, to profitable professions. Stable and predictable conditions would surely have a beneficial effect on the improved quality of decision making. This way we would not only achieve a higher level of respect for court decisions, but also a higher degree of regulation of society than has happened so far.

Stable and predictable conditions would surely have a beneficial effect on the improved quality of decision making. This would not merely lead to a higher level of respect for court decisions, it would also mean decisions would have a larger effect in regulating society than so far. The general impression is that court decisions objectively, and subjectively, deal with society's fringe issues, while the "right" questions are reserved for the legislator and government acts that can neutralize, or even annul, the effects of the courts' decisions.

The above stated can also provide a partial answer to the question of whether being a judge in Slovenia is harder than it was in the past. I confirm this with the general finding that the current path toward a correct decision, which has to be made in a reasonable time, is longer and more complicated than it once was. Due to the often changing legislation, we are also losing the healthy routine and predictability of proceedings, the efficiency of which increasingly depends on the individual efforts of each judge. If the judge was merely a component of a dominant, settled system before the changes, today they are the carrier, and not even by their own will, which is visible in an increasing workload for individual cases, and a wider social "draft" than in the past.

What is your personal philosophy as a judge?

The role of courts should remain as it is, that is, deciding on matters that cannot be resolved by legislative and executive authorities due to their close involvement. Courts should rule, not adopt laws, implement them, or perform tasks connected to the fulfillment of various politically legitimate goals, such as, for example, wishing to reduce the prison population, achieving a higher level of efficiency in implementing court decisions, etc. Any type of judicial activism challenges the court's impartiality and is, therefore, better suited for more qualified services to deal with. All this requires a complete and diversified social system, able to provide reliable information as a basis for possible legislative changes, for certain occurrences, or serve as relevant feedback in additional court rulings.

Generally speaking, it is hard to say that an individual part of the Criminal Court is not working according to previous projections, and is, thereby, redundant. Sometimes the efficiency of a particular component, which is the subject of frequent legislative intervention, is questionable. For example, I would like to mention the area of misdemeanors where processing is currently limited, due to the large number of cases (according to some calculations, there are over 4,000) and the courts' workload with new cases. This resulted in a partial amnesty and in reestablishment of the system in 2005, with the emphasis on efficiency. The number of misdemeanors remained practically unchanged, and the new system has already undergone six legislative changes, which is not exactly persuasive to the success of the changes.

The courts are an authoritative system, formalized, and rigid, expecting others to adapt to it. In relation to the community, they are part of the public service that has to operate efficiently. These two aspects are not always compatible. The first implies superiority and inaccessibility; the second suggests openness and flexibility. If these starting points were widely accepted, it would spare us many misunderstandings in executing judiciary power. This would also mean that we would have to find a way for the community to get the necessary insight into judicial work. A substantial part of this has been done by putting information on the Web sites of courts, so the interested public can find information on the state of cases, and perform individual actions electronically. There is still a certain information and communication gap in relationships with the media, although some courts have appointed public relations managers, and thereby the community should not be deprived of any information.

A special problem occurs when courts and other authorities do not coordinate work due to inadequate legislation. It is becoming a rule in Slovenia that changes to criminal legislation are not accompanied by changes in other related areas, which creates asymmetry and, consequently, inefficiency of the complete system. One recent example includes substituting enforcement of prison sentences, which is entrusted to social service centers to implement, without simultaneously changing the organizational legislation. The fear exists that substituting enforcement of prison sentences is not practically implemented, despite the courts' decisions, as the centers for social services do not have any internal regulations to base it on.

According to my ideas, the criminal legal system should have the form of a wedge. Authorities, or individuals handling the worst and most demanding types of crime, would be on top. I conditionally call this the repressive part. It is the most exposed part and, as such, it should have a special organization and be dissociated from other components. I mean it should have the best judges, support staff, stimulating working conditions, emphasized safety for family members, etc.

The second part (I call it the consensual model) should serve to hear other forms of criminality by finding various types of consensus between the accused and the injured party, and others involved, with the goal of establishing a new legal balance. I justify its existence for certain types of criminal offenses, such as negligent criminal offenses and perpetrators, especially those without a criminal record, and with more sympathy for the injured party whose lives are affected in the criminal proceedings. The role of judges should be controlling, while concrete tasks should be entrusted to others to implement as mediators, in the most general meaning of the word.

The third and most comprehensive part is the preventive part. This is the first membrane of the immune system, with the broadest inclusion and attraction of the largest possible number of individuals, and social organizations that provide peaceful symbiosis in society, in a rarely visible manner. I do not see judges in this third part, though exceptions are possible.

What are some of the accomplishments and problems that you have experienced in your career?

I honestly cannot think of a program that specialists would deem successful. A possible exception would be the introduction of consensual approaches for solving criminal cases (diversion). This would be planned in advance and developed in a positive direction. A negative exception would be the afore-mentioned alternative enforcement of a prison sentence, which has insufficient regulation and goes through many tests that could be avoided. The problem is bigger, as this type of enforcement of a sentence is generally accepted at the conceptual level, but the implementation system is not developed enough to ensure the concept can be implemented.

As in the rest of the world, Slovenia is in a period of validating human rights as the only instrument to curb any arbitrary action of the state. On the other hand, we are witnessing a transformation of old forms of criminality to other forms, or the emergence of new forms of crime that require special-ized responses. As we know, according to the demands of the European Court for Human Rights, all of this has to happen within a reasonable time period. Therefore, the fundamental question is how to achieve all of the above. I do not have the answer, but we will certainly have to work hard to build and establish a legal system that operates in all types of conditions, not merely the specific and most convenient ones.

What are some of the most difficult challenges that the courts face today?

Externally, the biggest problem for the Slovenian court system has to be case backlogs. If we observe the problem internally, we can discover that the accu-mulation of cases is a consequence of court overload. The number of cases assigned to a court keeps increasing every year, and—with some exceptions—the problem is being resolved merely by using programs that are primarily based on reducing the number of cases. This seems like a deteriorating form, reminiscent of working practices in socialist times. Courts are exhausting themselves, and every new program is accompanied by weariness. The con-tents and legal accuracy of the decision in an individual matter are no longer priorities. We do not need to warn what this means from the aspect of legiti-macy of the court system.

As the problem above has been present for over a decade, it is difficult for me to say how to resolve it. The trend of constant changes to legislation should be stopped, and we should try to test the concepts of laws on which life together is commonly based and which presently exist. This is a demanding task as Slovenian governments are coalitions where solutions are found by compromises, but, as concepts, they do not "quite" function.

Then there is the legislative procedure in which members of Parliament can change the contents of the law with amendments, and distance it from the original idea. As legal concepts are not fulfilled on their own, we must assess their reflection on the procedural, legal, and organizational areas, whereby the notion that these areas function, according to certain ideas, has to be considered. As well as that, their compatibility is an essential condition for the system's completion and its smooth operation. Besides the alternative implementation of a prison sentence mentioned above, our lack in success is also proven by house arrest, established in 2008, where we still cannot assess

whether it happened due to a changed perspective on the manner of enforcing a prison sentence, or merely due to overcrowded prisons. We do not have
a special procedure to assess the conditions for its imposition, and we do not
even have judges who deal specifically with these type of questions.

The situation was similar in other numerous changes to the laws on criminal proceedings, which usually brought more work to judges and few instru-
ments to perform the work faster or more easily. Much was tested at the
organizational level where changes can be made easily. This way, the chairper-
sons of courts were given higher jurisdiction and their decisions created faster
hearings of individual cases, the staff number in courts was improved, special
emphasis was paid toward their education, work, and technical conditions, so
their operations were improved.

The question is what else could we do to solve backlogs and their reoccur-
rence. We are in a position to have a relatively good racing car, but the track
keeps getting longer with every lap we make. Therefore, we are aiming our hopes
at out-of-court settlements and simplification of procedures, knowing that one
day we will be forced to answer the following questions as a broad social community: "Why do we need courts in Slovenia so much? Why do we go to courts?"
Considering my experience so far, these will be the most difficult questions.

Could you explain your theory and practice?

If we agree that the law is not a science, then there should not be many differences between theory and practice. Theory marks the way for practical
work, where theoretical findings are most efficiently tested. The most important thing for practices is to follow the newest theoretical findings, but, on the
other hand, theorists have to know what is happening in practice. I am optimistic about this. Court decisions that cite theorists are not rare anymore and
judiciary practice—at least in the highest courts—does not overlook the theoretical parts. The first has to be due to literature that judges receive to inform
them, and, secondly, it has to do with the available electronic databases that
considerably relieve the process of monitoring judicial work. I would like to
add the presence of theorists, as *amicus curiae,* in adopting decisions of the
Constitutional Court and principled legal opinions of the Supreme Court, for
specialized meetings and judicial training, where theorists are always present
as lecturers or moderators.

On the whole, Slovenian courts could benefit most from research dealing
with court efficiency, whereas Slovenian society would benefit from research
focusing on fixing the inflow of cases to courts. This could be followed by
research uncovering whether courts are working equally for all, or if someone is being discriminated against unjustifiably, and other questions aimed
at testing the court's functional adequacy. Excluding some exceptions, today
all of the above are relatively unknown. Research on special types of crime,
such as organized crime, white-collar crime, and other types of crime related
to the modern way of living, which challenge the courts today, would be the
most useful for criminal courts. Organized crime started in the 1990s, which

meant that relatively much time had to pass for things to calm down. With white-collar crime, it seems we do not even have a settled economic environment that would enable us to recognize and eliminate negative occurrences at a general level. Consequently, criminal courts appear to lack preparation and seem confused to the outside, all of which could be different if certain empirically confirmed findings were available to serve as a foundation for more specialized hearings, with results that would not disappoint us.

Finally, there is research dealing with the possible simplification of proceedings that could help make them more established, and also mean they would be used, with reservations, if they turn out to be a risk to the protection of human rights.

Where do you get your information on theory?

I almost always get the first pieces of information online. Then I check scientific and specialized publications. Books are also an important resource I use in my work. Access to these sources is good and has to be maintained. Finally, considering research—in the sense of scientific methods—I do not think courts would do this on their own, especially in open cases. There is supervision of the work of an individual judge, a department, or the whole court; not to supervise decisions, but rather the operation of the judge or the department. The aim is to record the situation and develop an estimation to serve as a basis for possible measures to eliminate established flaws in operations, and thereby improve the situation. However, these measures can mean the beginning of the end for a judge's career. This is [a] compilation of dates with specific internal intentions, but it does not exclude the fact that they can be an indirect indicator for other facts related to the work of judges or courts.

Is there any cross-border connections in your work?

Events abroad usually do not affect our work directly. If they do, then it has to do with decisions of the European Court for Human Rights, or the Court of Justice of the European Community, which have the largest effect, and are also part of valid legal regulation. Otherwise, events abroad are monitored merely for information purposes. Due to technical advances, the development of foreign judicial practices is increasingly present where, at least in the stages before decisions, possible solutions can be controlled. Personal cross-border connections are at two levels. Firstly, through an individual case that is becoming more frequent with the establishment of the European Arrest Warrant, and surrender, along with some other international acts, and then through various judicial training. The latter is increasing due to Slovenia joining the European Union, but many are omitted due to lack of time. This way the damage is doubled as we miss out on a opportunity for quality training as well the chance for better cohesion of the profession. Despite this, I was able to participate in a practical learning program in

Austria, attend seminars in Belgium, and training in a judicial school in Germany. A special network for judges exists within various professional organizations, such as the European Judicial Network, though their recognition is relatively weak in Slovenia.

Were there any effects on the work in your courts following the September 11, 2001, attacks?

The development of events following that date did not affect my work or the work of courts in Slovenia in any way.

Do you have any closing remarks?

Although we can detect certain positive shifts occasionally, I am not satisfied with the development of the criminal material and criminal procedural law, in general. The Criminal Code came into force recently in Slovenia, with many not-so-small changes, and probably the lowest consensus of specialists so far; and we have the Criminal Procedure Act, which is changed too frequently for a law system. It has undergone eight changes since 1995, not including the interventions of the Constitutional Court, and we are faced with new changes again. These are supposed to provide a new intermediate procedure—negotiations between the state prosecutor and the accused prior to indictment—and which should also eliminate the position of the investigating judge. We are a typical transitional country, lacking clear concepts in two main areas. That is, our concepts are rough and, therefore, more or less not functioning when it comes to implementation. This disease is then treated with a new dose of changes, until the next disappointment, when it is established that the idea could not be implemented, or it simply does not work.

Reservations of the judicial practice, toward changes, as a consequence of insecurity in using such laws, is not surprising. Ultimately, it is always the judges who have to conduct trials according to bad laws, and the ones who take responsibility for our actions before clients and the wider public. The situation described is bad for a modern legal system and its subsystem dealing with human rights, as a cornerstone of a democratic society, and it demands a return to a clear, simple, predictable system, which should be attainable, considering the degree of legal development and knowledge. My suggestion is not specific on purpose as the content of concepts—that they have to fit tested democratic standards—probably does not have to be emphasized separately. Nor is it as important, as it is a fact that they are enforced in an understandable and acceptable manner on a daily basis. That is why, as a judge and as a citizen, I want a firm and clear normative frame, upgraded with orderly judiciary practice, and a broadly theoretical background. This will make a judge's work considerably easier, and a citizen's fate more predictable.

Canada   V

RICHARD PARENT

Overview of the Canadian Legal System

The organization of Canada's judicial system is a function of Canada's Constitution. By virtue of the Constitution Act of 1867, the authority for the judicial system in Canada is divided between the federal government and the 10 provincial governments. The provinces are given jurisdiction over "the administration of justice," which includes "the constitution, organization, and maintenance" of the courts, both civil and criminal as well as the power to appoint "provincial court" judges. The power to appoint the judges of federal courts and the superior courts in the provinces is given to the federal government. All members of the judiciary in Canada, regardless of the court, are drawn from the legal profession. The independence of the judiciary in Canada is guaranteed both explicitly and implicitly by different parts of the Constitution of Canada. This independence is understood to consist in security of tenure, security of financial remuneration, and institutional administrative independence.

In Canada, the provincial governments have jurisdiction over both the Constitution, organization and maintenance of, and the appointment of judges to, the lowest level of courts ("provincial courts"), while the federal government has authority over the Constitution, organization and maintenance of, and the appointment of judges to, the Supreme Court of Canada, the Federal Court of Appeal, and the Federal Court. Authority over the superior courts in each province is shared between the provincial and federal governments.

Supreme Court of Canada

The courts in Canada are organized in a four-tiered structure. The Supreme Court of Canada sits at the apex of the structure and, consistent with its role as "a General Court of Appeal for Canada," hears appeals from both the federal court system, headed by the Federal Court of Appeal and the provincial court systems, headed in each province by that province's Court of Appeal. In contrast to its counterpart in the United States, the Supreme Court of Canada functions as a *national*, and not merely *federal*, court of last resort. In most cases, appeals are heard by the Court only if leave is first given. Leave will be given by the court when a case involves a question of public importance, or if it raises an important issue of law or of mixed law and fact. In sum, the broad scope of the Supreme Court of Canada's jurisdiction illustrates how it differs from that of many continental European and Latin and South American countries, where it is not unusual for there to be separate courts of last resort for both constitutional law and administrative law cases in addition to a general court of appeal.

Federal Courts

The Federal Court of Appeal and the Federal Court are historical successors of the Exchequer Court of Canada, which had jurisdiction only over revenue, the Crown in Right of Canada as litigant, industrial and intellectual property, admiralty, and a few other subject matters regulated by federal legislation. The Federal Courts now additionally have the power of judicial review with respect to decisions of federal administrative tribunals and jurisdiction over claims with respect to other matters falling within federal legislative jurisdiction.

Provincial Superior Courts

Superior courts exist in each province and territory. They include both a court of general trial jurisdiction and a provincial court of appeal. A significant feature of these courts is that jurisdiction is not limited to matters over which the provincial governments have legislative jurisdiction. In this respect, they are very different from the state courts in the United States. These provincial courts have jurisdiction over disputes arising in many of the areas over which the federal government is granted legislative jurisdiction in the Constitution Act of 1867, for example, criminal law and banking.

Provincial Courts

At the bottom of the hierarchy are the courts typically described as "provincial courts." These courts are generally divided into various divisions defined by the subject matter of their respective jurisdictions; hence, one usually finds a Traffic Division, a Small Claims Division, a Family Division, a Criminal Division, and so on. Provincial courts handle the overwhelming majority of cases that come into the Canadian court system. They deal with a broad range of criminal matters, much of the litigation in the area of family law, and all of the civil litigation in which the amount at issue is relatively small. If the average citizen has occasion to become involved in a dispute that requires adjudication on the part of a court, the likelihood is that he or she will appear before one of these courts.

References

Department of Justice. Canada's System of Justice. The judicial structure. How courts are organized. Retrieved from http://www.justice.gc.ca/eng/dept-min/pub/just/07.html

Supreme Court of Canada. Canadian Judicial System. Retrieved from http://www.scc-csc.gc.ca/court-cour/sys/index-eng.asp

Interview of Judge Wally Oppal, Queens Council, Supreme Court of British Columbia

RICHARD PARENT

Contents

Introduction

This interview explores the views of the Honorable Wally Oppal, retired Judge of the Supreme Court of British Columbia, and former Attorney General of British Columbia, on several aspects of law enforcement in Canada. As a practicing lawyer and later as a Supreme Court Judge, Wally Oppal went onto politics where he became the Attorney General of the province. Oppal discusses the various positions that he has held during his professional career, his insight into policing, and the future of criminal justice in Canada.

Among them were Queen's Counsel and Crown Counsel. The appointment to Queen's Counsel (QC) is a designation afforded to an attorney, recognizing individual merit, usually after years of community service and advocacy. The term Crown Counsel (CC) refers to attorneys that are prosecutors working for the provincial or federal governments in Canada in proceedings under the Charter of Rights and Freedoms and other federal statutes. Crown Attorneys are not elected and can be removed from their position only pursuant to employment agreements.

The interview took place on July 20, 2009, in Vancouver, British Columbia, Canada.

Career Highlights

Wally Oppal was born in Vancouver, British Columbia, in 1940. He attended the University of British Columbia's law school in the 1960s, graduating with a law degree. For over 12 years, he practiced law in the Vancouver area. Then, in the 1970s, he became a member of Crown Counsel, prosecuting cases for the government before being appointed to the Bench.

In 1981, Wally Oppal was appointed to the County Court of Vancouver and, in 1985, to the Supreme Court of British Columbia. In 2003, he was appointed to the British Columbia Court of Appeal where he served until he resigned to seek election to the provincial government legislature. He is the second Indo-Canadian in the province to have held the title of Attorney General (AG) of British Columbia.

Oppal served in the provincial cabinet as Attorney General of British Columbia and Minister responsible for multiculturalism. Oppal's dedication to the Canadian legal system is illustrated by the various positions that he has held throughout the years that include the president of the Law Courts Education Society of British Columbia, director of Family Services of Greater Vancouver, and the director of the B.C. Coalition for Safer Communities. One of the greatest achievements of his career has been as the author of the report of the Independent Commission of Inquiry into Policing in British Columbia. The document has served as a cornerstone for policing within the province of British Columbia. Throughout his career, Oppal has focused his time and energy on improving social justice and community safety.

The Interview

Honorable Wally Oppal, to start this interview and to better situate our readers, please describe your professional experience that led you from being a lawyer to a Supreme Court Judge to the Attorney General.

Well, I was born in Vancouver, grew up on Vancouver Island, and went to high school there. Later, I returned to Vancouver and graduated from the University of British Columbia, from law school. I was lucky in the late 1960s as there were lots of jobs for young lawyers. I ended up taking a job in a private law office in a suburb of Vancouver where we did a lot of prosecutions on behalf of the municipality as well as defense work. So, I was fortunate in that I learned to be both an advocate for the government (prosecutions on behalf of Crown Counsel) as well as an advocate for the accused (defense work). As time went on, I managed to be involved in some high profile cases that led me to work with the police, prosecuting major criminal cases. I guess you would say that I was at the right place at the right time.

Before I became a judge, I probably prosecuted 50 murder cases. I was also a special prosecutor on two of the police murders that took place in the province. They were horrible killings of police officers. I took the cases right from the bail hearings through to the Supreme Court of Canada. These cases were particularly challenging because they were given so much media attention. As

Crown Counsel, we had to thoroughly prepare and leave nothing to chance. Actually, one of the police murder trials resulted in the accused being the last person in Canada to be sentenced to be hanged. The laws in Canada have since been changed and the convicted individual is still alive today.

The early 1970s were a time of great growth in the Vancouver area, the city was expanding and, in 1972, they built a new courthouse in Delta. I was asked to do some of the Crown prosecutions, working alongside with police. Myself and another lawyer practiced law for approximately 12 years. In 1981, I was appointed to what was then the County Court of British Columbia, leaving my private practice behind. In 1985, I was appointed to the Supreme Court and then later to the Court of Appeal, the highest court in the province. I was quite happy as a judge, serving at all three levels of court. I had specialized in criminal law and felt privileged to be judge in these high courts.

After I had been on the bench for over 20 years, the premier of the province phoned me in 2004 and asked me if I would consider being the Attorney General in his government. I didn't think of myself as a political guy … so I had to think about it. I had never run for public office before. However, after giving it some thought I resigned my position as a judge on the Court of Appeal. I began knocking on doors and took part in all-candidates meetings. An election was held and I won. Shortly after the election, I was appointed as the Attorney General for the province. It has been a killer of a job, but it has been good. They never had a guy who was a judge and then went into the political field; nobody else in Canada had done this before.

As the Attorney General, I am considered to be the chief law officer of the province. I am there to give legal advice to the government. All of the laws that are passed in the province become my responsibility.

As a Supreme Court judge in the mid-1990s, you took on the enormous task of conducting an inquiry into virtually every aspect of policing. Could you please explain the mandate and scope of this inquiry and some of the resulting findings?

In the mid-1990s, the government of the day asked me to do a Royal Commission on policing. There had been a number of controversial issues that had occurred in the late 1980s and into the 1990s that included a police shooting incident that resulted in the death of a prominent young man. There were other outstanding issues that needed to be addressed, such as how police chiefs and police boards were chosen. Other issues included the governance of policing and the future role of the RCMP [Royal Canadian Mounted Police] within the province of British Columbia.

Since I had a background as Crown attorney (working alongside the police) and as a Supreme Court judge, the government felt that I would be the appropriate person to examine virtually every issue related to policing. The inquiry had a wide scope, examining issues that included the police use of force, training, recruiting, promotions, multiculturalism, women in policing, Aboriginal policing, and police accountability. The inquiry lasted over two years and resulted in a series of documents on these subjects that were filed within a government report entitled "Closing the Gap." Many of the Royal Commission's recommendations went on to be government legislation and policies that pertain to policing. You could say that the findings of the inquiry actually shaped many aspects of policing that we see it today in British Columbia.

Some of the significant changes that resulted out of the inquiry pertain to the police use of force and the establishment of a use of force coordinator for the province. The findings from the inquiry also assisted in establishing the types of firearms that police should use and the levels of force that are applied. For example, police transitioned from a revolver to a pistol since many of the criminals were carrying pistols and the police were at a disadvantage. Other issues, such as the lateral neck restraint and when it should be applied, were dealt with as well as how high-speed police pursuits should be directed within provincial polices and procedures.

We also recommended a process for resolving public complaints against the police as well as the establishment of an independent complaint commissioner that would oversee complaints that were made against the police. One of the issues that kept coming up during our inquiry into policing was the fact that the police were investigating themselves. While a Police Act and a Code of Conduct existed, the actual workings of the legislation and the investigation process were left up to the police. Police investigating themselves is a controversial subject. This is especially an issue when death results or the allegations of police misconduct are serious. As you are aware, this changed and now the Office of the Police Complaint Commissioner is firmly established, providing oversight to the municipal police in the province. Accountability and transparency for the police is a good thing. These things provide greater confidence in the police as well as greater professionalism in the organization. It is good for the police and it is good for the public.

What are some of the challenges that you see for police officers today? What are your thoughts on police frustrations with the court system and, in particular, working within the framework of the Charter of Rights and Freedoms?

I think the police are too sensitive about court decisions sometimes. I could fully understand the "police frustration" with the courts because the police often see the crime that has been committed. The police officers see victims, and they see them in an unvarnished environment. When the matter goes to court, by that time, it has been sanitized and things are seen in a clinical manner. Even the worst accused is cleaned up and presentable by the time he or she gets into a courtroom.

During the court process, there's a balancing exercise involved. It is important to emphasize that a fundamental aspect of our criminal justice system is being innocent until proven guilty and without a reasonable doubt. When a police officer observes a crime being committed, witnesses a terrible injustice, or is speaking to a victim of a crime, the procedures and safeguards involved aren't always readily apparent at that time. In a courtroom, because of the "Twin Pillars" of our criminal justice system (the presumptions of innocence and proof beyond a reasonable doubt), the courts must ensure that the state (which has the obligation of proof beyond a reasonable doubt) remains within the parameters of the law.

This is often seen by members of the public as a "technicality." For example, why do the police need to obtain a search warrant? The question may be asked, if the police find contraband in someone's home, who cares how they found it, and why do we have to dot every i and cross every t by getting a search warrant? The answer is, in a democracy, we have certain rights. One of our fundamental rights is to be guarded against unreasonable search and seizure. That's why we have a Charter of Rights and Freedoms that is guaranteed within our Constitution. The courts, and the police, have a duty to uphold these fundamental rights and freedoms.

Prior to 1982 when the Charter became law in Canada, it was easier to prosecute because we didn't worry about the legality of the evidence. As long as the evidence was relevant and it was probative, it was thus admissible. In fact, illegal evidence was admitted into court all the time with the exception of confessions. The voluntariness of confessions always had to be proved beyond a reasonable doubt. It has always been said that an involuntary confession obtained as a result of threats or torture was not reliable and, therefore, not admissible.

The reason we have all these rules in Canada, pertaining to police conduct, is to ensure that we do not have wrongful convictions in court. When I [was] working as a judge on a jury trial, I used to tell juries (during the jury hearings) that the reason we must have proof without a reasonable doubt is because we don't want wrongful convictions. What may be seen as a technicality in the eyes of the public is really a procedural fairness. We want to see people who have committed crimes prosecuted, convicted, and sentenced. But, we want to ensure that it is done fairly. When I say fairly, I do so within the framework of our Constitution. Since we live in a democracy, we all have certain rights. We have the right to be free of search and seizure, the right to be informed of counsel, the freedom of the press, the right to have a trial within a reasonable time. Those are fundamental rights. Prior to the Charter, while it was easier to conduct prosecutions, we didn't always treat people with fairness.

As you are aware, there has been a drop in public confidence in the Canadian criminal justice system. Opinion polls frequently indicate a general public dissatisfaction with court sentencing, the police response to organized crime, and a "revolving" correctional system. What are your thoughts on our criminal justice system as a whole?

Our judicial system in Canada works pretty well. That is in spite of the fact that the public confidence in the criminal justice system is at an all time low.

The fact is, when you compare our system in terms of fairness, transparency … it works well. It is important to emphasize that we have judges from all over the world and lawyers from all over the world who come here to be trained. Canada is a country that is looked on very favorably by many other nations.

The same can be said for our police in Canada. For example, I was recently at the training depot for the Royal Canadian Mounted Police and saw police officers from all over the world in attendance. There were even police officers from the United States at the RCMP academy. They were in Canada and being trained by our Canadian police officers. They had sought out our system of training and had come here to learn of our best practices. Why? Because we have a good system for training police. The other point to emphasize is that we have no systemic corruption of the police here in Canada. In many other places in the world, this is a real issue. We are fortunate in Canada to have a criminal justice system in place where others, from around the world, seek out, as a reference point, as a role model. We also lack many of the problems and issues that other countries face with their criminal justice system.

Yes, there are some aspects of our criminal justice system that we could improve upon here in Canada. People complain about our whole criminal justice system. It is true that we don't do a very good job of apprehending and sentencing chronic offenders. Hopefully, the new Community Court system that we are starting to implement in our country will address some of those things. Yes, there is an appearance that the police arrest many offenders only to find that they are back out on the street in a matter of days or, in some cases, hours. I can understand why some of our police officers get frustrated. They spend a lot of their time and effort apprehending these criminals only to see them released by the courts and back onto the streets.

It must be remembered that our bail laws changed in 1973. Up until the early 1970s in Canada we had cash bails. It wasn't a good system, as we found that too many poor people were in jail because they couldn't pay their bail. We also found that a lot of people who were in custody were not likely to commit crimes, yet they were being held in jail. In response, the government changed the law placing the onus upon the Crown prosecutor, in most cases, to reason why the person should be held in custody. Unless, of course, if a certain type of serious crime, like murder, has been committed, then the individual is held in custody. Today, the courts get blamed for releasing people that are placed in custody, but that's the law. However, in my view, individuals that breach their conditions should not be released again. That just brings the criminal justice system into disrepute.

You mentioned the concept of a Community Court System in Canada. Could you please explain how this model works and why do you see a need for this approach?

What we are seeing here in Canada is the chronic offender. We know that over 80% of street level crime is being committed by less than 10% of the population. In most cases, the police and the courts know who these individuals are as they continually come into the criminal justice system and then go out again. The cycle repeats itself. Typically, these offenders are addicted to some sort of substance—alcohol or drugs. They may be suffering from mental illness and many of them are homeless. A Community Court takes the time to look at the root causes that have led these individuals into the criminal justice system. Why are they committing crimes and how can we work towards helping them? How can we break the cycle of repeat offenders?

The criminal justice system cannot work in isolation. It needs to be part of the greater community that includes our healthcare system, our housing authority system, and our counseling centers. The courts, corrections, and the police need to work together with these other community providers to find out which offenders are good candidates for rehabilitation. Once identified, these individuals need to be directed towards treatment. They must also be provided with additional support from various aspects of the community so that they do not become repeat offenders. There has to be more of a collaborative approach. Those of us in the court system need to work with the Health Ministry because so many of the people involved in crime are sick or mentally ill. The criminal justice system has had too much independence in the past.

One of the biggest challenges has been getting our court people to work with the police. Drug courts, mental health courts and community courts have been tried in different fashions throughout the United States with success. I am confident that our new Community Court system in Canada will also have much success.

Are there other areas of our criminal justice system that need to change? Could you please comment on some of the changes that have occurred and some of the challenges that exist for the police and the legal system?

The Charter of Rights and Freedoms has had the biggest impact upon Canadian society. The impact has been huge. The other changes that have occurred are for the most part in the realm of technology. DNA and communications have vastly changed our world. The police have an advantage in that they can adapt to shifts in society and in some ways, the police of today have an advantage over police 20 years ago. However, the laws haven't kept pace with the technology, often leaving the police in difficult circumstances.

For example, most of our evidence comes from wire taps, but my message to the federal government is that the laws surrounding communications were last enacted in 1973. Since the early 1970s, society and technology has vastly changed. Cell phones, Blackberries, the Internet, and other technology are now part of everyday life. Some people that break the law use disposable cell phones that haven't been registered. The laws need to move forward with technology as it occurs. This really hasn't occurred. Governments and the legislation that they pass need to be reflective of the times. I think this would greatly help the police in dealing with street level and organized crimes.

The other challenge for the criminal justice system is in regards to multiculturalism. In Vancouver, roughly 40% of our city is made up of visible minorities and over 25% of the population is foreign born. In California, over 50% of the population is nonwhite. These are the demographics that we are dealing with. The police and our criminal justice system need to be in touch with these changes and realities.

I go to the high schools a lot and speak about gang violence and crime. When I am speaking, there aren't any white faces. If you are going to make inroads into those communities, then there needs to be more representation of visible minorities and women. Policing and all of our government institutions must reflect the societal makeup of the country. Minority representation within the criminal justice system has to be present for credibility issues and in order to make the system more effective. For years, women were excluded from policing. Women, visible minorities, and other identifiable groups need to be represented in all public institutions.

Another pressing issue that needs to be addressed is making the criminal justice system more accessible to ordinary people. For example, civil courts in Canada have become complex, time-consuming, and expensive. People are having a tough time getting access to our civil system. Issues, such as family law, resolving parental custody matters, and resolving smaller monetary disputes, are important to individuals. Members of the community need to easily access these areas of our legal system and they need to be user friendly. The law has to be approachable and of assistance to the community when they need it. Laws are there for the people.

Do you have any suggestions for operational policing? How can the police better serve the public? What can police do better?

There is not enough reform being done in policing. When we conducted our inquiry into policing, we recommended that police agencies adopt community-based policing. However, as you and I know, everybody says that they are doing community policing. The reality is they are not. Everybody is still riding around in police cars.

Look at New York as a perfect example. I have been there many times. One of the major reasons why the New York City police reduced property and personal crime is because they have police officers everywhere. When you walk around New York City, you feel safe. The police are friendly, too; they chat with you and are approachable. This is a great thing.

I don't think the police in Canada realize how loved they are. I've defended cops when they were charged with assault. I've never got any cop convicted and even when I prosecuted them, I never got a conviction. The courts never wanted to convict them. Why, because we in society give the police a leeway. People realize how difficult their job is. The vast majority of the public supports the police.

However, I think the police need to interact more with the public. I don't think they do enough of it. They tend to stay in their cars or in their offices at the police stations. For police to achieve greater success, they have to adopt more of a community-based policing approach. They have to get outside of their police buildings and their cars and interact more with the public. It is good for the police and it is good for the public.

The other aspect of operational policing that needs to be addressed is in regards to cyber crime. We need to find out where policing will be in the cyber world. This is a new area that is growing and changing very rapidly. There needs to be cooperation between jurisdictions within nations and also at the international level. Cyber crime is an international concern for all police agencies and will need to be addressed as it evolves.

In 1994, you headed the Commission of Inquiry into Policing in the province of British Columbia that made 300 recommendations that included several references to the Royal Canadian Mounted Police and their contracted/temporary status within the province. Some of these specific references to the RCMP included:

> "If the Royal Canadian Mounted Police (RCMP) is not prepared to participate actively in a process that engages open accountability, then the province will have to consider creating its own provincial police agency."
>
> "The RCMP remains a top-heavy paramilitary organization with little discretion given to members at lower levels. It operates within a closed system. There is no visible accountability. The inquiry believes that it is unacceptable that the citizens of B.C. are subject to one process for complaints involving RCMP members and another for complaints involving members of independent municipal forces."
>
> "Clearly, there should be one process for complaints against all police officers. There are several ways in which this can be accomplished. The first would be to have the RCMP, by moral suasion, consent to compliance with the provincial complaints systems. This could be affected by reopening the contract with the RCMP. This seems highly unlikely. The second way would be to enact provincial legislation, which would be applicable to all police officers in the province."
>
> "The commission recommends that the province begin the investigation of the establishment of a provincial police agency, so as to be prepared should the RCMP not comply with provincial policing policy."

What are your thoughts regarding the Royal Canadian Mounted Police and their contract to provide policing within the province of British Columbia? As you are aware, the contract with the RCMP will be expiring in the next couple of years and there is a reluctance to renew the contract due to the controversy surrounding the performance of the RCMP.

In particular, there have been several complaints pertaining to RCMP officers engaging in excessive force as well as unethical conduct. There is also a frustration by many members of the public who feel that the RCMP are unaccountable as they are not required to comply with provincial legislation surrounding public complaints and civilian oversight. Way back in 1994, you raised several concerns and many of those concerns remain unanswered today.

I really can't say too much on this as I am not responsible for this area and it falls upon another branch of the government. It is a complex issue. As I stated in my 1994 report that you quoted, there are drawbacks to restoring a provincial police force and replacing the federal RCMP with a provincial police force would be very expensive. Under our current contract, the federal government picks up about a third of the costs associated with the RCMP and those dollars would be lost. The province of British Columbia would face substantial outlays for start-up costs associated with police training and related equipment as well as shared services.

It is something that needs to be looked at and it is being discussed by other members of the government. The talks have begun and there is a negotiation process taking place that will hopefully address the concerns and issues surrounding the RCMP.

Can you share your thoughts on police leadership. What are some of the challenges facing contemporary police leadership?

Well, I think there needs to be more succession planning in police leadership. There also has to be more training. However, I think that the police leadership now is better than any time in the past. The police chiefs that are in place today tend to have postsecondary degrees and a wide variety of skills. For the most part, they are strong leaders. They tend to be well-educated and well-rounded individuals.

The other challenge facing police leaders is the modern police officer. We have seen some significant changes in police recruiting. For the most part, you cannot get into policing unless you have a university degree. The type of individual that is going into policing tends to be well educated. You even have individuals with law degrees doing patrol work in Vancouver.

As a result of this factor, I think the biggest impediment to policing, as far as individual police officers are concerned, is the paramilitary system. The young people coming into policing need to be given more flexibility and power as well as initiative to deal with issues. We give the police the power and authority to make split-second decisions on high-speed chases as well as life and death decision making. Yet, there is so much constraint from the top. There are too many levels of policing. Police organization need to be flattened out if we are to have real community-based policing. This would allow the police to interact with the communities more. It would also allow the smart and talented people that we are hiring today to utilize more of their abilities to reduce crime and improve service to the public.

The other issue that police leaders need to confront is ethical conduct and accountability. A few years ago, I met Detective Frank Serpico when we were on a panel at a conference. Frank Serpico is the retired New York City police officer from the late 1960s and early 1970s that confronted police corruption on the job. It is Frank Serpico's opinion that most police departments are corrupt. I disagree with him. I don't think that is correct. There is just no evidence. There will always be individual officers that engage in misconduct as well as issues that will occur from time to time within a police agency. The only thing that I would say is that there tends to be too much "cowboyism" in policing. People know the police have a lot of power. Police have an immense amount of power and respect in the community. If you use people skills, you can solve more crimes and the public will have greater satisfaction with the services you perform. This is something that police leaders must be aware of and must be able to deal with. Police agencies need to have a good system of accountability and transparency in place. They also need to ensure that the police are professional and worthy of the respect given to them.

Police leaders must also make use of the apology. When police make mistakes, they should apologize to the individual and to the public. Over the years, I have seen several examples where the police have made an honest mistake. When I conducted our inquiry into policing, there were individuals that came forward telling me how they had been stopped by the police with their guns drawn and commanding them to get onto the ground. Later, the police realized that they made a mistake and had checked the wrong individuals. However, rather than admitting they had made a mistake, the officers drove off.

Individuals would often tell me that all they wanted was an apology from the police officers. These were individuals that had typically been stopped or checked by the police in error or something had occurred where the police had made a mistake. An apology has an enormous impact. Most people will understand and accept an apology when a mistake is made. Police need to realize this. Legislation can be put in place to allow the police to apologize without the fear of civil litigation. The public has a lot of confidence in the police, and even more, if you are willing to admit that you make an honest mistake and to say that you are sorry. Police typically don't do this, but they really need to consider this when it is appropriate.

Finally, could you please comment on the types of crimes that police are dealing with and how they should best tackle the "war on crime"?

Any sort of "fight on crime" is not the sole responsibility of the police. We expect the police to do way too much. The problems that the police are dealing with are societal problems. They are often sociological or economical based and stem from a variety of social issues that include poverty, mental illness, and substance abuse. The police are not in a position to deal with these complexities. We expect a lot from our police when we expect them to solve these problems. The best crime fighting method is prevention. We need to have the foresight to deal with these issues before the crimes are committed. That is what we have to do as a society. We have to deal with children that are vulnerable before they engage in criminal activities.

The other thing that courts have to do is to give meaningful sentences. I know that as far as general deterrence is concerned, it is the principle of limited application. Most people don't look at the Criminal Code before they commit a crime to see what the penalties will be if they are caught. They just go ahead and commit the crime. What we need to do is to show that there are meaningful consequences for people that commit crimes. The courts must send out this message in their sentencing.

The marihuana grow-ops are a good example of that. It is not good to give a conditional sentence in these cases; it does little good. The fact is, in most cases, these individuals are growing marihuana for a profit. It is a business, it is an operation. As a result, there needs to be deterrence. We can start by seizing the property that it is grown on and using civil forfeiture laws. We need to do more of this and deal with the proceeds of crime, as deterrence. One of the best things that we have done to reduce impaired driving is by allowing police to seize motor vehicles. We have given the police extraordinary powers by allowing them to act as the judge and jury at the scene of an impaired driving incident. They can seize the car and suspend the driver's license for 24 hours. It takes the impaired driver off the road immediately and it acts as deterrence to others.

We also need to ensure that the police are supported, that Crown prosecutors work with the police. One of the greatest challenges that I had when I took this position was making sure that various ministries of government were working together. There was feeling among some of the Crown prosecutors that they were independent and they were not there to give advice to the police. A wall had gone up for some reason. This was something that I had to change. We are all on the same side. Crown Counsel and the police may have different responsibilities, but they must work together. Crown Counsel is there to give the police advice so that the evidence they obtain is not thrown out in court. There has to be more of a collaborative approach with policing and other government agencies as we all share the problems in society. We must all work together to solve crime and other social issues.

Epilogue

Shortly after the initial interview was conducted, Wally Oppal vacated his seat in government as a result of losing an election held in his constituency. Oppal had faced a close election in his riding; initially winning the election with a mere two-vote lead over his opponent. However, a recount of the votes revealed that Oppal had, in fact, lost the election by 32 votes and was forced to concede to his opponent.

Nonetheless, former Justice Wally Oppal was soon appointed to head a public inquiry into a controversial and horrific serial-killing spree that occurred in Vancouver between January 23, 1997 and February 5, 2002, when several women were reported missing from the downtown eastside area of the city. It was not until December 2007 that Robert Pickton was found guilty of six counts of second-degree murder and was sentenced to life in prison with no chance of parole for at least 25 years, which is the maximum sentence under Canadian Law for murder. He was also charged in the deaths of an additional 20 women, many of them prostitutes and drug users. It is believed that Robert Pickton took the vulnerable women to his farm located in a Vancouver suburb where he would kill and dismember the women, feeding their body parts to his emaciated pigs. The pigs were later slaughtered and sold to restaurants in Vancouver's Chinatown area. During the trial's first day of jury evidence, the Crown alleged that Pickton had confessed to 49 murders; however, the Crown could only achieve a conviction in six of the alleged murders.

Specifically, former Justice Oppal is to head the inquiry that will review the police investigations that were conducted into women reported missing from the Vancouver area and allegations that include that police agencies failed to direct adequate resources to locating the women because many were prostitutes and drug users. It also is alleged that the provincially contracted Royal Canadian Mounted Police failed to appropriately respond to the numerous missing women as well as investigate crimes occurring on Robert Pickton's farm that was located in their jurisdiction. Finally, the inquiry will also examine the January 1998 decision by Crown prosecutors to stay charges against the prime for the vicious assault of a Vancouver prostitute. It is speculated that had Crown prosecutors proceeded with the 1998 charges many of the deceased women would be alive today.

The Missing Women Commission's terms of reference include:

- Conduct hearings in or near Vancouver to inquire into and make findings of fact respecting the conduct of the missing women investigations between January 23, 1997 and February 5, 2002.
- Inquire into and make findings of fact respecting the decision of the Criminal Justice Branch on January 27, 1998, to enter a stay of proceedings on charges against the prime suspect for attempted murder, assault with a weapon, forcible confinement, and aggravated assault.
- Recommend changes considered necessary respecting the initiation and conduct of investigations in British Columbia of missing women and suspected multiple homicides.

- Recommend changes considered necessary respecting homicide investigations in B.C. by more than one investigating organization, including the coordination of those investigations.
- Submit a final report to the attorney general by December 31, 2011.

The current Attorney General, Mike de Jong, stated he picked Wally Oppal for the job because of his deep insight into the province's legal and law enforcement establishments as well as his sensitivity as a member of a visible minority. AG de Jong commented:

> Mr. Oppal comes to this assignment with an impeccable track record of public service. … As an individual, while serving on the bench and while serving as Attorney General, he distinguished himself in my view as having an ability to empathize in a very human way. He was a very human judge and as attorney general he brought those qualities to the task. I suppose the most difficult question of all is why a serial murderer was able to prey on his victims for so long while so many women went missing and ultimately were murdered. The inquiry is an expensive proposition, but I think a worthwhile one.

Attorney General de Jong said he hoped the inquiry would provide answers for the families of the many victims. As well, he insisted the government would take steps to commemorate the missing and murdered women in a formal and permanent way. Former Justice Wally Oppal is also to consider what changes if any should be made to the province's policing structure to prevent such an event in the future. As stated, the province of British Columbia does not have its own provincial police force and instead has opted to "contract" the services of the subsidized federal Royal Canadian Mounted Police (RCMP). This situation has resulted in the establishment of municipal and federal police agencies within the Vancouver area. At times, the differences between these policing agencies is highlighted in the lack of information sharing and a lack of coordinated efforts in solving regional and provincial crimes.

Oppal commented:

> I think an inquiry should only be held if we think we can learn something from the inquiry. We've had an exhaustive trial here. And a lot of evidence has come out. A lot of people have recognized that we could have done things a lot better. We know that there are multiple policing agencies in the Lower Mainland (Vancouver area). And are we going to learn anything by virtue of the fact that there were multiple investigations going on? Should the complaints have been received in a different way? So, those are things that sometimes the police can do themselves. Sometimes government can assist them doing those things. So, merely because things didn't go the way they should have gone doesn't necessarily mean we should embark on a lengthy inquiry.

I'm saying that if we're going to have an inquiry, let's put a proper focus on the inquiry. And, let's find out what issues we're going to inquire into.

Oppal added that the commission's terms of reference provide room to address the police response to the disappearances of women in the northern area of the province of British Columbia. Also known as the "Highway of Tears," the missing women of northern BC are believed to have been murdered while hitchhiking. Police reports note that more than 30 women have vanished since 1969 along this northern highway route of British Columbia. Many of the reported missing women are Aboriginal. Criticism has been leveled at the RCMP for a lack of progress in solving the missing person's cases with speculation that little has been done since the victims were largely Aboriginal and many involved in the sex or drug trade.

As in the Robert Pickton incident, vulnerable and marginalized women are believed to have fallen victim to one or more serial killers with police agencies failing to direct adequate resources to solving and preventing the crimes. It is speculated that civil litigation against the police in British Columbia will occur shortly after former Justice Wally Oppal reaches his conclusions and provides his recommendations regarding missing women in the province. The recommendations of the Missing Women's Commission also may provide insight into the future role and direction of the Royal Canadian Mounted Police in the Province of British Columbia.

India

VI

SANKAR SEN

Overview of Indian Legal System

By Sankar Sen

The Indian judicial system is one of the oldest judicial systems in the world. It has evolved gradually and bears the imprint of different periods of Indian history. During the British rule, serious efforts were made by the British rulers to tone up the judicial system. During the period from 1834 to 1947, as many as four Law Commissions and other committees were appointed for this purpose.

The framework of the current judicial system in India has been laid down by the Indian Constitution, which came into force on January 26, 1950. The Constitution of India is the supreme law of the country, the fountain source of law in India. The Constitution adopted a federal system of government, but it also provided for setting up of integrated systems of courts that administered both union and state laws. A notable feature of the Indian judicial system is that it is based on the pattern of adversarial system in which there are two sides, and, in every case, each side presents its argument to a neutral judge who then issues an order after an appreciation of the facts and evidence of the case.

Independence of the judiciary is one of the cornerstones of Indian democracy. The Constitution makes the judiciary independent of the executive and the legislative branches of the government.

Supreme Court

The Supreme Court is on the top of the judicial hierarchy in India. Below it, there are High Courts of respective states followed by subordinate courts. The Supreme Court of India comprises the Chief Justice and 25 other judges appointed by the president of India. A Supreme Court judge retires on attaining the age of 65 years. Article 124 of the Constitution provides that a person shall not be qualified for appointment as a judge of the Supreme Court unless he is a citizen of India and (a) has been for at least 5 years a judge of a High Court or two or more such courts in succession, (b) has been for at least 10 years an advocate of a High Court or two or more such courts in succession, and (c) in the opinion of the president, a distinguished jurist.

Provision exists in the Constitution for appointment of a judge of High Court as an ad hoc judge of Supreme Court and for a retired judge of the Supreme Court or the High Court to sit and act as judges of the court. The Constitution seeks to ensure independence of the Supreme Court by providing that a judge of the Supreme Court cannot be removed from office except by an order of the president, passed after an address by each House of the Parliament, supported by the majority of the total membership of that House and by majority of not less than two thirds of the members of the House present and voting has been presented to the president in the same session for such removal on grounds of proved misbehavior or incapacity. A person who had been a judge in the Supreme Court is debarred from practicing in any court of law or before any authority in India. Article 141 of the Indian Constitution provides that the law declared by the Supreme Court shall be binding on all the courts within the territory of India. The jurisdiction of the Supreme Court includes original, writ, and appellate. Appellate jurisdiction refers to the power of the court to hear appeals against any judgment or final order of any High Court. If the High Court certifies that the case involves a substantial question of law of great importance and in the opinion of the High Court the said question needs to be decided by the Supreme Court. The Constitution has conferred powers on the Supreme Court to issue orders or writs under Article 32 of the Constitution for the enforcement of any of the fundamental rights provided under Part III of the Constitution. This is referred to as the writ jurisdiction of the Supreme Court. The Supreme Court is also a court of record and has all the powers of such a court including the power to punish contempt of itself.

High Courts of India

High Courts of India are the supreme judicial authority at the state level. Article 141 of the Constitution provides that High Courts are bound by the judgment and orders of the Supreme Court of India. The courts have jurisdiction over the state, union territory, and a group of states and union territories. Judges in the High Courts are appointed by the chief justice of India and the governor of the State. The Calcutta High Court is the oldest High Court in the country, established in 1862. High Courts that get a large number of cases from a particular region have their permanent branches established there. Below High Courts there are subordinate courts like civil courts, family courts, criminal courts, and various other district courts.

One of the most important functions that have been assigned to the High Courts and the Supreme Court of India is that relating to judicial review. Part III of the Indian Constitution enumerates certain fundamental rights that have been granted to all the citizens of the country. According to Article 13 of the Constitution, all laws in force in the territory of India immediately before the commencement of the Constitution, insofar as they are inconsistent with Part III, shall to the extent of such inconsistency be void. This article further provides that the state shall not make any law that takes away or abridges the rights conferred by Part III and any law in contravention of this clause shall to the extent of such contravention be void.

All the High Courts have the same status under the Constitution. However, they do not constitute like a single all-India cadre. Each judge appointed to a particular High Court may be transferred to another High Court only by the Article 222 of the Constitution, which empowers the president to transfer the judge to another High Court after consultation with the chief justice of India. Each High Court is a court of record, which means that it has powers to determine questions about its own jurisdiction. The High Court is also the highest court of justice in the state on questions of law. It is the only court other than the Supreme Court that is vested with the jurisdiction to interpret the Constitution.

The High Court has the power to issue writs just as the apex court under Article 226 of the Constitution. There is, however, one difference. While the Supreme Court can issue writs in order to enforce rights provided under Paragraph III of the Constitution, the High Courts can issue writs for enforcement of rights under Part III of the Constitution "*or for any other purpose.*"

Certain other matters or issues may be heard by the High Court as part of its original jurisdiction if the law laid down by the legislature provides for it. Both the Supreme Court and High Courts are courts of record and have all the powers associated with such a court, which includes the power to punish the contempt. All persons convicted by the sessions judge are entitled to appeal to the High Court. Appeals by the states against acquittal also lie only to the High Court when the order of acquittal is passed by a sessions judge. A sentence of death can be confirmed by the High Court before it can be carried out.

The High Courts are also final courts of appeal in all criminal matters. An appeal lies to the Supreme Court against judgments of the High Courts as provided in the criminal procedure code and under Article 134 of the Constitution.

Subordinate Courts

District Courts are at the top of the subordinate lower courts. They are under the administrative control of the High Court of the state to which the District Court belongs. Decisions of the District Courts, of course, are subjected to the appellate jurisdiction of the High Court. Apart from these courts, which enforce laws and rules laid down by the legislature, there are many quasijudicial bodies, such as tribunals and regulators, which are involved in resolution of disputes. They provide another forum for redress of grievances or resolution of disputes other than the courts.

In recent years, a new class of litigation has developed that differs from traditional litigations in as much as there are no plaintiffs and defendants. Under this, people can bring action against, for example, exploitation of laborers by contractors, use of children as bonded laborer, illegal detention of undertrials, torture while in custody; even things, such as pollution of the environment, etc. This is known as Public Interest Litigation (PIL). It is less expensive and more efficacious. PIL has brought about a change in the traditional function of the Supreme Court and enable the Supreme Court to exercise affirmative action to vindicate those socioeconomic rights traditionally considered nonenforceable by the courts. Through Public Interest Litigation, judiciary has extended its jurisdiction and undertaken the responsibility to critique and monitor the government and its various agencies and to give socioeconomic justice to its underprivileged masses without interfering with the political and administrative field or legislative sphere.

Judicial Backlog

Indian courts have large judicial backlogs. The criminal justice system is slow moving. This is eroding people's faith in the judiciary, posing a grave threat to the constitutional and democratic governance of the country.

Interview of Judge Manmohan Singh, Delhi High Court, India

7

VIDISHA BARUA WORLEY

Contents

Introduction

> Population control and free compulsory education is the solution for India.
>
> **Judge Manmohan Singh**

India has a strong judiciary and the Supreme Court of India exercises more power than many parallel courts in the rest of the world. Not only does the court deal with significant constitutional issues like the death penalty, live-in relationships, and the rights of children born out of such relationships, it also keeps the Legislative Branch in check by entertaining important public interest litigations, as pointed out by Judge Manmohan Singh of the Delhi High Court. The High Court of Delhi, located in the capital of India, also plays an imperative role by addressing public interest litigations in its own right, a recent ruling of the court being concerned about the rights of the gay population in India. Judge Singh in an interview with Dr. Vidisha Barua Worley, assistant professor of Criminal Justice at the University of North Texas at Dallas, said that while advancements like the creation of electronic courts, introduction of plea bargaining, arbitration proceedings, and mediation

117

centers have marked an improvement in the criminal justice system, the high pending caseload and the low number of judges are continuing to take their toll.

The Interview

Career

To start out, please tell us a little bit about your career: length, organizations worked in, movements, specializations, etc.

Well, to start out at the very beginning, I lost my father when I was only a year old. My mother brought me up. It was my mother's dream that I join the legal profession, and perhaps one day become a judge. My maternal uncle, Anoop Singh, an intellectual property rights lawyer, had his practice in Peshawar, Pakistan, since 1940. He was my role model and guided me to become a trademark and patent lawyer. I started my career on August 12, 1980, under my uncle's guidance in the High Court of Delhi. I practiced independently for 28 years in Delhi, Bombay (Mumbai), Calcutta (Kolkata), and Madras (Chennai), specializing in trademarks, copyrights, and patents. On April 11, 2008, I became a judge of the Delhi High Court, India.

What about how your career developed surprised you?

I was very surprised when I was selected to become a judge. I got a call from the Delhi High Court requesting me to submit my papers in order to become a judge of the court. This was totally unexpected for me. A judge of the Delhi High Court is appointed by the president of India. A collegium of three senior judges of the Delhi High Court nominates a candidate for the position of a Delhi High Court judge. This candidate is then approved first, by a collegium of five justices of the Supreme Court of India, thereafter by the Ministry of Law, and, finally, by the president of India. After this vetting process, the president of India appoints a judge to the Delhi High Court. It was a matter of great honor and surprise for me that I was first nominated and then appointed a judge of the Delhi High Court, which is a very prestigious position and definitely the pinnacle of my career.

Did your work prove as interesting or rewarding as you thought it would?

This work is very different from that of a lawyer. The way you conduct yourself is very vital. It is very important to be able to maintain impartiality and neutrality in the court. Several old friendships get strained as judges have to follow a lot of written as well as informal rules in the way they conduct themselves.

As far as the work itself is concerned, as a lawyer I worked only in my area of specialization. As such, the work was restricted to a certain subject. After becoming a judge, it is totally different. I had never imagined that I would be exposed to such a wide array of subjects. It is very interesting and rewarding at the same time. Had I continued to be a lawyer, I would never have ventured into these areas of law, let alone rule on them. Now, I am gaining new knowledge every day and this is definitely increasing my horizon immensely. There are researchers who help us search the law and, now that everything is on the computer, it is very easy to quickly research a topic and read all related papers concerning a case with the click of the mouse. Fortunately, my court is an e-court, one of the few in the Delhi High Court, which has gone completely paperless. This has definitely added to the ease in handling cases.

Changes Experienced

What do you see as the most important philosophical changes that have happened in criminal justice over the course of your career?

Several important philosophical changes have taken place over the course of my career, more so in the recent past. There have been major developments in the areas of death penalty, live-in relationships, and homosexual relationships.

Death Penalty: The attitude toward the death penalty in India has undergone a tremendous change. As the Supreme Court of India observed, the capital punishment is now awarded only in the "rarest of rare" cases. This doctrine of using the death penalty only in the rarest of rare cases has evolved over several cases. Two seminal cases regarding the death penalty are *Kehar Singh v. Union of India* and *Machhi Singh and others v. State of Punjab.*[1]

Live-In Relationships: Also, the philosophy and the concept of the family and marriage as an institution have undergone changes. The Supreme Court has recognized the live-in relationship between a man and a woman. The judgment came in the case of *S. Khushboo v. Kanniammal & Another* (2010)[2] where there were several criminal cases filed against a famous film actress from South India, Khushboo, for her opinion on live-in relationships and premarital sex that was published in an entertainment magazine in India. The court observed that a live-in relationship was a matter of personal choice and criminal law could not interfere with the personal morality of individuals, which is a subjective matter. Later, issues of whether or not women who have been in a live-in relationship for a substantial period of time should be given the status of a "wife" and be entitled to maintenance arose before the Supreme Court in the case of *Chanmuniya v. Virendra Kumar Singh Kushwaha* (2010).[3] The court ruled that a woman who has lived with a man for a considerable period of time like a wife should be granted the status of a wife without her having to prove the status of her marriage and should be entitled to maintenance.

The law in this area is fast developing. Recently, the Supreme Court in *Revanasiddappa & Another v. Mallikarjun & Others* (2011)[4] has also recognized that children born out of a void marriage, considered illegitimate children, can claim rights to property that becomes the property of the parent, whether self-acquired or inherited, because they are innocent and should not be affected by the legal status of their parents' relationship.

Homosexual Relationships: The Delhi High Court in a landmark case, *Naz Foundation v. Government of NCT of Delhi* (2009)[5] decriminalized sodomy and held that homosexual relations between two consenting adults is a fundamental right protected by the Constitution of India. This decision invalidates parts of Section 377 of the Indian Penal Code of 1860 that was framed during British times and treated all forms of sexual acts except heterosexual vaginal intercourse as "unnatural offenses."

What changes have you seen in the organizational arrangements, specializations, policies and programs, equipment, personnel, diversity, etc.?

Besides the philosophical changes, there have been some organizational developments. The length of time needed for disposal of cases, which is a big issue in Indian courts, has changed in the recent past. I think this is one of the most important changes that I have noticed in the court system. Earlier, it took 10 to 15 years for a case to be disposed of. Now, it takes about one to two years.

There is computerized or e-filing available for petitions. Next, gathering evidence has become quicker. Today, this takes from six months to a year. Earlier, it took a long time to get copies of court orders. With the help of computers, pdf [portable document format] files of court orders are made available the same day. This is a huge accomplishment and a positive change. You can go to the Web site (www.delhihighcourt.com) to get judgments decided by the Delhi High Court. Cases have been expedited. Now, appeals can be filed the same day and can be heard within one day. These are some of the important changes I have seen in the judiciary in India.

What changes in external conditions (support from communities, legal powers, judicial relations, relations with minority communities, resource provision, political influence, etc.) have had a significant impact on criminal justice?

Development of technology has been a great resource that has impacted the criminal justice system. Unlike the United States of America, there is no political influence on the judiciary. Rather, the judiciary acts as a check on political corruption. Also, due to increase in public awareness of their rights, there is a high volume of public interest litigation that is instrumental in bringing about several policy changes concerning the public as well as exposing arbitrariness in the decision-making process of the government. Rather, the judiciary acts as a check on the other two limbs of the government, namely, legislature and executive through judicial review.

Overall, has the quality of criminal justice system improved or declined?

The overall quality of the criminal justice system has definitely improved.

In general, is it more or less difficult to be a judge or justice now than in the past?

The judiciary has always been considered by the public to be the last recourse for justice everywhere, including India. Therefore, rendering justice is a difficult task in the sense that one has to be very careful and circumspect in making decisions. In modern times, when the complexity of wrongs have increased, as the wrong doer has become more systematic with the advancement of technology, the issues arising before the court are comparatively newer than those presented before courts earlier. In that limited respect, one can say that it is slightly [more] difficult to become a judge in this era.

Personal Judicial Philosophy

What do you think should be the role of the judiciary in society?

The judiciary has a very active role to play in society. More specifically, tools like public interest litigation, judge made law, and the power of judicial review further enhance the scope of interpretation of laws and sometimes in rare cases, formulation of policies under judicial activism where there is inaction by the legislature or by the executive. Although I personally feel that the role of the judiciary should be limited to interpreting the law, judicial activism is sometimes quite useful. The object of India being a welfare state should not be forgotten while interpreting the law. My personal judicial philosophy is that judiciary is *tapasya* (meditation). It is different from any other profession. You work single-mindedly for the people.

What should be their job, functions, and roles?

In a democratic society when everything fails, the judiciary steps in and makes sure that the fundamental rights of citizens are protected and the rule of law is maintained. The judiciary keeps checks and balances on the other pillars of the government, the legislature, and the executive by virtue of the power of judicial review, so that no one oversteps the boundary and domain assigned to the respective pillars as envisaged in the Indian Constitution.

What should be left to others?

The remaining area of performing their roles like legislative roles and executive function must be left to the other two limbs of the government and that is what the separation of powers is all about. If we proceed in this direction, then the constitutional framework can never be shaken and the whole society will work in a peaceful manner.

However, whenever there are mistakes committed, the judiciary should intervene acting within the framework of the Constitution.

What organizational arrangements work and which do not?

There are several systems that have worked extremely well besides litigation in the courts. Our Delhi High Court Mediation Cell has been very successful. Within the span of a year or say a year and a half, about 100,000 cases were disposed of by mediation. Attorneys acting as mediators work for the best interest of their clients. As a mediator handles the proceedings like a judge would, the client feels confident that his or her grievances will be resolved in the best possible way. Such a system of mediation has worked very effectively in the Delhi High Court and I have personally witnessed several cases. Another system is the *Lok Adalat*, which is a Public Court wherein a retired judge disposes of petty cases and family matters. This system has really worked well where offenses are compounded and punishments are given in the form of fines.

One of the most significant developments in the criminal justice system in India is the introduction of plea bargaining,[6] which has done wonders in disposing of cases. While other countries have had plea bargaining for a long time, it is a new development in India and came into effect in 2006. Serious offenses that can be punished by life imprisonment or by more than seven years in prison cannot be resolved by plea bargaining. Plea bargaining was introduced in India to specifically alleviate the problems of delays in court proceedings, large pending caseloads, and the overcrowding of jails by pretrial detainees. The defendant, however, must voluntarily plead guilty and both parties must arrive at a mutually agreed upon settlement.

Besides these, in rural areas, organizations that are decentralized work better as they know the difficulties and the pulse of the people. The *Gram Sabha* (Village Assembly) and the *Panchayat* (five-member panel of village elders) are important elements of the rural justice system and local self governance. The central government is trying to make these bodies financially stronger so that there can be better governance at the local level. In some states like Bihar, Madhya Pradesh, and Maharashtra, the state governments have taken initiatives in improving the Panchayati programs by providing funds and by getting actively involved.

What policies on relations with the community, with political groups, with other criminal justice organizations work well?

India has a vast population where people with diversified cultures reside. Similarly, the level of crime and the frequency varies from state to state in India. There cannot be any uniform policy in every state to bring about a change in the criminal justice system. But, some endeavors can be made which, according to me, are in-built in the judiciary as a system wherein rotation of judges is already permissible under the Constitution. The chief justice of a state is always from another state for the better administration of the justice system. Likewise, there are other bylaws of the High Courts, which regulate the lower judiciary. The High Courts are given the power to transfer, and other powers that act as regulatory checks on the lower judiciary where judges handle civil as well as criminal matters.

What hampers cooperation with other agencies and groups?

The lack of connectivity and coordination among each limb of the government creates a kind of stagnancy in the system wherein the courts are also sometimes helpless and decide the cases with lack of proper guidance from the other branches of the government. This includes failure to get proper information from the government and its bodies even upon directions.

How should the criminal legal system in India be operated?

There should be more judges to handle the large number of pending cases in the criminal legal system. Also, the awareness about basic criminal law should be increased, especially in rural areas of states like Punjab and Haryana, where people kill one another over trivial matters. This can be achieved by introducing free mandatory minimum education.

What should be the preferred priorities and strategies: hard-edged crime control, prevention, or public services?

While all three are important and should be addressed simultaneously, keeping the future in mind, I would focus more on crime prevention. Crime prevention can be done by adopting preventive measures including some laws, imposing sanctions at the preventive stage like preventive detention laws, which act as a stringent measure against the suspect criminals. Furthermore, crime can be prevented by adopting the reformative theory of punishment where we have to reform the criminal, which India is following to a large extent. The concept of plea bargaining has set a benchmark in resolving a number of cases. These are measures for crime prevention. Crime control is also possible by following both preventive and curative measures, as stated above.

Problems and Successes Experienced

In your experience, what policies or programs have worked well and which have not? And can you speculate for what reasons?

The policies of introducing electronic media in the court system is working very well. More and more e-courts are being created, which is minimizing the processing time, and making the courts much more efficient. However, for lack of resources, it is difficult to make all courts electronic. So, the process is slow. However, I hope there will be more funds available to create electronic courts across the country so that there is faster filing and disposition of cases.

Also, the procedures for giving speedy justice like the mediation centers, *Lok Adalats* (public trials), arbitration proceedings, and plea bargaining have proved to be effective in relieving the caseload. Once again, because of illiteracy, ignorance, and a high population, the caseload keeps rising.

What would you consider to be the greatest problem facing the criminal courts at this time?

The greatest problem facing the criminal courts at this time is the plethora of pending cases and the low number of criminal courts. With cases pending for years, thousands of innocent people are behind bars waiting for their cases to be heard. Priority should be given to decide criminal cases, more judges should be appointed, and more criminal courts created.

What problems in courts do you find is the most difficult to deal with?

There is a huge population of pretrial detainees. For those detainees who are innocent and have children, their lives are shattered before they can get a hearing. There are no child protective services available for children whose parents are in prison. The fundamental rights of these children are repeatedly violated, in certain cases leading to the death of these children. As a judge of a criminal court, these are serious problems that I find very difficult to reconcile with. There should be child protective services for children of criminal parents.

What would be easy to change? Internal problems (culture of the organization, managerial deficiencies, allegations of corruption or gender related problems, etc.) or externally generated problems (resources, community support, etc.)? Is anything easy?

Internal problems are not seen in higher levels of the judiciary. These courts are very vigilant and very conscious of the high prestige attached to their office. There is no discrimination against women. In the Delhi High Court, out of 48 judges, 7 are female judges.

Externally generated problems are lack of funds. Basically, the problems are all related to high population growth, high case loads, low number of judges and courts, and lack of funds.

Theory and Practice

What should be the relationship between theory and practice?

In theory, we should have more courts and more judges, and more schools to educate and increase awareness amongst the populace. However, in practice we have a large number of pending cases, less time to decide so many cases, less number of judges than the permissible strength under the law and other practical difficulties like holidays, festivals, etc., which limit the scope of a human to go beyond his/her capacity.

What can practitioners learn from theory, and what theory builders from practitioners?

The problems are very clear. Theory builders can help in making policy changes if they focus on practical solutions to the problems facing India.

What is the relationship right now? Does it exist? Does it work? What holds collaboration or interactions back?

There are national and international seminars organized for judges where latest advancements are discussed. Alternate dispute resolution ways like arbitration and mediation, which have practical implications are discussed. Other interactions focus on women's rights and human rights issues.

What kind of research, in what form, on what questions would you find most useful for practice?

As a judge, I get the help of two researchers designated to my court. Internet sites that make available the latest judgments are especially helpful in conducting our research. Since case law and precedents are very important in the practice of law in India, legal Web sites that make these easily available are especially helpful for research.

Where do you find theory-based information? Where do you look? What journals, books, publications, reports?

Besides the legal Web sites, we refer, among others, to journals like the Supreme Court Cases, All India Cases, Criminal Law Journal, Labor Law Service, and, of course, the Constitution of India, for more information.

Do judges do research on their own outside of research dealing with pending cases? On what types of issues or questions?

Yes, I love to do research on trademark issues. The court is in session for 210 days a year. The rest of the days, I spend my time reading, writing articles, and traveling.

Transnational Relations

Have you been affected by, and how, in the work of your organization by developments outside the country (human rights demands, universal codes

of ethics, practical interactions with judges or justices from other countries, personal experiences outside the country, new crime threats, etc.)?

I regularly attend conferences for judges both nationally and internationally. Judges from across the world discuss issues that are important in their own countries and take advice and guidance from judges of other countries who have had more experience in handling similar issues. There is a healthy exchange of ideas. Indian judges are regarded very highly because most of them are older, more mature, experienced, and knowledgeable, especially as they deal with a large number of cases. Among others, issues concerning women's rights, human rights, latest advances in mediation and arbitration techniques are discussed.

Have those interactions been beneficial or harmful? What kind of external international influences are beneficial and which ones less so?

The most beneficial international interactions are those that discuss common difficulties faced and practical solutions if any. So, countries who continue to face similar problems in their judiciary can learn from the successful steps taken by others in addressing them. There are formal and informal interactions at these conferences that are immensely beneficial. Experiences of judges in less populated countries may not be as helpful to Indian judges, but there is always something you can learn.

How have developments post-September 11 affected your work?

The events of September 11, 2001, in the United States of America have not affected the judiciary in India.

General Assessments

Are you basically satisfied or dissatisfied with developments in criminal law and criminal procedure in your system?

I feel we have the best criminal law and the best judges any country could have. I am very satisfied with the quality of judges in India who go through a stringent process to be appointed. Unlike some other countries, the executive or political parties in India have no say in the appointment of judges. This ensures impartiality and integrity.

What are the most likely developments you see happening and which would you like to see happening?

In the next 10 to 15 years, with the advanced technology that the courts are now adopting, and new programs being introduced, the efficiency of the court system will increase manifold. This should definitely alleviate a lot of the current problems. In fact, it is possible that within 5 to 10 years, the pending cases will be cleared and the court system will be streamlined.

What is most needed now to improve the system?

To reiterate what I said earlier, the two priorities for the government should be to control the population and provide free education, and the priorities for the judiciary should be to create more criminal courts and appoint more judges as per the permissible strength.

References

Chanmuniya v. Virendra Kumar Singh Kushwaha (Supreme Court of India, 2010). Retrieved from http://judis.nic.in/supremecourt/helddis.aspx

Kehar Singh v. Union of India, 1989. All India Reporter 653.

Lawrence v. Texas (2003), 559 U.S. 538.

Machhi Singh and others v. State of Punjab, 1983. All India Reporter 957.

Murlidhar Meghraj Loya v. State of Maharashtra, 1976. All India Reporter 1929.

Naz Foundation v. Government of National Capital Territory of Delhi (Delhi High Court, 2009) Writ Petition (Civil) No. 7455/2001.

Revanasiddappa & Another v. Mallikarjun & Others (Supreme Court of India, 2011). Retrieved from http://judis.nic.in/supremecourt/helddis.aspx

S. Khushboo v. Kanniammal & Another (Supreme Court of India, 2010). Retrieved from http://judis.nic.in/supremecourt/helddis.aspx

Endnotes

1. Two important cases decided by the Supreme Court of India regarding the death penalty are *Kehar Singh v. Union of India*, 1989 All India Reporter 653 and *Machhi Singh and others v. State of Punjab*, 1983 All India Reporter 957. The case of Kehar Singh was related to the assassination of Indian Prime Minister Indira Gandhi on October 31, 1984 by Satwant Singh and Beant Singh. While Beant Singh died in the shootings during the course of the assassination, Satwant Singh, the second assassin, and Kehar Singh who was alleged to be a co-conspirator, received the death penalty. They were hanged to death on January 6, 1989. The death penalty for Kehar Singh was seen as problematic as he was not directly linked to the assassination. His clemency request was turned down by the President of India as trusting the judgment of the highest court of the country, even though the opinion of the Supreme Court clarified that the clemency power of the president did not interfere with the judiciary and in fact highlighted the separation of powers.

   In the case of *Macchi Singh*, the Supreme Court reiterated that the death penalty should be given only in the "rarest of rare" cases. The court also laid down the guidelines to identify the rarest of rare cases. While life imprisonment is the rule, the death penalty is considered an exception in India.

2. Giving validity to live-in relationships, the Supreme Court of India observed in the case of *S. Khushboo v. Kanniammal & Another* (2010):

> … the acceptance of premarital sex and live-in relationships is viewed by some as an attack on the centrality of marriage. While there can be no doubt that in India, marriage is an important social institution, we must also keep our minds open to the fact that there are certain individuals or groups who do not hold the same view. To be sure, there are some Indigenous groups within our country wherein sexual relations outside the marital setting are accepted as a normal occurrence. Even in the societal mainstream, there are a significant number of people who see nothing wrong in engaging in premarital sex. Notions of social morality are inherently subjective and the criminal law cannot be used as a means to unduly interfere with the domain of personal autonomy (p. 31–32)

3. In *Chanmuniya v. Virendra Kumar Singh Kushwaha* (2010), the Supreme Court of India ruled:

> We are of the opinion that a broad and expansive interpretation should be given to the term "wife" to include even those cases where a man and woman have been living together as husband and wife for a reasonably long period of time, and strict proof of marriage should not be a precondition for maintenance under Section 125 of the Criminal Procedure Code, so as to fulfill the true spirit and essence of the beneficial provision of maintenance under Section 125. We also believe that such an interpretation would be a just application of the principles enshrined in the Preamble to our Constitution, namely, social justice and upholding the dignity of the individual (p. 22).

4. Commenting on the changing moral values in society, the Supreme Court of India in *Revanasiddappa & another v. Mallikarjun & others* (2011) noted:

> With changing social norms of legitimacy in every society, including ours, what was illegitimate in the past may be legitimate today. The concept of legitimacy stems from social consensus, in the shaping of which various social groups play a vital role. Very often a dominant group loses its primacy over other groups in view of ever changing socioeconomic scenario and the consequential vicissitudes in human relationship. Law takes its own time to articulate such social changes through a process of amendment. That is why in changing society law cannot afford to remain static. If one looks at the history of development of Hindu Law it will be clear that it was never static and has changed from time to time to meet the challenges of the changing social pattern in different time (p.18).

In the same case, the Court further observed:

> The Court has to remember that relationship between the parents may not be sanctioned by law but the birth of a child in such relationship has to be viewed independently of the relationship of the parents. A child born in such relationship is innocent and is entitled to all the rights which are given to other children born in valid marriage (p. 23).

Accordingly, the Court ruled that "such children will have a right to whatever becomes the property of their parents whether self acquired or ancestral" (p. 26–27).

5. In the case of *Naz Foundation v. Government of NCT of Delhi* (2009), a writ petition was filed in the High Court of Delhi as a public interest litigation, challenging the constitutionality of Section 377 of the Indian Penal Code of 1860, which criminalizes all types of sex except heterosexual vaginal intercourse. Section 377 read:

> Unnatural Offences—Whoever voluntarily has carnal intercourse against the order of nature with any man, woman, or animal, shall be punished with imprisonment for life, or with imprisonment of either description for a term which may extend to ten years, and shall also be liable to fine.

> Explanation—Penetration is sufficient to constitute the carnal intercourse necessary to the offence described in this section.

The High Court of Delhi ruled that Section 377 of the Indian Penal Code to the extent that it criminalized sexual acts of consenting adults in private was unconstitutional. These decisions show how old conceptions of morality in India are changing in keeping with the progress in the rest of the world. The court also observed that such a decision was necessary as Section 377 was discriminatory and adversely affected the homosexual population of the country and deprived them of basic human dignity that is assured under the Constitution of India. This decision is similar to the case of *Lawrence v. Texas* (2003), which decriminalized sodomy in the United States of America.

6. Plea bargaining was introduced in the Criminal Procedure Code of 1973 in India in 2005 as Chapter XXIA and came into effect in 2006. It applies only to offenses that can be punished by up to 7 years in prison and does not apply to offenses affecting the socioeconomic condition of the country, and against women, and children below 14 years old. There is no right to appeal after a defendant has pled guilty and a judgment has been finalized.

Earlier, plea bargaining was frowned upon by the Supreme Court of India. In a case related to a white-collar crime, *Murlidhar Meghraj Loya v. State of Maharashtra* (1976), the Supreme Court of India observed that, in the United States of America, white collar criminals enter into plea bargains and get a compromised deal in criminal cases, which helps clear the court docket. The white collar criminal defendant can plead guilty in exchange for having to serve time in prison. Such a practice in the case of white collar crimes, the court noted, can benefit everyone involved in the transaction, the offender, the prosecutor, and the judge, but not the remote victim and society that suffers in silence. However, this stand in India has now changed with the introduction of plea bargaining, albeit with restrictions on the kind of cases, unlike the United States.

United States

VII

MICHAEL M. BERLIN

Overview of United States Legal Systems

The United States has a dual federal and state court system. The vast majority of criminal cases involves violation of state laws and are tried in state courts. Crimes involving violation of federal statutes are tried in federal court, but federal courts also play a critical constitutional role with regard to state cases.

The U.S. Constitution created the federal court system. Article III, Section 1 provides for "one Supreme Court" and "such inferior courts as the Congress may from time to time ordain and establish." State court systems originated independently in the 13 colonies.

State court systems typically have a four-tier structure that includes two trial courts (a court of general jurisdiction and a court of limited jurisdiction) and two appellate courts. Trial courts adjudicate cases, hear testimony from witnesses, review evidence, rule upon applicable law and procedure, and make decisions of fact. Trial courts hear both criminal and civil cases. Criminal cases involve charges brought by the state against one individual or multiple defendants, provide for sentences that carry the possibility of incarceration and require proof beyond a reasonable doubt for conviction. Civil cases typically involve disputes between individual parties, provide for an award of money damages or decrees of specific performance, and require proof by a preponderance of the evidence.

The court of general jurisdiction is usually located in the county seat. It hears serious criminal cases, primarily felonies, as well as substantial civil cases. Courts of general jurisdiction are known by a variety of names in different states, including Circuit Courts, Courts of Common Pleas, District Courts, Superior Courts, and, sometimes, Supreme Courts.

State courts of limited jurisdiction hear less serious criminal cases, often misdemeanors, as well as smaller civil cases. Like courts of general jurisdiction, courts of limited jurisdiction are known by different names in different states, including County Courts, Magistrate Courts, Municipal Courts, and District Courts, among others. A recent trend in state court systems has been the development of problem-solving or specialty courts.

The vast majority of criminal cases are disposed of through plea bargaining and preliminary dispositions. Given enormous caseloads and limited judicial resources, this practice is likely to continue at both the state and federal level.

Appellate courts review decisions of the lower courts, generally based on the record, which includes trial transcripts, docket entries, and exhibits. Their caseloads are dramatically lower than those of trial courts. Most states have a two-tier appellate system, consisting of an intermediate appellate court and the highest court (or court of last resort). Intermediate appellate courts are often called Courts of Appeal. Defendants convicted in courts of general jurisdiction usually have an appeal of right to the intermediate appellate court. To prevail on appeal, the defendant must typically demonstrate that the trial court made an error of law or otherwise abused its discretion. Errors of law most frequently involve trial court rulings on the admissibility of evidence, jury instructions, and other technical issues. If the defendant prevails on appeal, the case is typically reversed and remanded back to the trial court for a new trial consistent with the findings of the appellate court. In some instances, however, the appellate court may simply reverse the decision of the trial court.

The states' highest appellate courts are often known as Supreme Courts. Relatively few cases are appealed to the state supreme courts, especially in the vast majority of states, which have intermediate appellate courts. Some state statutes provide for automatic appeals to the state's highest appellate court in death penalty and certain other cases. More often, states require the petitioner, or appealing party, to file a writ of certiorari requesting permission to appeal. For permission to be granted, the petitioners usually must demonstrate that the appeal involves either an unsettled area of law requiring the court's guidance or an important public policy issue.

The federal trial court is the U.S. District Court. There are 94 U.S. District Courts, with at least one in each state and U.S. territory. In addition to the District Courts, there are additional specialized federal trial courts. U.S. District Court judges are appointed by the president and confirmed by the U.S. Senate. Pursuant to Article III of the U.S. Constitution, they have lifetime tenure in office. U.S. District Courts adjudicate both civil and criminal cases and have original jurisdiction over violations of federal criminal statutes. Cases tried at the state level may enter the federal court system only after all state appeals have been exhausted.

The intermediate federal appellate court is the U.S. Circuit Court of Appeals. There are 12 Circuit Courts of Appeal, divided by geographical region, plus one additional Federal Circuit for a variety of specialized appeals. These courts hear appeals of federal civil and criminal cases. Criminal defendants convicted in the U.S. District Court are typically entitled to an appeal as of right to the U.S. Circuit Courts of Appeals.

The U.S. Supreme Court is the highest court in the land and the court of last resort. While the U.S. Supreme Court has original jurisdiction in a few special types of cases, the vast majority of its cases involve judicial review of lower court decisions that raise important federal questions or issues.

Critical constitutional issues often arrive at the U.S. Supreme Court from the state's highest court by way of a writ of certiorari. Landmark criminal procedure cases such as *Miranda v. Arizona* 384 U.S. 436 (1966), involving the right to counsel prior to a custodial interrogation; *Mapp v. Ohio* 367 U.S. 643 (1961), establishing the exclusionary rule, which prevents prosecutors from using evidence obtained in violation of the Constitution; and *Terry v. Ohio* 392 U.S. 1 (1968), setting forth the standard for stop and frisk, were brought to the U.S. Supreme Court as a result of this process.

Consistent with the U.S. model of dual federal and state court systems, most civil and criminal cases are tried in the state courts. The federal courts typically hear cases arising under federal statues or involving federal questions or constitutional issues. Diversity jurisdiction involving citizens or corporations from different states is another major source of federal jurisdiction.

Interview of Judge Robert M. Bell, Maryland Court of Appeals

8

MICHAEL M. BERLIN

Contents

Introduction

Career Highlights

Judge Robert M. Bell is the chief judge of the Maryland Court of Appeals, Maryland's highest court. Judge Bell's judicial career spans nearly 40 years and includes service on all four tiers of the Maryland state court system.

Judge Bell graduated in 1966 from Morgan State College (now Morgan State University), a historically black college in Baltimore, Maryland. He entered Harvard Law School later that same year. After graduating from Harvard Law School in 1969, Judge Bell returned to Baltimore, where he became an associate at Piper and Marbury, a prominent law firm. At Piper, he worked on cases involving a wide variety of issues, including labor law, zoning, hospital discipline, legislative relations, and charities. Piper encouraged its associates to perform volunteer work and, as a young attorney, Judge Bell had the opportunity to represent pro bono clients in both criminal and civil cases. He became personally acquainted with William L. Marbury, one of the founders of the firm and a descendant of the William Marbury of *Marbury vs. Madison* fame. Marbury's philosophy was one of civic responsibility: Do well for yourself and give back.

Judge Bell remained at Piper until January 1975, when he was appointed as a judge of the District Court of Maryland for Baltimore City. He served on the District Court bench for five years until his appointment to the Supreme Bench of Baltimore (now the Circuit Court for Baltimore City) on January 22, 1980. He ran for office in the next election and served on the Supreme Bench until his appointment in 1984 to the Maryland Court of Special Appeals. In 1991, Governor William Donald Schaefer appointed Judge Bell to the Maryland Court of Appeals. He was named chief judge of the Court of Appeals by Governor Parris Glendening on October 23, 1996, and still holds that position today.

As an African American who grew up in a segregated society and went on to become chief judge of the Maryland Court of Appeals, Judge Bell has a unique perspective on the legal system. At the age of 16, he participated in a civil rights era lunch counter sit-in to ensure equal access to accommodations for African Americans in Maryland and found himself a criminal defendant. Following his conviction for trespassing, his case was heard by the Maryland Court of Appeals and considered by the U.S. Supreme Court. His conviction was overturned.

Brief Overview of the Maryland Legal System

Maryland's court structure is similar to that of many other U.S. states. Maryland has two trial courts. The Maryland District Court is the court of limited jurisdiction, which hears less serious criminal cases, generally misdemeanors, and smaller civil cases involving (with limited exceptions) amounts under $30,000. The Circuit Court is the trial court of general jurisdiction, which hears more serious criminal cases, generally felonies, and larger civil cases. Each of Maryland's 23 counties and Baltimore City has multiple District Court locations throughout the county, as well as a Circuit Court, typically located in the county seat.

Maryland has two appellate courts. The Court of Special Appeals is the intermediate appellate court to which litigants are entitled to an "appeal as of right." The Maryland Court of Appeals is the state's highest court and has a mix of discretionary and statutory jurisdiction, which will be discussed later. The Court of Special Appeals and Court of Appeals are located in Annapolis, Maryland, the state capital.

State courts generally have a similar four-tier system of two trial and two appellate courts, although other arrangements are possible. There is usually a trial court of limited jurisdiction, a trial court general jurisdiction, an intermediate appellate court, and a court of last resort. However, the names of the courts vary substantially from state to state.

The Interview

Judge Bell was interviewed in his Baltimore office in Court House East. The interview lasted approximately two hours and the atmosphere was very relaxed and comfortable. We covered a wide range of topics beginning with general background questions concerning career highlights and then went on to discuss early experiences and influences that contributed to Judge Bell's decision to enter the legal profession; questions of judicial philosophy and administration; and the judge's insight on a variety of specific legal and criminal justice issues.

Do you remember when and why you decided to become a lawyer?

I don't know precisely, but I know I wanted to be a lawyer for a long time. I made the decision when I was a kid, probably in elementary school. I did a lot of reading and one of the books I used to read was Erle Stanley Gardner's books on Perry Mason. I was very intrigued by the portrayal of a lawyer by Erle Stanley Gardner and was particularly impressed by the good that lawyers did and the excitement. So, I think, I decided back then to become a lawyer. That is, after I had determined my first love, which had been drawing art, wouldn't work for me because I couldn't draw.

Is there anything in particular about growing up in North Carolina and Baltimore that influenced your career choices?

I noticed significant differences between growing up in Baltimore and growing up in North Carolina. For example, the difference in schooling. My cousins did not go to school as often as we did. I remember being down there during the winter and I remember once going to school with them, but then the next several days they didn't go because they were working.

I also noticed there was a difference in the social interaction between the races. In Baltimore, we were segregated as they were, but the difference was our segregation was almost complete, we had our part of town and only ventured out to the other part of town when you really had to. We had a shopping area to which black folk went. In East Baltimore, it was on K Street and in West Baltimore it was on Pennsylvania Avenue. While the merchants were white, you were pretty much insulated from the kinds of day-to-day interactions that were going on in the South.

There were signs and we knew we could not go into certain places, but we were not in a position to see them as often as when we went to North Carolina. We had our own movie theatres so you didn't have to go to a segregated movie theatre. The segregation here was less obvious because of the protectionism of parents and the community. They kind of shielded us from parts of it. Now, there were times if you ventured off and you went downtown to buy a suit or something, then you would run into it.

I remember very vividly having to go to the back door of the Friendly Grill in Infield, North Carolina, where we went to get something to eat. I remember sitting up in the balcony in the movie theatre in North Carolina. There was only one movie theatre; it was segregated so that white people sat on the first level and we sat on the balcony. Quite frankly, I could never understand because I liked sitting on the balcony and besides I could dump stuff on them. I also recall having to change busses going south once you got to D.C. Trailways was the only bus that went south, the Greyhound didn't.

Are there any other experiences that influenced career choices beyond what you have already discussed?

I don't know about anything that influenced career choices, but I mean there was a difference in the influence of society structure then as opposed to now. For example, you had doctors, lawyers, ministers, and teachers in the neighborhood because of segregation. My teachers, for example, the ones that I remember most vividly, lived about two or three blocks up the street from me and I had to walk by their house to get to school. We had that neighborhood, [but it] was not a homogenous neighborhood in that you only had blue collar or white collar and what not. There was a kind of community feel in a sense that everyone pretty much knew each other. If they didn't know each other, they recognized everyone and there was a sense of vigilance in the sense that there were no restrictions placed on anybody in the neighborhood when it came to disciplining somebody. If my mother saw somebody doing something he had no business doing, she was tacitly authorized to do something about it. So it was a real sense of community and I have often said that, when somebody celebrated a success of some kind, it was something that everybody knew about and appreciated and pretty much joined in, if not physically, at least spiritually.

You have to talk about what happened in school because we had a segregated school, no question about that, and the teachers were very involved with their students in terms of trying to motivate them to do better and do as well as they could. We were always told about black folk who had done well, it was a sense of pride and we were always told about focusing on "p's and q's" because you were being watched and what you do is not only affecting you, but it affects the entire group of us. This was a theme that was rather consistent for everyone. The teachers were very dedicated to teaching. The class sizes were double classes and we would have half days because it was such a large number of students, but that didn't stop the teachers from spending as much time as they thought was necessary nor did it stop them from stopping by your house if you didn't act right.

You described a sense of community amongst African Americans. What do you think has happened over the past decades?

Success. The more affluent you are, the more you feel that you can take advantage of that affluence. So, you move out and better yourself. When everyone was in the same boat as a result of blatant segregation, you didn't have a choice and didn't see the flight. You also have the social issues, in the old days if anybody got pregnant, nobody ever heard about it. The kids went away to someplace and came back and nobody knew exactly why, but it was not something that anybody celebrated, and it was not something that anybody talked about. With the advent of the disclosure of the pregnancy and the lessening of the shame involved in it, it became more and more acceptable. I expect that had some impact because young people having kids they were unable to parent put the burden on the grandparents who, while they were tougher on their own kids, tended to be less tough on the others. With success, you started seeing people drawing lines between themselves and people who were less fortunate. After moving out, they saw no continuing responsibility for those who were left.

Can you describe for me your involvement in the *Bell v. Maryland* case and the lessons you learned as a result of your involvement in the case?

The lesson that I tell kids about all the time is a very simple one and that is that you are going to have a whole lot of choices that are going to be thrown at you and you can make those choices based on one's own self-interest or you can make them on the basis that it's the right thing to do. My lesson is that you make them on the basis for what is right and, in the end, everything is going to work out fine. You'll see the fruits of that decision.

I was the student government president at Dunbar, so I was the point person for contact by the students at Morgan who really were the organizers of the demonstration and the sit-in. I was asked to help recruit high school students to participate in a demonstration to occur the last day of school in 1960. When the day came, we got on the bus and the leader of the bus was a fellow named Quarrels. His wife was with him; they were both Morgan students. The first thing we did was to go down to Baltimore Street and picket a couple of establishments. After an hour there, we ventured up the street and found Hooper's restaurant. We went in and sat at different tables, one student to a table. The restaurant said they were not going to serve us; we refused to leave. The manager came in and asked us to leave and we refused. Eventually, they called the police. An officer read the trespass statute and we again refused to leave. At that point, the officer placed us under arrest. Quarrels negotiated a deal. We were not taken off in a paddy wagon to the old Central District, which at that time was at Fayette Street and Fallsway. The deal was that we would report on Monday morning to the old Central District for processing, fingerprinting, and charging.

We reported on Monday morning, were charged with trespassing, and later tried in Circuit Court, the old Supreme Bench in the Mitchell building. We were tried by Joe Byrnes, John Carroll Byrne's father, and were convicted, sentenced to a $10 fine, which was suspended, and offered probation without verdict, which we refused because we wanted to take the appeal.

The case went to the Court of Appeals; there was no court of Special Appeals at the time. The Court of Appeals affirmed the conviction. Maryland was represented by Lawrence Rodowsky. We were represented by Robert Watts, who later became a judge, and Juanita Jackson Mitchell. Thurgood Marshall, who later went on to become a U.S. Supreme Court justice, was involved in the case for a brief period of time.

The U.S. Supreme Court granted certiorari. However, the case was not decided on the merits. In the interim, a public accommodations law was passed for Baltimore City and the State of Maryland. Justice Brennan who wrote the opinion for the plurality of the U.S. Supreme Court sent it back to the Maryland Court of Appeals for review in light of the changed circumstances. There were, of course, those on the Supreme Court that would have affirmed the Court of Appeals decision. That group was led by, believe it or not, Hugo Black, and there were those that would have reversed outright on the merits. That group was led by Justices Douglass and Goldberg. The case went back to the Maryland Court of Appeals, which initially reaffirmed its earlier decision. On a motion for reconsideration several months later, the court reversed itself. With the reversal, I was no longer a convicted misdemeanor. Robert Charles Murphy who represented the state at the time was chief judge of the Maryland Court of Appeals when I joined the court.

Do you recall what influenced your decision to go to Harvard and did your experiences there shape your legal philosophy?

I chose Harvard based upon its reputation as the best school. I was influenced by my professors at Morgan. I always wanted to go to Harvard because of the reputation. It was supposedly the best school going and recognizing that and being encouraged by professors at Morgan, that's where I set my sights to go. Paul Sarbanes, who later became a U.S. senator, and his wife, Christine, also reinforced my decision.

I am not sure that anything at Harvard influenced my philosophy or anything else. The times that I was living in, probably more than anything else, had a lot to do with how I turned out. In those days, everyone was about saving the world, remember it was the 60s. So, you had that sense that there was a mission to be accomplished and you had to be a part of it. In fact, I often think about one of my buddies in Detroit at a large law firm there. He started out in the Legal Aid Bureau up in Brooklyn, New York. We all had the sense that there was something for us to do that had little or nothing to do with making money.

I ended up at Piper for an interesting reason. I figured that rather than going out and hanging up a shingle, I should probably get as much experience as I could from those that could afford having me mess up. That's how I ended up going with Piper. I intended on staying there only a short time in order to get my bearings and underpinnings. But Harvard was interesting experience. I always tell people it was a trade school. Unlike what I understood Yale was like, Harvard was really not about trying to look at the broader picture, it was focused on being a technician. Law school is a conservative institution and one should look at it that way. But, I understand that at Yale, for example, they really did get into the humanistic aspect unlike Harvard. The movie *Paper*

Chase was set at Harvard. One of the guys on whom it was based was a fellow named Clark Byce. As scary as he could be, this was just intimidation. It was one of the things he did and it was not the most pleasant experience.

You were at Morgan State University in the 1960s. Did the fact that it was a socially active time influence your educational experiences or career?

I was student government president and we were very active at Morgan. I remember participating in a political convention right around the time that Johnson was running. We were very active in trying to change the rules of the game on campus. In those days you had very restrictive rules on dorm visitation, on visitors on campuses, and on student involvement in university policy. We were able to put students on various academic committees and able to expand some of the rights of students through activism.

The same thing happened at Harvard when we were there. Kennedy was assassinated while I was there. The Black Law Students Association formed while I was there and that led to some activism on our part. In fact, one of the things that I was involved with was the recruitment of the first African American tenured professor at Harvard, Derek Bell, who just recently died. In fact, Derek was then the dean of a law school and I went out to California to recruit him. This was done as the result of the creation of the organization of BALSA. In those days it was the Black American Law Students Association, now it's the Black Law Students Association, BLSA, without the American in it. We cannot lay claim to having founded it; Jay Cooper at New York University did this.

You legal career spans about 42 years thus far, if I calculated correctly. Did anything surprise you about how your career developed?

The fact that I am a judge. I never intended or thought about becoming a judge. In fact, once I got out of law school and went to Piper, I intended to go out and practice law on my own. Actually, at the time I didn't have the requisite experience to be a judge, but things were changed because there were very few African American judges on the Circuit Court in Baltimore before the early 1970s. You had Joe Howard who had run for office and won in 1968, Harry Cole and Robert Watts, as I recall. George Russell had been a judge, but left the bench. In the District Court there was William Murphy, senior, and I believe Jim Bundy, or maybe Bundy came a little later, I'm not sure, but that's about it. No appellate judges. There were some concerns that we didn't have anyone in the pipeline either, so I was approached because of my background, the degree from Harvard, the associateship at Piper, they figured I could make the list. I was asked to apply. Among those who did the pushing was John Hargrove, so I agreed to do it and became a judge on January 2, 1985. Of course, that was almost 30 years ago.

Did your work prove as interesting and rewarding as you thought?

Oh, yes. I don't think there is any doubt about that. It has had its moments.

How does your life as an appellate judge differ from your life as a trial judge?

The degree of involvement in each case is totally different. You're a member of a committee that gets the cases on the appellate level, either a three-person committee or a seven-person committee, whereas in the trial courts you were actively engaged in all of the decision making and it's your call, right or wrong, your call. In addition to that, the focus is different. In a trial, you're looking at issues as they affect that particular case; you're trying to resolve an objection on the basis of the facts and the circumstances that exist in that case. On the appellate level, you're looking at a more broad resolution of the matter. What you are looking at is not how it is going to impact this case only, it is also the ramifications of any ruling that you make on subsequent cases. When you change the facts a little bit, does the decision hold up? When you take it to its extreme, does it make any sense?

   In addition on the appellate level, especially on the Court of Appeals, you're dealing with trying to anticipate issues as well. You're looking down the road determining whether or not there are issues that need to be resolved in order to move this thing called law and the rule of law along. So, you're much more engaged in a much broader level than you are at the trial level. You are not dealing just with the litigants in the case, you're dealing with litigants, broadly speaking, and you're dealing with the system, broadly speaking.

As chief judge of the Maryland Court of Appeals, the state's highest court, you and your colleagues are able select your cases. Can you briefly describe the process and factors the court takes into consideration in whether or not to accept a case?

Well, first of all we need to make clear that's not entirely true that we select all of our cases. There are categories of cases that we have to take. One, of course, that everybody knows is the death penalty. If a person has been sentenced to death, that person has an absolute right and, in fact, has nothing to say about review of that case, it has to be reviewed by the Court of Appeals. Now, recently, the legislature has given us jurisdiction over innocence cases, those cases in which it is alleged that technological advances can demonstrate the person didn't do the deed. Those cases are reviewed by the Court of Appeals.

   Obviously, because we regulate the profession, cases involving the discipline of lawyers and the admission of lawyers to the bar, are cases that we have to hear. Of course, when the issue is of Maryland law, it is the Court of Appeals that is the voice of last resort, and any issue that arises outside of the Court of Appeals can be certified by the Court of Appeals for resolution and those cases can only come to the Court of Appeals. Then, there is, of course, the 10-year deal where every 10 years the apportionment of the legislature comes before the court. These cases are in the Court of Appeals as a matter of original jurisdiction. They are all ours, whether we want them or not.

With regards to those other cases, we've got two ways of doing it. We have petitions of certiorari where lawyers, having filed the appeal, believe the case is of such interest and such importance to bench and bar that it ought to be finally decided by the Court of Appeals, they file that petition with the court. In that instance, the court is looking to the extent in which the case presents a novel issue, which will have an impact beyond the parties in the initial case and whether or not it is something that has the kind of notoriety that requires final resolution by the highest court. So what we are really looking at is whether it is in the public interest for the Court of Appeals to decide the case. For example, if it is a case involving the interpretation of self-defense, something that has happened time and time and time again over the last hundred years, the court will not accept that as a case to be decided by the Court of Appeals unless it presents a little twist in which we have never got involved. When we first addressed imperfect self-defense, it was a self-defense case, but the attorneys put enough twist in it because they added in that the person really believed it was self-defense even though the facts didn't support it. Does that at least mitigate it? Well, that caused us to look at that because that does have some impact on how these cases will be tried in the future.

I'm talking about two different ways of getting there. One is by filing a petition of certiorari and it is this whole business about whether it's in the public interest or in the benefit of the bench or the bar to have this issue resolved. When a petition is filed, the petition requires the concurrence of at least three of the four judges on the court and hopefully those three judges aren't just voting on the case just because they think it was wrongly decided. The reason for the three is that it shows it has a significant interest, but it's not enough to decide the case. So, it takes three votes and the way we do this is we start with the junior judge voting then we move up to the most senior judge with the senior chief judge voting last. Judges can either say, "I vote to take it," or you can say or give a reason why you want to vote for it. There is no set way of doing the vote.

The other way we take cases is that we have committees of the court; we have three committees of the court that view every yellow brief that's filed in the Court of Special Appeals. The yellow briefs are filed by the plaintiff's lawyers, who are the petitioners. What we are doing is having those committees, which are made up of two judges, look for cases that are ultimately going to end up in the Court of Appeals, cases with novel issues. Cases involving legislation, for example, where constitutionality is an issue and it's an issue that has never been decided before. Or, its new legislation that we need to have a definitive determination made as soon as we can. If those two judges agree that the case is one that merits consideration by the court, that particular case is presented to the court and, if it gets another vote, it's put on our docket.

By the way, there is another category of cases. There are certain election cases that the legislature has required us to resolve as opposed to having it go before the Court of Special Appeals. Most are done through writs of certiorari. To be perfectly honest with you, there was a time that we would do more of the bypasses, but there is a danger with bypasses, to the extent that [if] cases have not been fully briefed, they may end up presenting problems that you can't anticipate because there has been no response to the petitioner's brief. So what you're doing is flying blind in many instances and so we cut back on the use of the bypass as a means of getting the cases.

What do you see as the most important changes that have happened in criminal justice over the course of you career? (Criminal justice = police, courts, corrections, parole and probation, juvenile justice, etc.)

It varies, actually. There was a time when we had a flurry in the death penalty issues we had to resolve, not constitutionality, because that decision was made by the U.S. Supreme Court, but we had to resolve how our statute comported with the guidelines laid down by the Supreme Court. We had a large number of cases dealing with every aspect of the death penalty statute, which passed. At some point, we considered an issue about lethal injections, the extent to which it was a constitutional punishment or whether it was cruel and unusual.

We've had issues with regard to right to die and every 10 years we do get involved in this reappointment stuff and that is critically important. And, throughout the years, we're dealing [with] issues of discipline of lawyers, which is critically important to the public at large.

Other possible changes include changes in philosophies, organizational arrangements, specializations, policies and programs, equipment, personnel, diversity, etc.

I really have not thought about that. When I started out, this was a Warren court dealing with the rights of defendants. Very expansive rights and they went on to reach a high point and what I have been noticing in the last part of my career is, having reached that high point, they are on the way back down. Interposed within that equation are victim's rights. Maryland has passed a constitutional amendment on victims' rights and the number of cases raised on the issue of what rights victims have, have risen and are much more active and have become a part of the legal or criminal jurisprudence. It's not just defendant and state, it is defendant, state, and the victim. So, I'm noticing, first of all, a dismantling, to some extent, of a number of the rights that were accorded to defendants; if not a dismantling, at least the moderation of them and the rise of another branch of the jurisprudence dealing with the victim's rights.

What changes in external conditions, such as support from communities, changes in legal powers, judicial relations with the community,

generally, and minority communities, specifically, resource provision, political influence, have had a significant impact on the criminal justice system? Especially the judicial system.

After I became chief judge, we started trying to deal with outreach and do a better job of it. For example, we now have in the Maryland judiciary a court information office. We call it the *office of communications*. In that way, we are able to communicate with the public at large and with the media. What the court is doing is trying to maintain a degree of transparency on our operations. In addition to that, we have put into place and have had it in place for a long time, a speaker's bureau that allows our judges time off to educate the public on what the judiciary does, how it does it, and why. Our court information office is involved and engaged in putting together brochures and pamphlets and other forms of media to deal with aspects of the judiciary's core function and it helps judges with communicating to community groups, schools, other agencies, and branches of government.

In addition, we have had mediation in place for about 12 years now. We are looking for alternatives to courts. We are looking at how we can best maximize access to the justice system by empowering people to resolve their own disputes. We have an Access to Justice Commission, the function that is to look at those issues which present barriers to access and suggest ways of dealing with those issues, tearing down those barriers. So we have more active engagement with [the] public than we had 15 years ago. I should mention the fact that we are now involved, we've now put together problem-solving courts. There was a time when we experimented with summary judgment in divorce cases. That was a way to try and allow people to navigate the system in that particular area without having to invest in a lawyer and make it easier for them.

The problem-solving courts are another way of trying to deal with the problems that society is facing on a broader scale than it ever has before. We've got drug courts, we've got drunk driving courts, we're on the verge of doing veteran's courts, we have mental health courts. All of these courts are supposed to deal with an issue that is of some concern to the public and has an impact, a disproportionate impact, on members of the public. These courts are at both District and Circuit Court levels. We have approximately 40 of those courts now across the state at both levels. We've got juvenile courts, which have always been specialized courts, but we've supplemented the juvenile courts with a family, a holistic approach. That's another thing, family courts, that's something we didn't have. What we tried to do is fashion a remedy so that people are dealt with more as a group, as a family, as opposed to individuals separated from each other even though all of their problems interconnected. So, we have all of those things that we have put into place in the last 15 years.

How do you think the public perceives the courts?

Better than the executive and legislative branches. I don't know, it varies. We've done surveys and we do better than the other two branches of government. We do not do as well as we would like. Our best ambassadors are those who have been involved with the courts, for example, former jurors have a much better understanding of what we're doing and what we're trying to do and can, therefore, appreciate the job we're doing better than the average person who only sees us maybe as a traffic case, who gets most of their information from the television; you know, where the judicial system is portrayed as entertainment.

The last survey we did a number of years ago showed that we were above the other two branches of government, but were significantly below some other groups, like plumbers, which is somewhat disheartening, but, of course, one has to understand that there is a dissatisfaction across the board with government and it is something that has been going on over time. It didn't just happen. The survey results may be on the Web site.

Can you tell me a little bit about the role of the Administrative Office of the courts?

Well the Administrative Office of the Courts is really what it is, the administrative office. It is the state court administrator who is my appointee. His responsibility is to perform administrative functions for every aspect of the judiciary. We have separate Circuit Courts, 24 of them. We have a Court of Appeals, a Court of Special Appeals, and we have a District Court. Servicing the Circuit Courts are clerks of the court. There is an information system, which deals with all of them and, of course, there has to be an Human Resources (HR) system. The Administrative Office of the Court houses all of these things and it is the role of the state court administrator to be the one who oversees getting these things organized and coordinated.

I have chosen to pull some things out of the Administrative Office of the Court because we have a District Court system that is co-extensive with the state and it has a chief judge. Now, you can't have a court administrator administering the District Court chief judge. That causes something of a logistical issue, so what we have done is to make sure the Administrative Judicial Information System (JIS) Office of the Court handles everything that is statewide, that is not a core District Court function. So all of JIS is an administrative office, all of finance is an administrative office, all of HR is an administrative office, even though there is some duplication in the District Court, but the function is to make sure all of those things operate well and function together.

What we've done is to develop a cabinet so that the chief judge of District Court, the chairman of the Conference of Circuit Judges, the chief judge of the Court of Special Appeals, and the chief judge of the Court of Appeals sit as a body along with the State Court administrator to consider and address issues that affect the system statewide and issues that transcend the various boundaries of these various courts. The Conference of Circuit Court Judges is a group; there is no Circuit Court chief judge, there are 24 separate ones. What we have done is created a system, a conference wherein each Circuit Administrative judge is represented and there are eight circuits plus one representative from each of the circuits, so that's 16 members and they choose from amongst themselves the chair of that body and that person functions essentially as the chief judge of that group. We sit together as a group to consider all of these issues.

There are certain functions that do not fit comfortably in that format. The Office of Communications is one of them. Its function is co-extensive with the state, but it's not subject to the same boundaries. In other words, it has as much responsibility to communicate with the District Court as it does with the Circuit Court, Court of Appeals, and Court of Special Appeals. So, it ought not be; it can't be supervised or overseen by a District Court chief judge or a State Court administrator because its boundaries are a lot more extensive. The same thing is true of the internal audits system, trying to figure out what we're doing with our resources. That is something that has to report directly to the head of the organization. It cannot go to one of the minor players. The same thing is true of the government relations person and lobbyists. So, all of those people are placed under my direct oversight. The State Court administrator has the responsibility for coordinating most of the issues except for the District Court. The chief judge of the District Court has the District Court and I have these other special things.

Did you design this system and when was it implemented?

Kind of, over the last 15 years, because when I took over we had two internal auditors, one would report to the District Court and the other would report to the State Court administrator. You can't have the internal auditor report to the person that you're auditing, so I changed that to make sure that they report to me. When we did the Office of Communications, which has been about 13 years now, it struck me that it had to be responsive to everybody and not just one aspect of the system, so we didn't put that under the State Court administrator or the District Court. The same thing is true for the government relations person. Their function is much more extensive; it's across the board.

What do you see as the biggest challenges in the court system?

Well, there are a couple of them. One of the big ones, of course, is the financial, the economic system, the ability to fund the courts adequately. It hasn't been as big of a problem in Maryland as it has been in some places, but I can see it becoming a real issue. As things get tight, you start cutting. I can see them start cutting into the judiciary's core functions, so we've got to be vigilant against that.

What do you see as the judiciary's core functions?

Our core function, bottom line, is to the extent that we are going about what we do, we will be enhancing the rule of law and the adherence to it. But, the way we do it is by providing justice in its broad sense to those who are seeking it and seeking relief from the other two branches of government and from private entities. So, we resolve disputes consistent with the mandate of the Constitution of Maryland and the United States. Our core function, therefore, is to resolve those disputes between individuals, states, institutions, private entities, and, in the process of resolving those disputes, we are supposed to be providing "justice" in its broadest sense to those persons seeking it.

Right now what is the biggest challenge?

The other one is, of course, something Alexander Hamilton talked about—the danger of the legislative branch of government because of the power of the purse, the danger of encroachment by the legislative branch into the affairs of the judiciary. It hasn't happened as much here, but one can look at what has happened in other states where they start to limit the jurisdiction of the courts, when they start to change rulings, or they start looking at the rulings by the court and passing laws aimed at overruling them simply because of a philosophical disagreement with the court as opposed to looking at what the law is and how the law has been interpreted by the court.

Iowa is a good example. That's the same-sex marriage issue (three Iowa Supreme Court Justices were removed by voters in a 2010 judicial recall election led by conservative activist groups following the Iowa Supreme Court's unanimous vote to legalize same sex marriage in 2009. See *Varnum v. Brien* 763 N.W. 2d 862 (Iowa, 2009). These events pre-dated the U.S Supreme Court rulings in 2013 which struck down portions of the federal Defense of Marriage Act which denied federal benefits to legally married same-sex couples *U.S. v. Windsor* (2013) Slip Opinion # 12-307 and upheld the lower court rulings that California Proposition 8 which defined marriage as between a man and a woman was unconstitutional. *Hollingsworth v. Perry* (2013) Slip Opinion # 12-144), politicians start dealing with those kinds of issues and looking at whatever the court does from philosophical perspective. They are going to do what they want to do, whether or not the law is consistent with it or not, and they are using the referendum to do it, which undermines constitutional government because the whole point of the constitutional government is to protect the minority and if you're going to use referendum to have majority rule on every issue, that undermines constitutional government and does not protect the minority at all. So, those are two of the big ones I think: money and encroachment.

Is there anything you would like to say about your personal philosophies as a judge?

I don't have one. Well, to the extent that the closest I come to a philosophy is that I believe in strict construction, that if you are going to interpret a statutory enactment *you ought not be bringing to the table your own personal views on it*, and the way you get your personal views in is by expanding the scope of review. If you're going to define ambiguity in a broad way, then you get a lot more room to bring biases to bear. If you are looking at ambiguity very strictly, you recognize that a legislative enactment can make no sense at all and yet can be exactly what the legislature has passed and you must give effect to it, even if it's stupid. That's the way I look at it. I just don't believe in opening up the doors to interpretation so that I can bring to bear my own point of view and, thereby, as an activist, change the law.

Can you say something more about expanding the scope of review?

My view is if you've got a statute and the legislature said A = B and that's all they said, you should not try to find A = B + 1. Now if A = B doesn't make a whole lot of sense to you, so be it. Now some people will say, "Well, it doesn't make any sense, I have got to give it a meaning that makes some sense." Makes sense to whom? If it's me that it has to make sense to, then it seems to me that I run the risk of usurping the legislative intent or its prerogative to pass the statute. Now if I say A and B is what they said and it doesn't make any sense, the legislature has the right to say, "Well, that's not what we meant, this is what we meant." But if I say that A = B doesn't make any sense and I believe that it equals this, then what I have done is forced the legislature to take an action, which it may not be able to do because it may not have the necessary votes. I have put the onus on the legislature to do something that it should not have the onus on it to do.

So, you don't think the scope of review should be expanded?

I think it's a narrow scope of review. I'm strict construction. I would not see myself as an activist judge. In fact, those of us who are strict constructionists are not activist judges; it is the opposite. I submit to you that those who are determined to be activist judges are generally those who, when you talk to the average person about activist judges and legislatures, they are talking about liberal judges. They're not talking about activist judges because an activist judge that does what he/she wants done is not an activist. I mean if you take a position that is consistent with the conservative position, however you got there, you're not going to be called activist. If you're liberal and you take a position, no matter how you got there, you're going to be called activist no matter what. So, I don't buy this liberal and conservative. I'm not always sure I understand what it means. But, I do believe that judges ought to give effect to what the legislature intended and they ought to be very careful in the process of trying to do that; not to interpose their own views for that of the legislature.

There has been a debate in the criminal justice and legal system about the harder versus softer approaches; harsher sentencing versus rehabilitation. How do you address these issues?

Well, the truth is that you are supposed to be fashioning sentencing so as to fit the crime and the person. You ought to be looking at what is particularly appropriate for this person in light of facts and circumstances that have occurred. As far as I'm concerned, that is punishment, and that is appropriate punishment. It ought not be an extra amount just because you want to send a message. So, I believe that what you ought to do is look at the crime, how serious was it, and the prospects of this particular person benefitting from what you do. If your answer is that 20 years will benefit and have the desired effect, then 20 years it should be. If your answer is that it will not, then it ought to be whatever you think will do the job.

The desired effect is a combination of punishment and rehabilitation?

Yes, to me the desired effect is a combination of punishment and rehabilitation. I consider myself to be a rehabilitative person, because otherwise I don't understand how you would have a punishment fit the crime if you're not looking at some result down the road. If all you're trying to do is exact retribution, there is no such thing as trying to individualize punishment. If you really are interested in trying to individualize punishment or sentencing, then there ought to be some end result in mind and that end result should be a change in behavior.

Do you think that the Maryland sentencing guidelines are pretty effective in accomplishing what they are intended to do?

They are not intended to be binding, they are supposed to be helpful and to the extent that they provide the necessary information for comparisons sake so that people in one part of the state know what's going on in the other part of the state and with the idea that they will try to make sure that the discrepancies or the differences are not so great, I think the extent that they provide information is good. Whether or not judges are responding to it, I have no clue. I guess that sentences are still going and I haven't heard any complaints here recently. I suspect that it must be having some desired effect. I'm optimistic from that perspective.

How do you feel about mandatory minimum sentencing and mandatory sentencing?

Well, see that's the problem. The judiciary always opposes mandatories. The reason for it is because it limits discretion. It is the antithesis of individualized sentencing. I mean if all you're going to do is mandatory minimums and mandatory maximums, then you don't need a judge to do that, you just need a judge to do the fact finding and the conclusions of law and let anybody else do whatever you want after that and I don't think that's very useful, particularly in the harsh case. It may work for a large number of cases, but there are going to be some cases where it's going to be the greatest injustice you can imagine and there is nothing you can do about it. That is why we are so intent on making sure that we have the utmost discretion to deal with these unusual cases and deserving, I guess that's the key to it, deserving cases.

Do you think the courts do a reasonably good job with balancing the rights of defendants with the rights of the state to investigate and prosecute?

I think so. I think that all judges take it seriously and they understand the way in which the founding fathers intended it as interpreted by the U.S. Supreme Court. They recognize that there is supposed to be a burden on the state beyond that that is placed on the defendant and for the most part we try to adhere to that. So, yes, I'm satisfied that we do.

Have there been significant changes as a result of 9/11?

No, I don't think so. Not for us. The most significant change for us is that we have in virtually every courthouse, including the Court of Appeals, a police presence that we did not have before. That's something that did not initiate with me, it initiated with the governor. I did not countermand it because I did a survey of the people in the building, the judiciary employees, and found that they felt safer and so recognizing that, I acquiesced, but I am not one that believes that it really is anything more than a show.

When you say police presence, do you mean beyond just the sheriffs in the local court?

We have in the lobbies of all these buildings these machines that people come through and they have to sign in and they have to show the ID and that didn't used to be there. Well, it was in some buildings, but in the Court of Appeals, no. So, we've changed that. In fact, I didn't find out about the police officer being in the building because I don't go down there every day and even when I go to Annapolis, I don't go in the front door, I go through the back door, so I had no clue that we had police officers in the lobby until I got a call from one of the judges who was raising holy hell about why this law clerk was asking to see his ID. The executive branch has had significant changes, I'm sure of that. They've got their equivalent of homeland security and I suspect the legislature is a recipient of that, too, but we have not.

What do you think the relationship should be between theory and practice? What can practitioners learn from theory builders and what can theory builders learn from practitioners?

I learn what the theory is, but I have to apply it in real life situations, so therefore it's no longer theory. And I suspect that it is the same thing with police. I mean you sit there and you think about theory. That's fine until that situation presents itself, when you have to make a decision of hard choices based on what you have in front of you. So, to the extent that you are applying it, necessarily you can learn from theory and vice versa. Quite frankly, the actual doing of it informs the theory the next time you discuss it. I have difficulty understanding how that relates at all.

Do you think their perspective is mostly that many police executives are focused on the day-to-day, what they have to do, and don't necessarily focus on theory or the bigger picture?

No, that's different, though, I can understand that. If you're talking about an executive sitting behind his desk saying, "I'm going to make decisions for you," and then you as a police officer must apply it. You are away from the decision making in the field. To the extent that we are away from the game in terms of a trial, that doesn't change the fact that we still have to apply those same rules on the level where we are because we are in a sense providing them the template. So, to the extent that we do what we do becomes their theory that they have to apply. But, our theory comes from those books that we are reading all of the time, and our application on our level cannot be said to be in the same sense that a police officer that is a captain at a precinct is going to be as he relates to his line officers. It's not quite the same thing. It's not a perfect analogy, but I think ours is more application of theory on a more consistent basis.

Many of the police executives, especially at the top level, stay up on the theories, but many at the midlevel really don't.

Well, they really don't need to because, if the policy is made by the commissioner and his command staff writes the policy, which is then passed down, all these other folks have to do is read the policy. They don't have to worry about whether or not the policy makes sense or not. See, for us, we've got to make sure that it makes sense in the time we write it. Of course, the next level below us, the Court of Special Appeals, is continually retesting it and whatnot and the other folks are applying it because they have no choice but to do it. They can't make it, but they have to apply it.

Any particular policies and programs that you think have worked pretty well for the Court of Appeals as opposed to ones that you don't think have worked?

You mean in terms of the adjudication process? Our system is not a new system. It hasn't changed over the years, but it continues to be responsive to our needs, that is to say, the way we process the cases … the way we conference the cases at the end of the day and the way we discuss the decision of the cases. I don't think we would change it. The only other thing we have done is how best to utilize our resources when we are down a judge or two and what we've done is to use a seniority system in order to avoid any perception that we're trying to comment on decision in a particular case. For example, if we have a judge that is out of a case for some reason, in years past, we had a system of selecting a judge that would come in and decide the case. My theory has been [that] you ought to do it on a seniority basis so the same judge sits every time whether it's a case that has a liberal potential leaning or conservative. You're not choosing the judge on the basis of what the nature of the case is and no one can perceive that's the case because it's the same guy. And if you do that in a rotational basis, that I think works to our advantage and also avoids the disadvantage of having the public think that we're manipulative. That is one change that we have made and I think that works pretty well.

Has the changing technology impacted the way the courts do business?

We all have laptops. When I first started, we had electric typewriters and only the secretary had those. It was not until 1997, I think, when we started giving every judge a computer and now every judge has a laptop and we've got the research online through Lexis/Nexis and/or Westlaw and it's available to all of the judges. We are getting ready to try to obtain a single case management system so we are going to be able to communicate from one court to the next.

This would be for all the courts?

Yes, for all four courts. And with add-ons for the ancillary agencies, which feed into the system so that everybody is able to utilize the same information and, therefore, be on the same page. You could avoid a situation [like what] happened in Prince Georges County where a fellow was let go on reduced bail when the state didn't know that they were talking about the same guy. If we had a system where everybody talked to everyone else with the same information, you wouldn't have that issue. Technology has been quite helpful to us and our information system has grown quite significantly over the years. In fact, we're now looking at potential tablets for our judges as opposed to laptops. And, of course, we've all got smartphones. I'm not sure that's a good thing.

Has the foreclosure crisis impacted the Maryland court system?

Both trial courts and us because we have had over 1,200 lawyers involved in trying to help people with the foreclosure crisis. Of course, the other piece of it is that legislature has been involved in passing legislation that has changed the foreclosure process in order to slow it down and that has helped some, too. But Maryland has had an influx of a number of cases. We have a number of cases, which must be processed, particularly in Prince Georges County and Baltimore City.

Do you think the courts do a reasonably good job in providing access to disabled individuals?

We're working on it. That's why we have the access to justice commission, that's why we have the self-help centers, that's why we've got these outreach programs I told you about. We do a fairly good job. Of course, nobody ever does a perfect job, but the key, I guess, and the thing to keep in mind is that we are aware that that is an issue and being aware of it means that we keep looking at it and trying to improve our response to that issue. So, if you force me to, I think we do a pretty good job. We're not where we want to be, but we are much farther along than we once were.

Have you been affected by international developments and treaties?

My point here is that if you're deciding a case where a treaty or foreign law is at issue you have got to deal with it. And I don't have a problem as I do research accepting the wisdom of a judge from another jurisdiction even outside of the United States if what the judge says under the circumstances in the case that judge is deciding makes good sense. It is persuasiveness that you're dealing with, it is not about their system, it is not about their judge, it is about whether or not the proposition that you are citing makes sense in the context in which you're using and did it make sense in the context in which it was said. If that's the case, you use it. What you're doing is constructing an argument, not an argument, an opinion, and that opinion must hang together. If the proposition advances the opinion for the proposition you're trying to espouse, for goodness sake, you use it. To say that because something was said by somebody in another place, under a system that is not quite the same as yours, that it has no value, that is ridiculous.

Postscript

Chief Judge Bell remained in office until July 6, 2013, when he turned 70, Maryland's mandatory judicial retirement age. Judge Bell was honored by the Maryland State Bar Association and the Friends of the Robert M. Bell Committee which hosted a two-day statewide Gala and Legal Symposium called Access to Justice: Five Decades of Change in Maryland and the Impact on America in April, 2013, several months prior to the effective date of his retirement.

Interview of Stephen N. Limbaugh, Jr., District Judge, U.S. District Court, Eastern District of Missouri

9

DIANA BRUNS
JEFF W. BRUNS

Contents

Introduction

Stephen N. Limbaugh, Jr. (Judge Limbaugh) is a U.S. District judge working in the Eastern District of Missouri. His primary responsibility is to hear criminal and civil cases that fall under the jurisdiction of the U.S. federal government. Judge Limbaugh started his law career working in private practice, but shortly thereafter was elected as a State Prosecuting Attorney of Cape Girardeau County in Missouri. After serving his four-year term, he returned to private practice for the next four and one half years. He was then appointed as a Circuit Judge in the 32nd Circuit of Missouri. He served in that capacity until he was appointed to the Missouri State Supreme Court five years later. He served 16 years on the Supreme Court of Missouri (including serving a two-year term as the Chief Justice) before he was appointed to U.S. District Court, Eastern District of Missouri. Judge Limbaugh was sworn in as a federal judge on August 1, 2008 (and occupies that position today). He earned an undergraduate degree in history and a Juris Doctorate both from Southern Methodist University, Texas. In addition, he earned a Master of Laws degree in Judicial Process from the University of Virginia.

The U.S. District Court and Federal Court System

The federal court system in the United States is made up of the 94 Federal Judicial Districts to hear trial cases. In addition, there are two appellate levels in the federal court system: U.S. Circuit Courts of Appeal and U.S. Supreme Court.

The U.S. District Courts are organized into 94 federal judicial districts located throughout the United States. Federal judges located in each district hear trial cases (criminal and civil) that originate from the counties located within their boundaries. There is at least one district court per state (Missouri has an eastern and a western district court). Federal Judge Stephen Limbaugh, Jr. is one of 677 federal trial judges in the United States. He is located in the U.S. District Court for the Eastern District of Missouri.

The U.S. Circuit Court of Appeals is organized into 12 (13, if one includes the U.S. Court of Appeals for the Federal District) regional circuit courts. There are 179 Court of Appeals judges located in one of the U.S. Court of Appeals. The U.S. Circuit Court of Appeals hears cases that are appealed from federal trial courts located within their geographical jurisdiction. Their locations are diversified based on the geographic breakdown of their district. There is the Federal Circuit (along with the D.C. Circuit) located in Washington, D.C. The other court locations are:

The 1st Circuit Court: Boston, Massachusetts
The 2nd Circuit Court: New York City
The 3rd Circuit Court: Philadelphia, Pennsylvania
The 4th Circuit Court: Richmond, Virginia
The 5th Circuit Court: New Orleans, Louisiana
The 6th Circuit Court: Cincinnati, Ohio
The 7th Circuit Court: Chicago, Illinois
The 8th Circuit Court: St. Louis, Missouri (this is the appeals court for
    Judge Limbaugh's court)
The 9th Circuit Court: San Francisco, California
The 10th Circuit Court: Denver, Colorado
The 11th Circuit Court: Atlanta, Georgia

The second (and highest court) of appeals is the U.S. Supreme Court. There are nine justices of the U.S. Supreme Court and it is based in Washington, D.C.

The Interview

Will you elaborate on your career path and highlights, such as being young in the field and in the right place at the right time?

I graduated from law school a semester early from Southern Methodist University in Texas and took the Texas bar in February of 1977, having graduated in December of 1976. I passed the Texas bar in April, but to join my family law firm I also passed the Missouri bar, which granted me reciprocity. So, I had to take the Missouri-specific part and passed it in September. I practiced with my family firm for a year and a half in general practice. It turned out there was an opening in the prosecutor's office, so I was elected prosecuting attorney for Cape Girardeau County in November 1978, having never tried a jury trial; I was 26 years old and did not have much experience. The opportunity arose and it had a lot to do with my career from start to finish—I have been in the right place at the right time. People just do not get those opportunities very often. Another thing was that a public defender was my opponent, and not many people were amenable to having a public defender being the prosecutor.

I was elected and took office at age 26 and was one of the youngest prosecutors in the state, especially as an elected prosecutor. I served a four-year term, and the first two years were difficult because I was still learning. The more you do something the better you become at it. At the end of my four-year term, I was very competent at criminal law and felt I could go up against anyone in the state and give a credible performance in the courtroom. However, I decided to go back into private practice after that four-year term. Salary was low for prosecutors; I think it was $19,000 a year back then. I went back to my family firm. The last three to four months of my tenure as prosecuting attorney, we had a very strange case that required the prosecution of several not-for-profit, charitable, and even religious organizations, for gambling. The Division of Liquor Control brought the case to me against the Knights of Columbus, the Veterans of Foreign Wars, the American Legion, the Elks Lodge, and an assortment of other entities. I sent a letter and that did not stop them. So, they were shut down, and I would probably not have been reelected anyway. I rejoined the family firm and engaged in general practice for the next four and a half years. As it turned out, four months after I rejoined, my father was appointed by President Ronald Reagan to the federal bench and [he] left the firm. He became a U.S. District judge and, at the time, was the president of the Missouri bar, with a huge caseload in both state and federal court. By and large, I took over his case load.

What are your career specializations?

I was 31 years old and thrust into federal court trying significant federal cases that nobody my age would hardly have been allowed to do; however, I tried all sorts of different cases—mainly civil cases—but I was active in state court as well. This is the second time in my life that I was getting significant exposure in the courtroom. By the time I was 30, I had tried more jury trials in Southeast Missouri than anyone my age or younger. I went from a prosecuting attorney in state court to having a significant federal court case load in civil cases. I did that for four and a half years, along with the general practice.

Furthermore, I involved myself in all sorts of civic activities as well. When I was 35, Judge Stan Grimm, who was one of the circuit judges here for the three counties of Cape Girardeau, Bollinger, and Perry, went to the Missouri Court of Appeals. I had to make a career decision on whether I wanted to go into the judiciary or stay in private practice. I had to decide if I wanted to stay in private practice, doing the things that I could do in private practice that being a judge would not allow.

I was appointed by Governor John Ashcroft to fill out the remainder of Judge Grimm's unexpired term, and I was twice re-elected to the position. I served there for five years and when another event happened. There were several vacancies on the Supreme Court of Missouri. During my five-year term as a circuit judge, I did everything from juvenile court all the way to presiding judge over the entire circuit. I had a huge case load of both civil and criminal cases. I was doing litigation all the time. I presided over 50 jury trials and I also became involved in the activities of the judicial conference and started teaching some of the continuing legal education programs that were sponsored by the judicial conference at the annual judicial colleges. That helped me gain even more attraction for career advancement.

In 1992, there were several vacancies before the Supreme Court because of the unprecedented situation that five Supreme Court judges turned 70 (which is mandatory retirement) within a two-year period. So, I applied for each of the last four and was the last one selected—the last one of the [Governor] Ashcroft appointees in 1992. I went to the Supreme Court at age 40; another example of being in the right place at the right time. I went on the Supreme Court at age 40 in 1992, and served 16 years on the court, including two years as chief justice from 2001 to 2003 (that was at the time of 9/11). I had been chief justice for just two months when 9/11 occurred. I remember that to this day, because we had court on that day; by a 4 to 3 vote, we decided on proceeding with court on that day.

I served 16 years on the Supreme Court and heard hundreds of cases, although we had a case load similar to those of the U.S. Supreme Court, because we pick and choose cases that we hear. We choose the cases that are worthy of being heard by the highest court in the state. Meaning, they usually have some legal issue that is presented or there is legal conflict between the different divisions in the court of appeals. To qualify, there are some cases that we did have mandatory original jurisdiction; all death penalty cases are appealed to the Supreme Court. All judge and lawyer disciplinary cases, as well as any challenge to the constitutionality of the state statute goes straight to the Supreme Court and bypasses the state court of appeals.

For 16 years, I was on the court hearing all the difficult and sometimes nebulous cases that do not have any good answer to them, so it was a wonderful and enlightening experience. During that time, I also went back to school (in my mid-40s) attending a special program at the University of Virginia, and received a Master of Laws degree in the Judicial Process. That is a special program for appellate judges nationwide and some federal trial judges.

It was a full 36-credit hour program that was concentrated because all the classes were done in two consecutive summers. We took 12 hours of classes each summer and then we had to write a thesis. I went through that program and got it published in a major journal. It helped a lot because, not only did I learn about modern trends about the law, but also the things I should have learned in law school, but did not. For instance, constitutional law was very difficult in law school, but we had six credit hours in American constitutional history (in the Master of Laws program), and I learned everything regarding the American constitution that I should have learned in law school.

I finished 16 years and it was time for a change. Then another event occurred, with a vacancy on the U.S. District Court. I attempted to get on the U.S. Court of Appeals of the 8th Circuit, which would have been a natural progression, coming from the highest appellate court in the state, but was not successful. I had two White House interviews and I just could not get over the top. Then a district court judgeship came along and I applied and I was the first in line. My service on the Supreme Court, as well as the trial experience, put me at the top of the list. I was appointed and went through the grueling confirmation process. In the end, it turned out that my nomination was not contested and it just went through three and a half years ago on a consent calendar in the U.S. Senate. I was sworn in on August 1, 2008, three years and one month ago. Unfortunately, unbeknownst to me or anyone in my family, there is an obscure federal statute that prohibits two [family] members from serving on the same court, even though one member was senior status (which my father was at that time), so he had to retire after 25 years of service and signed up with a major law firm in St. Louis. I have been here three years [*at the time of this interview*] in this new job, and I think it is beneficial to have different careers; it keeps you fresh. This job, I could do the rest of my life. There is no mandatory retirement coming from the state court to the federal court. The state did not have much money, but the federal court has a lot of money. Anything I want, they bring it to me. The courthouse is brand new—another point about being in the right place at the right time. When this position became open, the federal courthouse in Cape Girardeau was brand new and I came right into a brand new U.S. courthouse that is state-of-the-art. The courthouse is very high tech and I have the additional honor of serving in the courthouse named (by an act of U.S. Congress) after my grandfather, Rush H. Limbaugh, Sr.; that is truly impressive. I have just been blessed by all the wonderful things that few people ever dream of.

What have been your ideals as a judge? Also, what advice do you have for future judges?

My family has been involved in the law in Cape Girardeau, state wide, and even nationally, for 50 to 60 years. Their reputation and mentorship have helped me immensely. I was able to practice law with my grandfather for 10 years, and it was a wonderful experience. Both my father and grandfather were the best mentors imaginable. I also tried to cultivate friendships with other judges and lawyers in the bar throughout the state, and tried to follow their examples. I understood early on that if I wanted to make good on the opportunities, it is not enough just to be a competent, ethical, professional lawyer, you have to do more than that. You have to be the ethical, public citizen. You have to use your special abilities as a lawyer, but also you need to do pro bono services. You need to use your special skills as a lawyer to the betterment of the community, for public service. You also should devote your time to civic and charitable events: everything from the Salvation Army to Red Cross or homeless shelter programs. That was the way I was taught. I involved myself in everything there was in Cape Girardeau that benefited the community. I tried to build my career and résumé to be worthy of these opportunities that got dropped on me. I have told others that want to be a judge that it is not just enough to be a good judge, you have to get involved in everything, politics as well. Politics has gotten a bad reputation, but politics is a noble profession.

What are some of the career developments that have surprised you?

I came out of law school terrified about going to court. I was going to be a probate trust lawyer, doing corporate work because I was fearful of the court and public speaking. Law school is not very beneficial, in the sense that it is designed to be intimidating to you. When I went to law school, we were required to stand up and recite in front of all the other students, when we were called. That was a terrifying experience for someone who was 22 years old. In addition, whatever you said to the law school professor was not going to be sufficient, and so one way or another, you were going to be humiliated or at least put back down in your chair without much positive reinforcement. There is not a lot of positive reinforcement in law school; it is designed to intimidate you so you can stand in front of mean-spirited federal judges in court. Anyway, that was the mindset I had coming out of law school. When the opportunity came up to be a prosecuting attorney at age 26, I had to change my outlook of what I wanted to do. It was terrifying at first. The first trial I did made me so nervous that I had to go outside and walk about the courthouse three times, just to get the courage to go inside. The more you do it, the more confident you become in yourself and your abilities. I worked through all that and I learned how to try cases. By the end, I felt like I could go up against anyone in open court.

How did you build confidence as an attorney?

The four years I worked as a prosecuting attorney. I was okay at first, but because of a lack of experience, there were some cases that I might have won, but did not. The last two years, I won every case—I knew what I was doing. It is a healthy experience in a way, because it is good to be a little nervous and, if you are not consumed by what you are doing, then you will not do a very good job.

What have been some of the interesting and rewarding aspects of your career?

From day one, you do not get bogged down in one type of case (you are working criminal, civil, etc.). I have prosecuted everything from DWI to murder. We had a variety of crimes and I was able to prosecute the full gamut of criminal offenses—personally. All of that was exciting, especially for someone as young as I was. It was hard work, but it was always interesting. When you go into the courtroom as a lawyer, and you are the prosecutor, you have command of the whole place. Everyone is there to see what you have to say. It is a lot of power within the courtroom.

How has forensics helped or hindered prosecutions?

Forensic stuff (DNA)—had we had DNA, there would have been more prosecutions. It works both ways: it frees people who are not guilty, and it also convicts people who would have gotten away with crimes. I was at the ABA [American Bar Association] meeting last month, and had an excellent CLE [Continuing Legal Education] that my group co-sponsored. It was about forensic evidence, everything from eyewitness identification to fingerprint identification to arson techniques. The panelist showed how so many unlawful convictions were obtained by faulty science. There have been so many advancements in the last generation, as it relates to this field of evidence. Fingerprint identification has so changed with several different comparisons that a lot of the old way of doing it has been debunked. We had a prominent judge from Canada and discussed forensic science advancement from an international perspective. DNA, in particular, and the advancement of forensic science, in general, have been the major changes.

What has the impact of drugs had on the courts?

The drug situation has been overwhelming, probably 80% of the current cases that I have are somehow drug related. In our part of the country, it is the poor black population with crack cocaine and the poor whites with methamphetamine. Both of them are low-end socioeconomic populations. There is so much of it that it is hard to believe. Even for the defendants who are not charged with possession or sale of controlled substance, a lot of offenses they are charged with are a direct result of their drug use. For instance, the feds will charge an individual with possession of a firearm as a convicted felon, instead of some kind of drug conspiracy, because the firearm cases are so much easier to prove. The elements are just that, you have a firearm and you are a convicted felon, and the firearm crossed a state line. It is so easy to prove, they will either plead the defendant to that case instead of the drug conspiracy, or possibly even let the drug conspiracy go to trial and plea out the firearms conviction. You get other things, like fraud related to gambling addiction (which has drugs at its foundation). Even child porn and fraud cases often involve substance abuse. Nobody knows the answers to the substance abuse problems. It has been bad for a long time.

What has been the significant impact of sentencing guidelines upon the criminal justice system?

Most recently, there have been reductions in sentencing guidelines for things such as crack cocaine, so that crack is more in line with marijuana, which is the benchmark by which other illegal substances are measured. However, this has caused some problems with methamphetamine because their sentencing guidelines are way up there, and they have not been rolled back. Those charged with methamphetamine get "hammered" by the sentencing guidelines.

Has the quality of the criminal justice system improved throughout the course of your career?

I think the criminal justice system has improved because of the advancements in forensic sciences. It has also improved because there are more resources for defendants. Despite all the concern about underfunding to public defenders, there are more resources available to public defendants than there was a generation ago. It is a change from that perspective. Defendants are afforded, in both state and federal court, rights and liberties that are just amazing to most people. The courts bend over backwards to make sure that all constitutional rights are afforded to them. There is not a judge or prosecutor that I know that would not be sickened by the fact of a wrongful conviction. When you see a case that involves prosecutorial misconduct, that is very rare.

Is it more or less difficult to be a judge today than in the past?

I think it is about the same. I remember in my time as a state trial judge, the federal court is much more formal; we have to write opinions on almost all decisions we make.

What do you think is the proper role of the judiciary in society?

Its purpose is to make sure every citizen is afforded the liberties they are entitled to under the constitution and statute; this is high responsibility. It is an honor to have that responsibility. I do not know any judge who does not take the responsibility very seriously.

In preferred strategies in the criminal justice system, what works best?

I think all of it is worthy of our attention. There is a big push for drug courts; I do not think they are as cost-effective as some think. The reason I do not is because of being in state and now federal trial court, the probation officers, and even the people who supervise release after incarceration, are afforded every kind of rehabilitation tool that is offered to anyone in society. There are treatments available, but there are not enough probation officers. The ones that go to drug courts are "cherry picked" and are the ones that will usually make it through the system anyway. Additionally, it is very expensive, and they only have one or two people go through every six months. For the upfront cost, the return is not effective.

How are resource problems dealt with in courts?

On the federal level, we do not have resource problems, especially compared to the states. The states are in bad shape. They do not have the resources to maintain the prison system in an effective way. The federal courts have been funded adequately and funded very well. I suppose the same holds true for the federal prisons as well. There is not a resource problem in the federal courts. With one exception, there is a shortage of resources on the borders, they need more judges, more probation officers, and they need more everything in the border states (where all the immigration cases are coming from). I could not do the job if I was a judge in the Southern District of Texas. The Southern District of Arizona is another area where the case loads are three to four times higher than here. It is unbelievable; with that exception, the federal courts are well funded.

In your opinion, what is the relationship between theory and practice?

You could write page after page about that, but the practice is more important to me. As I go through my career, I start to see that the practice is consistent with the theory.

As appellate judge, I studied at length over the years, both in formal settings, as well as on my own, the art of appellate judicial decision making. I have my own beliefs in that and abide by the tenets that Justice Scalia, Justice Thomas, Justice Alito, and Justice Roberts espouse in their originality thinking; it has its faults, but it is the least bad alternative in appellate judicial decision making. The thing that bothers me about some appellate judges is that they are outcome-orientated. That is the worst criticism you could level at me as an appellate judge, and yet there are a lot of people who think that it is exactly the way that appellate judges should act. All judges say that the foremost criterion is to pledge to follow the constitution of the United States. Well, some of us do it better than others. In our judicial decision making, when you are outcome-orientated, anything goes. That is not a proper role for an appellate judge. I could talk to you for a long time.

Have you been affected by new crime threats from other countries?

Not at all. Here in the Midwest, it is not a major factor, except for one exception. That is, we do get a significant amount of the drug traffic coming up from Mexico.

Have there been any effects of 9/11?

We are not located in a big city, so we do not have the kind of international terrorist threats that might impact New York, Chicago, or elsewhere. However, in response to 9/11 and all the law enforcement measures that were taken at that time on an emergency basis, we do have changes that have come about from wiretap cases. I have had quite a few of those that might not have been available or present before 9/11. Those types of investigative techniques are much more prevalent than they were before.

Are there areas for improvement with the development of criminal law and criminal procedures in the United States?

If it were up to me, there are certain areas of the sentencing guidelines in the federal courts that are too harsh. However, there are other areas that are too low. For instance, Tuesday, I had a case in St. Louis, involving a couple who had defrauded the government out of over $100,000. The sentencing guidelines allowed for 18 to 24 months. It was a Medicare fraud case where they opened a business-related in-home nursing care, and they provided nursing care to a lot people who did not exist or did not need it. There was little question related to their guilt. They stole over $100,000 dollars from the federal government, from taxpayers. The sentencing guidelines were 18 to 24 months.

The next case was a drug case for a person who did not have any felonies on her record; just a couple of minor misdemeanors and the sentencing guidelines were way higher than the people who had stolen $100,000. Her sentencing guidelines were 68 to 80 months, instead of the 18 to 24 months. That is something that I think is a problem as well as child porn cases, too, that have mandatory minimums that have high sentencing guidelines. That is a separate area of the criminal law that is undergoing a serious debate on both sides. With drug cases in particular, the sentencing guidelines are very high.

Let me give you two examples: my transition from state to federal court. What I have found in federal court is that the sentencing is so terribly harsh. In the state system, if you are sent to prison, you will serve a third of your time before you become eligible for parole, unless you are a career criminal. If you are a Class X felon, then one would have to serve as much as 85% of his/her incarceration before being eligible for parole. The federal system is just the opposite. Everybody serves at least 85% of their incarceration before they are eligible for supervised release. The second thing is that after three years, I have sentenced almost 200 felons in federal court; of those 200 sentencings, about a dozen were illegal alien charges that got time served and were deported. With the next 188 cases, maybe four or five qualified for probation under the sentencing guidelines. Point of the story: Do not get caught by the "feds."

What is most needed to improve the system?

I think adjustments to the guidelines, and much more importantly, is federal criminal sentencing standards altogether. As I say that, I do not mean to diminish the importance of prosecuting drug offenses severely if necessary, but there is an inconsistency in the harshness those people face and the lack of harshness that people who commit fraud (like the example from St. Louis).

Glossary of Terms

Chief Justice: Each appellate court has a chief judge who is not only responsible for hearing cases but must also have oversight over the operations of the court. Usually, the chief judge is the judge who has been serving on the court the longest (although, this is not always the case: Justice Roberts is the chief justice of the U.S. Supreme Court, but has not been the longest-serving member) (Neubauer & Fradella, 2011).

Class X Felon: A Class X Felon is someone who has been convicted of a Class X Felony. Class X felonies are usually considered to be the worst type of crimes (minus first degree murder) and the punishments are usually severe when it comes to prison sentences. Under most circumstances, if someone is convicted of a Class X felony, he/she is not eligible for probation. Some crimes that fall under this classification are aggravated kidnapping, home invasion, aggravated battery, armed robbery (Schmalleger, 2012).

DNA: DNA is an individual's genetic code that is unique to each person (although, identical twins can have some of the same markers). DNA samples can come from a variety of places, such as saliva, semen, blood, or even small skin samples. A DNA profile can be established from the sample(s) and will appear as a bar code on a film negative that will allow for comparison to the individual who is charged with a criminal violation. DNA can be used to exonerate a suspect or used to convict him/her of a crime (Brightman, 2009).

Drug Conspiracy: A drug conspiracy is when someone conspires or agrees with someone else to do something which, if actually carried out, would amount to a drug crime or offense. It is an agreement or a kind of partnership for criminal purposes, in which each member becomes the agent or partner of every other member. It is not necessary to prove that the criminal plan actually was accomplished or that the conspirator was involved in all stages of the planning or knew all of the details involved. The main elements that need to be proved are a voluntary agreement to participate and some overt act by one of the conspirators in furtherance of the criminal plan. If a person has an understanding of the unlawful nature of a plan, and knowingly and willfully joins in that plan on one occasion, that is sufficient to convict him for conspiracy, even though he had not participated before and even though he played only a minor part (Schmalleger, 2012).

Drug Court: Drug courts were established to handle the exceeding large number of drug-related cases that were "clogging" up the court system. These courts were usually used for nonviolent offenders who might be helped by something external to incarceration. The eligible participants were offered the ability to stay out of prison by completing supervised treatment and submitting to random drug testing. The idea was to find a way to change the patterns of the defendant and thereby keep him/her out of the prison system (where he/she would receive little help with the drug-related behavior). The participants who completed the program might be eligible for a reduced sentence or even a dismissal of charges. The judge who presides over the court is responsible for monitoring the positive or negative outcomes from each defendant and deciding on what course of action to take related to the defendant's actions (Siegel, 2012).

DWI: DWI (driving while intoxicated) is a legal description related to alcohol consumption and the operation of a moving vehicle. The measurement of alcohol in the system (BAC: blood alcohol content) is the set legal definition to establish where an individual is operating a motorized vehicle under the influence of alcohol. In the United States, the legal limit is .08, which is a percentage of alcohol in the blood by weight. The conviction of a DWI can have different consequences based on the jurisdiction in which the offense occurs. The outcome of a DWI can be anything from loss of license and a fine, all the way to imprisonment in a jail or state prison (Brown, Esbensen, & Geis, 2010).

Federal U.S. Court of Appeals: There are 94 judicial districts that are organized into 12 circuits. Each of the circuits has its own U.S. Court of Appeals. The main directive of each court of appeals is to hear appeals from the District Courts located within its jurisdiction, as well as possible appeals from federal administrative agencies (Neubauer & Fradella, 2011).

Forensic Sciences: Forensic science is a generic term used to analyze different investigative techniques while examining a crime scene. Forensic scientists use a variety of techniques (chemical analysis, DNA analysis, etc.) to help establish in a court of law the possible guilt or innocence of a defendant (Marsh, 2011).

Mandatory Original Jurisdiction: Mandatory original jurisdiction is the term used to signify which specific court has the first level of jurisdiction over a case. For example, the U.S. Supreme Court has mandatory original jurisdiction over cases between the states. This signifies the court that hears the case for the first time, as well as the venue in which the case should be heard (Neubauer & Fradella, 2011).

Medicare Fraud: Is a generic term that relates to an individual or organization trying to collect payments from the federal government (via Medicare) without complying with all the legal provisions required to receive said distribution. This fraud could include a healthcare provider billing Medicare without any services actually being offered. It also can include a supplier billing the Medicare system for equipment that was never used or to continue to bill the system for rental equipment after it has been returned to the supplier. In addition, this type of fraud can occur when one person uses another person's Medicare card for medical services that they are not entitled to receive. Finally, it is also fraud if an individual or organization uses false or misleading information to convince someone to join a Medicare plan.

Missouri Court of Appeals: The Missouri Court of Appeals is the first court of appeal in the state of Missouri. The court of appeals for the state of Missouri can hear state cases that are appealed from the trial courts within the state. Each state has its own court of appeals to hear state cases (criminal and civil) in nature.

Outcome-Oriented: Outcome-oriented is usually part of a performance review process. The process is set up to allow for the measurement of goals to see if they are being met, utilizing some component of outcome assessment. Does what you are measuring truly reach those goal(s) and is the measurement instrument reliable in helping the organization achieve their end results? The outcomes that the organization wishes to achieve are the focus of the planning process that goes into the benchmarks used to measure whether the goal(s) are being met (Maxfield & Babbie, 2011).

Red Cross: The Red Cross is an international organization that is designed to help in humanitarian crises throughout the world. It was started to provide human relief to all, without any discrimination based on sex, religion, nationality, and/or political opinion (Barton, 2011).

Rehabilitation: Rehabilitation is usually associated with criminal defendants and/or drug abusers. The idea is that the individual can be changed to make sure that in future times he/she will not fall back on illegal behavior and, therefore, will become a productive member of society. The goal is to use a therapeutic method, as opposed to punishment, to help individuals change their ways, not become recidivism and fall into their past ways of things. The goal is to break the habit and make sure that the defendant does not return to his/her criminal activities after already being convicted of a criminal offense (Bartol & Bartol, 2011).

Salvation Army: The Salvation Army is a religious organization that operates thrift shops and does charitable work throughout the United States as well as the world. It is one of the world's largest providers of social aid and comfort, especially when disaster strikes (Lamb, 2010).

Sentencing Commission: The body responsible for developing the U.S. sentencing guidelines.

Sentencing Guidelines: Sentencing guidelines are a set of rules established by the United States.

Supreme Court: There are two types of Supreme Courts in the United States (state and federal). All 50 states have their own final court of appeal (Supreme Court), as well as the one final court of appeal (U.S. Supreme Court). The Supreme Court (state and federal) has a chief justice who is responsible for the overseeing of the court. A Supreme Court has the ability to pick and choose which cases to hear based on nature of the case and its time constraints. A case may be appealed from the Supreme Court of a state to the U.S. Supreme Court (Neubauer & Fradella, 2011).

U.S. District Judge: A U.S. District Judge is responsible for hearing trial cases on the federal level. The federal judicial system was created by the U.S. Congress via the U.S. Constitution (Article III: they are appointed for life and can only be removed through an impeachment process). There are 94 federal judicial districts (including at least one in all 50 states), as well as the District of Columbia and Puerto Rico. A district judge is appointed by the president of the United States and must be approved by the U.S. Senate. U.S. District judges can hear all types of federal cases, including criminal and civil (Neubauer & Fradella, 2011).

References

Bartol, C., & Bartol, A. (2011). *Criminal behavior: A psychological approach*, 9th ed. New York: Prentice Hall Publications.

Barton, C. (2011). *A history of the Red Cross: Glimpses of field work*. Charleston, SC: Nabu Press.

Brightman, H. (2009). *Today's white collar crime: Legal, investigative, and theoretical perspectives.* New York: Routledge.

Brown, S., Esbensen, F., & Geis, G. (2010). *Criminology: Explaining crime and its content*, 7th ed. New Providence, NJ: LexisNexis Publications.

Lamb, E. (2010). *The social work of the Salvation Army*. Charleston, SC: Nabu Press.

Marsh, I. (2011). *Crime and criminal justice*. New York: Routledge.

Maxfield, M., & Babbie, E. (2011). *Research methods for criminal justice and criminology*, 6th ed. Belmont, CA: Cengage Publications.

Neubauer, D., & Fradella, H. (2011). *American courts and the criminal justice system*, 10th ed. Belmont, CA: Cengage Publications.

Schmalleger, F. (2012). *Criminology today: An integrative introduction*, 6th ed. New York: Prentice Hall Publications.

Siegel, L. (2012). *Criminology*, 11th ed. Belmont, CA: Cengage Publications.

Interview of Chief Judge Wilson Rambo, 4th Judicial District Court, State of Louisiana

10

ROBERT HANSER

Contents

Introduction

Selected for interview was the Honorable Wilson Rambo, chief judge of the 4th Judicial District Court of Louisiana. The interview itself took place in the judge's chambers at the Ouachita Parish Courthouse, in Monroe, Louisiana. The entire experience was quite pleasant and informative. Staff was introduced and demonstrated professionalism that was both serious yet approachable in nature. Judge Rambo was relaxed and made a point to have arrangements that were comfortable and conducive to effective interviewing. Upon learning some of the key areas of inquiry that would be relevant to students wishing to gain insight from a practicing judge, he made a point to find materials and documents that would ensure accuracy of information provided. This ensured that the interview itself was productive and that students would be given appropriate and adequate information regarding judicial proceedings in this practitioner's court.

Brief Overview of Legal Structure in Country and Region

In the United States, the court system is one that is a dual system. This dual system of judicial processing includes both the federal- and a state-level court system. While each court system has jurisdiction over certain types of cases, neither of these systems are completely independent of one another. To further complicate matters, these two systems do often interact. For both systems, the desire to solve legal disputes and to vindicate legal rights are key goals.

Both systems have, as a general rule, at least three layers of court jurisdiction. In the federal system, there are 94 District Courts throughout the United States. Each state has at least one federal district court and some states may have as many as four district courts. These courts are trial courts that have original jurisdiction and will have anywhere from 2 to 28 judges, and hear both criminal and civil cases. The next layer, the Courts of Appeals in the United States (called Circuit Courts), consists of 13 courts, 12 having jurisdiction over assigned regions of the United States, with the 13th being located in Washington, D.C., which has jurisdiction over the Federal Circuit. Lastly, the United States Supreme Court is the highest court of the federal system. This court includes nine justices, presides in Washington, D.C., and hears various cases of original jurisdiction as well as cases from the federal Courts of Appeal and, when requested, petitions from state supreme courts.

As noted, the state court systems (consisting of a separate court system for each of the 50 states in the United States) is separate from the federal system. The location for the subject of this interview was in the state of Louisiana, where there are 40 district courts that preside over both civil and criminal cases within their jurisdiction. In addition, there are five Courts of Appeal in Louisiana, which process cases appealed from the lower district courts. The Supreme Court of Louisiana, consisting of seven justices, addresses cases that meet specified criteria. The Louisiana Supreme Court is required to hear cases involving disciplinary actions against lawyers and judges as well as all cases where a law is thought to be unconstitutional or when the death penalty is imposed. For other cases, where one or both parties are not satisfied with the outcome of their case in lower court, a writ for review must be submitted and a majority of the justices (at least four out of seven) must agree to have the case brought forward.

It is perhaps important to note that the legal traditions in the state of Louisiana are unique from most others in the United States. Indeed, Louisiana is the only state to have based much of its initial judicial structure on what is referred to as the **Napoleonic Code**, which reflected the French cultural influences upon that state's early history. This was somewhat different from other states, which tended to use precedent and structures similar to the English common law customs. Thus, the judicial process in the state of Louisiana, to some extent, has been distinct from other state court systems, mainly in terms of French cultural influences on legal precedents. Lastly, as a reflection of the influence of French culture on this state, legal jurisdictions will include at least one or more parishes; *parish* being a term that is synonymous with *county* in the other 49 states. The 4th Judicial District Court includes, within its jurisdiction, both Ouachita and Morehouse Parishes, which are located in the northeast section of Louisiana.

The Interview

Career Overview

Judge Wilson Rambo currently serves as chief judge of the 4th Judicial District Court for Morehouse and Ouachita Parishes. He earned his Bachelor of Arts in Political Science from Louisiana State University in 1979 and his Juris Doctor from the LSU-Paul M. Hébert Law Center in 1982. While working on his Bachelor and Juris Doctor degrees, Rambo served on the staff with the state legislature. He also worked as staff with the Louisiana 2nd Circuit Court of Appeal as well as an assistant district attorney for the 4th Judicial District in that same state. While in private practice, Rambo served as in-house counsel for the City of Monroe's Marshal's Office and as local counsel for the Southern States Police Benevolent Association. He likewise worked as a public defender with the 4th Judicial District and served as a past president and founding member of the Louisiana Public Defender Association. Judge Rambo presently serves as a hearing officer for the Judiciary Commission, which deals with ethical violations relative to the conduct of judges and justices of the peace. He also presents continuing education regularly on behalf of the Louisiana State Bar Association and other professional organizations on a variety of topics including ethics and professionalism for both lawyers and judges. Among his community service activities are participation in the American Inns of Court as a past president and master of the Fred Fudicar local chapter, service on the Access to Justice Committee of the Louisiana State Bar Association, membership on the steering committee of the Family Justice Center, work as a trustee for Our House, service as a CASA Advocate, as well as membership in various Chambers of Commerce in his jurisdiction.

These career experiences have provided Judge Rambo with both breadth and depth in understanding and applying criminal law as well as civil law considerations. His experience as both a public defender and as an assistant district attorney has provided him with legal experience and knowledge along both sides of the judicial fence. In other words, Judge Rambo is experienced with both the prosecution and defense of those accused of crimes. This is particularly important given the adversarial nature of the United States court system where the defense and prosecution (district attorney's office) compete to present their case in an attempt to obtain a verdict that is in their favor.

Rambo noted that throughout his career, he was aware of his own humble roots, not having come from a family of great financial means. Though this was the case, it would seem that this characteristic is what makes him so approachable and well liked by those within his community. This is important as a judge's role in the community is a reflection on the courthouse, in particular, and the legal profession, in general. Being integrated in both the day-to-day workings of the courthouse as well as various aspects of the community has made his position both demanding and rewarding, at the same time.

Further, Judge Rambo expounded on his role as chief judge, a position that rotates every three years among the judges of this jurisdiction. Currently, Judge Rambo is fulfilling that duty and noted that this was a very serious responsibility that entailed a good deal of time and effort. In this role, Judge Rambo leads the other 10 judges of the judicial district, with 5 of these judges being assigned to criminal proceedings and 5 being assigned to civil proceedings. Among the five judges assigned to criminal courts, one is assigned to handle misdemeanors, arraignments, and 72-hour hearing. Among those five judges assigned to the civil arena, one is assigned juvenile cases, child adoption cases, and also presides over drug courts at both the juvenile and adult level. It is clear then, that as chief judge, Rambo must be conversant on many facets of the law and its application to a variety of circumstances.

What changes have you seen and experienced?

I have seen quite a few developments take place in the law during my 30-year career. There have been a variety of rulings from the U.S. Supreme Court that have changed the state-of-affairs in the nation and in Louisiana. Likewise, Louisiana has gone through changes that have impacted its legal precedents and the rulings that have been determined by judges and juries alike. This means that, on the one hand, case law at both the national and the state level has impacted Louisiana. On the other hand, the cultural nuances and social mores of Louisiana also have impacted how the law has developed in that state.

The trend toward result-oriented approaches in addressing legal issues has been a key change that I have seen. It is interesting to point out that, in many cases, a judge's likelihood to adhere to a results-oriented approach has little or nothing to do with the judge's political affiliation. Instead, this has more to do with the function and purpose of the law as well as his or her personal view of the role in implementing the law.

The "results-oriented" approach is a judicial philosophy that differs from the "rule of law" approach. With the results-oriented approach, judges will tend to take an expansive view of the law. These judges are more likely to fashion innovative legal remedies as a means of rectifying perceived injustices or to expand the ability of a plaintiff to recover damages in civil court against a defendant who is liable. The judges also believe that they should play a role in shaping public policy. In essence, this is a form of **judicial activism** that seeks to ensure that justice is actually obtained in the legal system. These judges, therefore, will occasionally interpret their state constitution or laws passed by their respective legislatures in a manner that seeks to achieve specific policy outcomes. This may or may not always be consistent with the actual intent of the law.

The rule-of-law approach, on the other hand, is attributed to judges who tend to be strict minimalists in the interpretation of the law. They are more prone to exercise **judicial restraint** and are generally more conservative in their legal interpretations. Judges who adhere to a rule-of-law approach, are likely to emphasize prior case precedent in Louisiana and they are also likely to defer to the state legislature when broad questions of public policy are at issue. They are usually less prone to read new meanings or derive innovative solutions from legislative statutes or the state constitution.

While the distinction between these two approaches exists, in reality, no judge falls neatly within one philosophy to the complete exclusion of the other. In truth, both are practical approaches and judges may switch their view depending on the nature, facts, and circumstances of the case. Nevertheless, the philosophical orientation of a judge can be important, particularly if the judge is influential in both the courtroom environment and his or her broader community. The results-oriented approach has demonstrated that judges throughout the state recognize that, given limited resources and hard economic times, alternate solutions to addressing cases in the criminal justice and civil system may provide viable options that produce better outcomes for all parties concerned.

The Shift toward Reentry

Judge Rambo also noted that he has observed, in the past few years, more of a focus from incarceration to reintegration.

This shift from incarceration as retribution and deterrence toward an emphasis on reintegration of offenders into the community upon their release, has been in the interest of lowering recidivism by providing or giving offenders a stake in the community into which they are released. This emphasis on reintegration has been adopted as an initiative by the Louisiana Department of Public Safety and Corrections (LDPSC).

Indeed, the LDPSC Web site notes that approximately 15,000 offenders are released each year from prisons in Louisiana into outlying communities throughout the state. Prior to implementing this initiative, many of these offenders were released with only a bus ticket and a small amount of cash. Upon being released into the community, the expectation is that they will be able to get a job, earn a living, fulfill familial responsibilities, remain law-abiding, and also get along in society with little or no difficulty in adjusting from their release experience. However, within five years, nearly half have been found to return to prison for either violating conditions of their release or committing new crimes. This process simply translates to more victimization in society, more dollars spent, and more frustration and diminished success when offenders are released.

Further, it is clear that offenders are constantly cycling in and out of probation and parole offices, jails, and prisons, in a seemingly hopeless ability to work their way out of the criminal justice system. In Louisiana, the recidivism rate has been reported by the LDPSC to be right around 50% after five years (LDPSC, 2011). Reducing this recidivism rate by even 10% would result in significant dollar savings for the state and would improve public safety conditions in Louisiana's communities.

In other contexts, Judge Rambo has given credence to the importance of reintegrative efforts as well as the natural connection to the increased use of community corrections sanctions, rather than those that utilize incarceration.

Community sanctions and the reintegrative approach, in actuality, can help to alleviate a number of social problems that are corollary to problems encountered among the offending population. For instance, if the offender is successfully reintegrated, it is more likely that the offender will produce something of material value (through gainful employment) for society. The mere payment of taxes, coupled with a lack of further cost to society from the commission of further crimes, itself is a benefit extending to the whole of society. Further, offenders who are employed are able to generate payment for court fines, treatment programs, and victim compensation—none of these benefits are realized within the prison environment.

Likewise, a truly reintegrated offender can provide contributions through effective parenting of one's own children. This is actually a very important issue. Female offenders are often the primary caretakers of their children (with at least 70% of such offenders having children) while male offenders are often absent from the lives of their children (further adding to problems associated with father absenteeism). The social costs associated with foster homes are staggering, not to mention the fact that these children are likely to have a number of emotional problems that stem from their chaotic childhoods. Offenders that are reintegrated can stop this trend and can perhaps counter intergenerational cycles that persist in some family systems. This alone is a substantial social benefit that makes reintegrative aspects all the more valuable.

More Diversity on the Bench

Judge Rambo also has noted that, at around the midpoint of his career, significant changes occurred with respect to increased diversity on the bench resulting in the greater inclusion of women as members of the bench.

Similarly, there also has been more inclusion of African Americans to the bench throughout the United States, in general, and, more specifically, in Louisiana. These two changes overall have produced very positive results for citizen, laypersons, and professionals working in the judicial system.

In expounding on the integration of these two groups into the legal profession, it is important to consider that throughout history, women have had a limited role as judges in the judicial system. Indeed, it really was not until the 1980s when women truly did experience substantial increases in their access to the courts as employees of the courthouse, practicing attorneys, prosecutors, and judges. This era led to more attention being given to women in the legal professions, with the National Association of Women Judges and the National Organization for Women Legal Defense and Education Fund working to encourage state and federal systems to address bias and discrimination against the activity of women in the court system. Throughout the 1980s, significant developments would take place that eventually aided women to be active players within the judicial system.

Nowadays, it is not uncommon for women to practice law and there is even a higher proportion who make it to the position of judge within their jurisdiction. Indeed, it is perhaps the role of judge that is the most prestigious position within the courthouse. When considering this, it is clear that women are represented in the judiciaries of all 50 states, but their representation is less than a 50/50 split that one might expect between men and women. Indeed, according to the National Association of Women Judges (2010), there were 4,521 female judges out of a total of 17,108 total judges around the nation. Essentially, this means that women accounted for only 26% of all the state-level judgeships around the country. When examining the specific types of judgeships, it would appear that the representation is only slightly higher in appellate courts (about 31%) and is a bit lower in general jurisdiction courts (24%) throughout the nation (National Association of Women Judges, 2010).

In regard to diversity in the legal profession specific to Louisiana, the Louisiana State Bar Association Diversity Statement recognizes that achieving diversity in the legal profession is an evolutionary process that requires the association's continued effort and commitment. The Diversity Committee for this organization provides extensive training and resources on diversity issues related to the judiciary in Louisiana. These events are sponsored in the state capital and also in various cities throughout the state. Due to these and other efforts, there have been continued efforts throughout the years to include African Americans in the judiciary, including the bench.

Technology

During the past few years, it has become increasingly clear that technology has improved in the criminal justice field, including the judicial segment. For instance, Judge Rambo was interviewed regarding the implementation of electronic warrants (Eddington, 2011).

It is likely that the use of such technology will increase the number of warrants due to the ease with which they can be obtained. The Vsigner Program, as it is called, is part of a broader array of electronic legal document software designed to be secure, efficient, and streamlined. The program eliminates the need for law enforcement officers to physically report to a judge to get documents signed, such as search and/or arrest warrants. Further, this technology allows for effective tracking of legal documents as they are processed. Thus, the speed by which they are processed is not the only benefit, but the security and data management of these documents is also enhanced.

Technological advances such as these have been developed in other areas as well. For instance, the 4th JDC Probation Department has implemented the use of case management software that has greatly improved the process of creating weekly court dockets. The use of JustWare/Probation & Parole, from New Dawn Technologies, has been hailed as a success among courthouse officials, for providing effective tracking of offender records and aiding in accounting for offender fee payments and other financial obligations through the use of a bar coding system. This and other advancements in the courthouse process, not to mention potential innovations in security technology, show how far we have come in the past 30 years.

Additional Comments

Aside from the specific topics outlined regarding changes in the judicial system during his 30 years of service, Judge Rambo had some other remarks to add regarding changes that have occurred throughout his career. When asked about the state of affairs regarding the courts and the criminal justice system in Louisiana, he stated the following:

> In my opinion, the overall quality of the Criminal Justice System and its operation has improved. We are becoming more adept at handling a greater number of cases more efficiently and we now address many sub issues and layers of sub issues, which went unresolved previously.

He also noted that:

> In general, it is more difficult to be a judge now than in the past because there are what should be extraneous issues that now have a greater potential for impact on the handling of any particular case. The judge must fight against and remove these factors from consideration by him and others in order to handle the case properly. Among these concerns are economic and budgetary constraints that are often urged in support of or opposition to a particular resolution of a criminal case when, in fact, these factors should be relatively minor considerations as far as the merits of the case is concerned.

His comments reflect the difficult financial challenges that impact many judicial court systems.

Indeed, this has impacted the 4th Judicial District, like many other court systems around the nation. Further still, as a means of demonstrating how the courthouse impacts other aspects of the criminal justice system, it has been noted that a backlog of pretrial detainees (persons awaiting their court appearance) has been very costly to Ouachita Parish. This has resulted in a very costly expense to parish taxpayers and it has been noted that, despite the work of additional judges, there has been little or no effect on the number of detainees held in the parish jail. Not only does this cost taxpayers to house these detainees, but the jail system itself, run by the Ouachita Parish Sheriff's Office, loses revenue that, in Louisiana, is provided to jail facilities that house state inmates. One of the key means by which the jail facility is able to stay solvent is through the housing of state prison inmates. This arrangement, not completely peculiar to Louisiana, provides the parish sheriff's office with revenue to offset costs of maintaining the agency and the facility, and it saves the state correctional system dollars due to the lower expense of running such a facility as compared to state institutions. This win–win situation is compromised when the jail facility, known as Ouachita Correctional Center (OCC), is filled with pretrial detainees who are housed there simply due to their court appearance being delayed. This backlog then costs the parish through various means. This can, and likely does, impact enforcement decisions for surrounding law enforcement, particularly with minor crimes.

What is your personal judicial philosophy?

The role of the judiciary in our society is to follow the law provided by the legislature. The legislature is the formal expression of the people's will on any particular topic and the judiciary is obliged to implement those expressions in a meaningful and reasonable manner. Naturally, some aspects of the situation are not accounted for and could not have been envisioned at the time a particular statute was written. The court must make every effort to make that piece of the puzzle fit well by reasonable interpretation that gives effect to the expressed intent provided by the statute.

In a broader sense, the judiciary is called on routinely to address what are societal rather than legal problems. Oftentimes, the tools available to us as judges are somewhat inadequate to accomplish this task. It is a constant struggle and a challenge, which must be met by finding a way to work within the legal framework that currently exists to address these problems and to pinpoint and fashion programs of change that will provide a better general framework to address these issues.

What problems and successes have you experienced?

The problems mentioned above are the biggest challenges facing our criminal legal system. In other words, how to effectively address societal problems in a system, which is designed and intended to work on a case-by-case basis is a primary concern and a constant challenge. Along with budgetary constraints, addressing societal problems within the framework we presently have is the greatest challenge facing our criminal courts at this time.

What problems in Court do you find are the most difficult to deal with?

I find it equally difficult to deal with internal problems, such as the culture of the organizations and agencies involved in the process, their resistance or disfavor of change, and their willingness to maintain their zeal in performing their jobs effectively. Other problems, such as limited resources and budgets, lack of community support, and political pressure exerted on the legislature, among others, are equally hard to deal with. I do not find allegations of corruption or gender-based complaints to be significant or frequent problems with respect to how our system works.

What do you see as the relationship between theory and practice?

The relationship between theory and practice should be such that practice is grounded in theoretical underpinnings, which reflect the general consensus and will of society. Practitioners can learn how to better impact cultural mores and public perceptions by understanding the theoretical underpinnings associated with crime and punishment. The sentencing process and the rationale behind different types of sentences often have theoretical origins that should be kept in focus by practitioners. A failure to do this can result in attorneys and judges becoming nothing more than legal technocrats. Understanding and appreciating theoretical elements can also aid judges who, as I noted earlier, face as many social situations as they do legal ones.

Theory builders, on the other hand, can and should engage practitioners in the field as often as possible. This will allow them to optimize the utility of their theoretical constructs and to improve the explanatory power of their theories. Further, when conducting research, they will better be able to design and test theories due to their understanding of the pragmatic and day-to-day realities inherent to courthouse operations. Further, it is more likely that their theories will be more applicable to a wider array of social and legal circumstances if they keep a foot in the world of the practitioner.

Lastly, I would say that the relationship between theorists and practitioners in our judicial district is very good. I can give clear and specific examples that corroborate this point. On October 21, 2011, our court provided training for local practitioners, scholars, and community members, related to sentencing laws and their application to correctional populations. Among the presentations, I myself presented on sentencing issues and discussed, in detail, the goals of criminal punishment along with the theoretical underpinnings behind those goals. Further, among the persons who attended this training was none other than Dr. Rob Hanser with the University of Louisiana at Monroe (ULM), the person who happens to have interviewed me and who has compiled the notes and comments that I have provided. As a professor of criminal justice at that university, his work with our judicial district represents a clear connection between theorists and practitioners. Our hosting the sentencing training and welcoming him to that training is all the more indication of how, in our judicial district, we have a nearly symbiotic relationship between theorists and practitioners in our area.

In 2010, another judge from our judicial district hosted the Northeast Judicial Juvenile Justice Summit, which featured the collaborative efforts between institutions of higher education, the legal system, and service providers in our state's juvenile justice arena. This partnership and the projects involved helped to improve our model juvenile drug courts, parenting programs, and our district attorney triage screening. This partnership also included our Models for Change juvenile justice reform initiatives that were developed and implemented for use in courts across the state. The bringing together of so many different community players as well as the direct inclusion of university professors and legal practitioners from the courthouse is a prime example of how theory from the academic realm impacts (and I would say improves) the work of practitioners in the field. Further, researchers and theorists from surrounding universities gained specific insight and understanding as to the day-to-day operations of the courthouse and the means by which juvenile services are delivered, both in a legal environment and a social service environment.

I have, in the past, also had Dr. Hanser's classes come to our courthouse and observe court in session. This was particularly useful for his students in his Courts and Criminal Justice course at ULM. Further still, in another text that Dr. Hanser authored, my court provided input and photos to aid in the teaching and learning process. This, to me, again shows how we work in a collaborative manner with scholars and theorists in our judicial district. Add to this that Dr. Hanser also works in partnership with our misdemeanor probation department as well as the 4th JDC Drug Court, providing therapeutic services to domestic batterers and drug offenders who are court mandated, and it becomes clear that this partnership is multifaceted in nature.

What are some of the types of research that might be useful?

This is easy to answer, with a direct and to the-point approach probably being best. I usually do not do comprehensive theoretical research; my research usually has to do with case developments as well changes generated from the legislature. We do sometimes do research on our own, but usually simply defer to the many contacts that we have with universities in the area, if the issue is more theory-based. Otherwise, most of the research that we develop and are in need of having completed has to do with the evaluation of administrative aspects of running the courthouse. For instance, in 2009 and in conjunction with the National Center for State Courts, our jurisdiction published the Louisiana 4th Judicial District Court *Criminal Case Processing Improvement Manual*. This document provided an assessment and a variety of recommendations regarding the day-to-day operations of the courthouse. In particular, this group provided recommendations that emphasized better communication and information sharing between the court, the district attorney's office, and area law enforcement and community corrections officers (probation and parole).

This, to me, is consistent with how we have continued to build community and academic partnerships and, as I noted earlier, how we implemented technological advancements into our operations to improve collaboration among the various criminal justice players who work with our judicial district. Likewise, presentations like the one that I gave just a few days ago, utilized information from the Center for Community Alternatives in Syracuse, New York, which shows how I have used outside sources on criminal punishment goals—to include deterrence, retribution, incapacitation, restitution, and rehabilitation—as a platform for training practitioners in the region. This, to me, exemplifies how my court uses outside theory-based research and how this research is integrated into the training that we provide our practitioners.

Has there been an impact of transnational relations during your tenure as judge?

For the most part, we are not overly impacted by transnational relations, at least on the surface level. However, we have observed some issues with immigration, from time-to-time, particularly in regard to populations who work in seasonal industries. While this may not greatly impact our courthouse, I do suspect that, like in many other states that are west of our own, we will see this become a more frequent issue of consideration. I say this because we do see this becoming more of an area of concern in the southern section of our state and, with that in mind, it is only a matter of time until the issues start to trickle upward to our area on a more frequent basis.

Likewise, it has been thought, by some of our officials, that problems with our pretrial detainees—something that I had mentioned earlier—started to escalate in early 1994 when the North American Free Trade Agreement (NAFTA) relaxed borders between the United States and Mexico. This is thought to have also allowed for easier trafficking of drugs by Mexican drug cartels. Since that time, the amount of vehicular traffic coming into the United States has grown exponentially at a more rapid rate than would historically be normal otherwise. Because our district sits on one of the two major routes of drug trafficking from Houston to Atlanta, where illegal drugs are frequently distributed throughout the country, we get quite a bit of transnational traffic and drug traffickers who are from Mexico and other nations south of us (Eddington, 2011). Interstate 20, along with Interstate 10, serve as major drug trafficking routes in the United States and our own local, regional, state, and federal law enforcement are required to patrol Highway I-10 in a vigorous fashion (Eddington, 2011). This results in quite a bit of criminal activity that is apprehended and this translates to even more pretrial jail detainees in our regional correctional facilities.

In addition, there have been reports of various criminal gangs, some from El Salvador and Mexico, such as MS-13, who have been found in the New Orleans region, particularly after Hurricane Katrina. This gang, as is well known, has operations in numerous countries throughout Central and South America as well as various regions in the United States. In our own region, law enforcement personnel have come into contact with suspected members of this gang. Though the numbers are small when compared with a larger, more urbanized region, this still demonstrates how our jurisdiction is impacted by transnational events and criminal enterprises.

Lastly, the Louisiana Commission on Law Enforcement (LCLE) entered into a partnership with the Louisiana Sheriff's Association (LSA) to implement the Louisiana Human Trafficking Task Force (HTTF). As many international researchers and criminal justice practitioners are aware, human trafficking concerns have risen to the forefront in the past 5 to 10 years throughout the global community. This has also impacted Louisiana, and the Louisiana HTTF focuses its law enforcement and victim rescue efforts on the Interstate 10 (I-10) corridor from the Texas border on the west to the Mississippi border on the east (LCLE, 2006). Interstate 10, which serves as a major route for drug trafficking, also has been a longtime major avenue of illegal immigration activity (LCLE, 2006). Further, this I-10 corridor, as it is called, is a major avenue for human traffickers to supply various labor needs in hurricane damaged areas of the state. In fact, our state passed a new law just a couple of years ago, LSA-R.S. 14:46.2, the Louisiana Human Trafficking Law, in response to this emerging issue.

I would say that interactions with external agencies, including those with members who come from abroad, have been helpful. While these interactions are more common in the southern area of our state, they do occur here, particularly as the world becomes increasingly more globalized. Midsized cities, such as ours, are now being impacted by criminal activity that was once thought to be a large-sized city problem. In more recent literature, there is more attention to suburbs, mid-sized towns, and rural areas where crime, having both international and local influences, seems to be recognized as a noteworthy problem.

What is your general assessment of the region's justice process and developments?

Overall, I am fairly pleased with the innovations in our region's criminal justice process and with our state's development of the criminal law and criminal procedure. I think that our state and our judicial district are at least on par with other regions throughout the United States. While there is always room for improvement, it is my own view that, considering the state of the world economy and other social challenges that have impacted the United States, we are doing fairly well in our response to crime in our region.

Conclusion

From the interview with Judge Wilson Rambo, it was clear that he had an excellent grasp of how the judicial district in his region impacted various components of the criminal justice system in that area. Further, it also was clear that he took serious the collaborative nature that exists between the courthouse and the field. This was true as well regarding partnerships between theorists and legal practitioners in the field. His insights made it clear that developments in criminal laws, as well as procedural issues, had a direct impact on the day-to-day efforts of crime fighting. The means by which this is formally implemented along with the social issues that judges also must consider, illustrate the complicated nature of their role, both within the judiciary and the communities that they serve.

References

Eddington, S. (2011). Judge: Warrant process streamlined. *The News Star,* July 25, Monroe, LA.

Louisiana Commission on Law Enforcement (2006). *Louisiana human trafficking task force.* Baton Rouge, LA: Louisiana Commission on Law Enforcement and Administration of Criminal Justice. Retrieved from: http://www.cole.state.la.us/programs/human_trafficking.asp

Louisiana Department of Public Safety and Corrections (2011*). Reentry initiatives overview.* Baton Rouge, LA: LDPSC. Retrieved from: http://doc.la.gov/pages/reentry-initiatives/overview/

National Association of Women Judges (2010). *The American bench: Judges of the nation,* 2010 ed. Dallas, TX: Forster-Long, Inc.

National Center for State Courts (2009). *Louisiana 4th Judicial District Court criminal case processing improvement: Assessment and recommendations,* July. Denver, CO: National Center for State Courts.

New Dawn Technologies (2009). Fourth District Court probation. Logan, UT: New Dawn Technologies. Retrieved from: http://newdawn.com/our-customers/probation-parole/fourth-judicial-district-court-probation/

Interview of Judge Eugene C. Turner, Collier County Court, Florida

11

CLOUD MILLER
LANDON MILLER

Contents

The Florida Court System

For anyone considering legal action, an understanding of how our legal system works is essential. As you may remember from civics class, the U.S. system of government, on both the state and federal levels, is divided into three separate and competing branches: the legislative, executive, and judicial. The legislative branch creates the laws, the executive branch enforces the laws, and the judicial branch interprets the laws. State government maintains control of state and local affairs, while the federal government oversees those areas important to the national interest.

Florida State Courts

Which court system hears your case depends upon three factors: the subject matter of the dispute, the amount of money in controversy, and the location of the parties. To get into federal court, a lawsuit must either involve some issue of federal law, raise a question of constitutional interpretation, or involve parties from different states and more than $50,000. If a lawsuit does not meet one of these criteria, it must be heard in state court.

State Courts

The Florida court system consists of the Florida Supreme Court, District Courts of Appeal, Circuit Courts, and County Courts (Table 11.1). As the name suggests, the Florida Supreme Court is the highest court in the state. Located in Tallahassee, the **Florida Supreme Court** is composed of seven justices. Five justices must be present in order to conduct business and at least four justices must agree on a decision in each case.

The jurisdiction of the Florida Supreme Court is both mandatory and discretionary. The Florida Supreme Court must hear all judgments imposing the death penalty, district court decisions declaring a state statute or provision of the state constitution invalid, bond validation judgments, and actions of statewide agencies relating to public utilities. The Florida Supreme Court has discretion in hearing decisions of District Courts of Appeal that expressly declare a state statute valid; questions certified by the District Courts of Appeal as being of great public importance; or decisions where the District Courts are in conflict with one another. The Florida Supreme Court also may

Table 11.1 Florida Court System

Supreme Court	
• Located in Tallahassee • Each justice serves a six-year term, but can remain in office if retained in a general election • Seven justices	• Justices are appointed by the governor • Decisions of the Florida Supreme Court can be appealed to the U.S. Supreme Court where the validity of a federal law is in question

District Courts of Appeal	
• Five districts: • 1st District: Tallahassee; 15 judges • 2nd District: Lakeland; 14 judges • 3rd District: Miami; 11 judges • 4th District: W. Palm Beach; 12 judges • 5th District: Daytona Beach; 9 judges	• Each judge serves a six-year term, but can remain in office if retained in a general election • Cases are reviewed by a three-judge panel • Judges are appointed by governor • District courts of appeal hear appeal from circuit and county courts

Circuit Courts	
• 20 judicial circuits • 442 judges, each judge serves a six-year term • Different number of judges in each circuit	• Judges are elected into office • Judges sit individually • Trial court

County Courts	
• At least one judge in each of Florida's 67 counties, 254 in total • Judges sit individually	• Judges serve four-year terms and are elected into office • Trial court

issue advisory opinions at the governor's request concerning interpretation of the state constitution regarding the governor's powers and duties.

To become a Florida Supreme Court justice, a person must reside in Florida and have been admitted to the Florida Bar for the preceding 10 years. When there is a vacancy on the court, the governor appoints the next justice from a list of three qualified persons prepared by the state Judicial Nominating Commission. Justices serve for six years, after which they can have their name put on the general election ballot if they wish to remain in office. The court hears oral arguments on the first Monday through Friday of each month, except in July and August.

There are five **District Courts of Appeal** in Florida, each covering a geographic district. Judges sit in panels of three and decide appeals from circuit courts in most criminal and civil cases. They also have jurisdiction to decide appeals from county courts when a state statute or provision of the state constitution is held invalid, or for orders or judgments certified to be of great public importance. As a practical matter, the District Courts of Appeal are the final appellate review of litigated cases. Someone displeased with a District Court's decision may seek review in the Florida Supreme Court or in the U.S. Supreme Court, but the overwhelming majority of such requests are denied.

Most civil and criminal cases in Florida originate at the **Circuit Court** level. The Circuit Courts are courts of general jurisdiction, handling such matters as domestic relations, major criminal offenses, probate issues, civil cases involving amounts greater than $15,000, and appeals from county courts.

The **County Courts**, which occupy the lowest rung in the Florida court system, are sometimes referred to as "the peoples' courts," because a large portion of the County Courts' work involves citizen disputes like traffic offenses, county and city ordinance violations, less serious criminal offenses, and civil cases involving less than $15,000, such as landlord/tenant disputes.

The **small claims division** of the County Court permits members of the public to bring their own lawsuits without an attorney (provided the amount in dispute is less than $2,500). The clerk of the local County Court can provide information on how to file a small claims lawsuit.

The state of Florida pays the salaries of all judges and their secretaries. The state shares with the counties most of the remaining expenses. The facilities for the appellate courts are provided by the state and the counties provide facilities for the trial courts.

Background and Career

Judge Eugene C. Turner graduated from the University of South Florida, attended law school at Stetson University, and received his JD from the

University of Baltimore in 1974. Judge Turner served as assistant state attorney in the 20th Judicial Circuit of Florida from 1974 to 1977, then entered into private practice. He remained in private general practice until 1983 when he was appointed to the Collier County Court.

Judge Turner has been a county court judge for 29 years and is highly respected by the community and the legal profession as a fair, dignified, open-minded, and **deliberative jurist**.

Judge Turner was born in Virginia and moved to Immokalee, Florida, with his parents. His mother was a teacher and his father was a civil engineer. He was raised in Immokalee, which is a small rural community of approximately 700 residents located in the Florida Everglades. As a child, he had a reputation in the community as a "good boy" because everyone knew everybody and, if you did something wrong, your parents would know it by the time you got home. He also knew that he wanted to be a lawyer and that limited his bad behavior. Judge Turner's first interest in the legal arena was at age 10 when his aunt told him that she thought he would make a good judge. At that time, he did not know what a judge was; however, it sparked his interest in the legal profession. He would visit the court as a young man for entertainment watching the proceedings and making notes of the events. Knowing subsequently that he wanted to become a lawyer, he finished high school and entered the University of South Florida where he obtained his BA degree in Economics. Thereafter, he moved to Maryland and attended the University of Baltimore School of Law receiving his JD Degree in 1975.

Judge Turner started his legal career serving three years as a prosecutor before entering private general practice including the defense of criminal defendants. While practicing law, Judge Turner became active in local politics serving on numerous boards including the County School Board. His law partner was appointed a Circuit Court judge and Turner then put his name in for an appointment to serve as a County Court Judge as well. He was appointed in 1983.

Dynamics of Change

Judge Turner views the defendants before him as individuals and not merely a defendant that he has to deal with. In other words he is interested in their background, who they are, where they came from and what is their potential for lawful productive citizens. He is of the opinion that the judicial system in Florida is becoming a system of statistical numbers, which dictate the outcome of sentencing dispositions. He is of the opinion that this merely becomes a system of noninvolvement by the judiciary because the main decisions are already made and printed in black and white for the judge to follow. Judge Turner, in his county court sessions, attempts to get personal with the defendants in order to understand the characteristics of the defendants in order that they, the defendants, know that he is evaluating their demeanor and social attitudes.

His technique is to find something unique about the defendant (e.g., clothing, hairstyle, posture, physique, or other individual characteristics) that he can comment on to the defendant who will recognize that the judge has studied him as an individual and not just another "defendant." Judge Turner stated that he can take time to personalize the judicial encounter rather than to "run them through" a judicial gauntlet.

> At the county court level, I am able to interact with the defendant, on a one-to-one basis, whereas in Circuit Felony Criminal Courts, I cannot do that. Most of my effort is to consider youthful offenders and their potential for lawful lifestyle. Most cases are handled by private counsel and that, in my county, it is the exception rather than the rule to not have an attorney.
>
> Collier County is one of the wealthiest counties in the state of Florida and the public believes that representation by counsel is a positive impact. The Florida Judicial System has developed into an academic event rather than a personalized event. Judge and jury during the early formative years of my practice were dealing with the individual, and a change has occurred that the judicial experience is more academic and sterile, failing to discuss the salient factors of the individual and substituting in statistical analysis predictors.
>
> The judge who wants to be independent and interject his own philosophy of law more than likely would be reversed due to the appellate process, which applies the salient factor guideline system rather than individualizing the outcome based on personal observations and examination. Every judge brings to court his or her own interpretation and philosophy of law. Some judges choose to disbelieve law enforcement agents as a matter of practice while others believe that the law enforcement officer is the authority of the criminal events.
>
> The Florida legislature, in my opinion, has gone too far by removing discretion. What do you need a judge for, if you don't have discretion—rubber stamping? However, I believe ultimately the law will reverse its guideline system providing judges to use more discretion. I am pleased with the legal defense bar who practice before me due to the fact that they bring personalized recommendations and information regarding their client. They provide the court with the defendant's background and any attempt to become involved in counseling or rehabilitation programs before they stand before the court for sentencing.
>
> I believe that the different areas of population specialize in their judicial demeanor in order to meet the different ecological, cultural, and societal factors. For example, in the high density metropolis areas, you would not have to deal with a DUI defendant driving a tractor as compared to my jurisdiction that has a high concentration of agriculture enterprises. There was no increase in case loads as a result of the terrorist attacks on September 11, 2001. However, the Rodney King incident affected the jury decisions with a number of "not guilty" verdicts.

I try to get personal with the client, try to attach a characteristic to the defendant so they know I am looking at what they bring to the courtroom with pride or distinction; something that I use as an identity as to what he is or who he is, whether it is clothing or hair, or posture or physique, if he is a weightlifter. I try to pick an identity to let that person know I am talking to him. At my level of County Court, I can do that. I don't do it at certain courts. At the county level, it is more one-on-one between the defendant and the court. There is an attorney there, but at the county level I can speak to the defendant; at least in my jurisdiction I can speak to the defense. In Circuit Court frequently you will always have an attorney. In Circuit Court, 99.9% have an attorney; however, in my court, 50 to 60% of the time we don't have an attorney. Lot of times they just walk in and plead without attorneys. In Collier County, enormous quantity of defendants have private attorneys, not public defenders. How Collier County developed that way, I'm not sure.

Local peer pressure, if you go to Lee County, you don't get as many DUIs up there represented by private counsel percentage or numbers. Collier County has a high percentage and numbers that are represented by counsel. Why? 80% of them are convicted, and 90% of those have the same exact sentences as those represented, and the perception of the community is that you hire private counsel.

The judge also recognizes that, if there are family members, he brings mom and dad to the podium as well. It is almost like a family counseling session and I am trying to make the young adults recognize what the parents are doing for them and that they should not put parents through this type of situation.

In County Court, there is a perception different from Circuit Court. Circuit Court is a different level of activity. County court has high levels of negligence on their part, irresponsibility, procrastination, anxiety of not knowing how to do it, therefore I don't do it. "Well, there was nothing wrong with driving under the influence; I really wasn't that drunk." Whatever the level is, it's not the level of Circuit Court where they break into houses, knowing it's wrong to retrieve money to go buy drugs. County Court is mainly irresponsibility, lack of education, and ones who don't know how the system works. They aren't bad people, we get bad people in there, but most of them aren't bad people. They're just people that let life get ahead of them—"I forgot to get the tag or I didn't have money buy or renew the tag or I got drunk."

The Interview

Would you describe your background?

I began as a prosecutor for three years, and then went into private general practice, which included being a criminal defense lawyer. I became politically active and ended up getting an appointment to the school board as an attorney, in a very Republican area, and I was a Democrat supporting the democratic state nominee for governor. I did not get on the school board for political reasons, I did it because my mother was a schoolteacher and I was well educated, but by the time you become a lawyer, you have 19 years of school and I thought I could help the community on with education. I absolutely loved it, probably the most rewarding job that I could get. It was a dead-end job and it was one that could be eliminated any moment. My law partner became a county judge and I looked at him thinking about, what the heck, thought it must be one of the most boring jobs because he used to be a prosecutor. He then became circuit judge, so I put my name in for the appointment. I was making a lot of money, but I was getting older fast because I was on the school board, 12 other boards, was politically active, and I was running a one-man law firm. I was exhausted and I thought that the appointment would get me off the boards, so I put my name in for the county court judgeship and got the appointment. That gradually got me off the boards.

When there was an opening in Collier County, the Circuit Court judge in Charlotte County moved to Collier County closing the opportunity. He was invited to go to Charlotte County; however, he would have had to move there and he didn't want to relocate.

I enjoy doing what I do, but I never thought I'd end up here. I never thought County Court judge was the epitome of a legal career. Did I think I was going to do more? Probably. Quite frankly I think I do more as a county judge than I would as a circuit judge. I like the personality of the County Court more than the sterile Circuit Court judgeship. "Sterile," meaning an academic Harvard style of speaking to the lawyers. I would have liked to have gone farther, but it isn't a disappointment. I enjoy where I am and the people I work with; they are quite a good group.

Have there been any legal changes? If so, do you have confidence it's in the right direction?

Getting back to where I grew up, we had a judge and I would end up [visiting?] in his courtroom. He was a travelling circuit judge. I would go listen and it was always fun in terms of what was going on. My father was an engineer and he also was the juvenile court judge. You did not have to be an attorney to be a juvenile judge back in those days. What I can remember from growing up … in 1974, it had moved from a personal event to an academic event, where the judge was dealing with individual and the jury was dealing with an individual and the consequences were to the individual. Now I think everything has been made almost sterile and academic. We aren't talking to a person, but talking to an action. We eliminate the identity of the person who is doing the action. We are just esoterically and philosophically discussing the action. I think that's not necessarily in the best interest of society. One of the reasons I guess I do my court the way I do is because I try to make it personal to the defendant. I can't (I wouldn't) attempt that in Circuit Court; you would be reversed quickly. It wouldn't work well there. I think that is where we are going. I don't think it's going to change and I think we are going to have to go that way.

Everything is appealable and the staleness of the black lettering on a white page read by a distant 200-mile-away judge from the event of a local community removes the reality of the consequences. Not just from the individual, but for the community as a whole. It has gone that way not just by the judiciary, but by the legislature that has insisted that a judge in one area of the state must sentence a defendant to the same exact action equally as a defendant for the same action in another area of the state, although the focus of the local community may need a different response for the same action. Some areas may be severely involved in drugs and other areas not. Some areas may have a higher tolerance of alcohol, such as a rural community where they drive their tractors drunk, and other areas, such as downtown in a city, you can't drive your car drunk, you will kill people, but driving a tractor drunk at 20 mph in Lafayette County is not quite the same event. But, you have to sentence them the exact same way. The legislature has removed what we call discretion, in an effort to be uniform. I understand the philosophy of doing so, which is to avoid abuse of discretion. But, I think direction is more and more the same trying to do everything with the cookie cutter, and not allowing subjective judgment of another human shows itself most horribly in the juvenile justice system where a judge has lost the ability to evaluate the attitude of the defendant as a juvenile and sentence him in accordance with his conspicuously defiant, hostile, rebellious, rejective attitude. We have to sentence him according to a mathematical formula. To do that to the juvenile, to me, is impersonal and that's where I think the law is going and I think it isn't going to change. I think juvenile court will change. Philosophy is going to move more and more toward an academic approach.

Can you explain your theory and practice?

When I first joined the judiciary, I went to one of our educational conferences in 1983, and one of my first impressions was a disappointment of the judiciary when I heard a particular judge in Manatee County say, "I don't give a dam what the law says, I'm going to do what I want to do." To me, that is an old school, Judge Roy Bean attitude, but it just surprised me as a fledgling academic just getting into the judiciary and I was appalled that he would not follow the law. His response: "I don't give a dam what the law says, I'm going to do what I want to do," well, that doesn't exist much anymore I don't think because we have too many opportunities for appeal. So, there are negative things from the appeal process and you simply cannot do the things you want to do anymore in defiance of the rule of law. It is shocking to me and I saw it in the older judiciary systems. I believe the judiciary has moved away from that philosophy because none of us can do what we want to do, write the law as we would choose it to be; we don't do that anymore. I think it has moved in a very positive way from where it was when I first began.

Every judge not only brings his academic interpretation of what is written on the black and white paper, but brings his philosophy of life as well. An example I'm thinking of is: Do you distrust government? Or, do you have faith that people attempt to do the right thing? And will do the right thing given the opportunity to do so. And that is where some judges will choose to automatically disbelieve law enforcement. Because law enforcement is a strong government entity with a powerful hand that isn't often covered with a nice fuzzy glove, but cold metal, and defendants are disrespectful of that power and they disbelieve that the power of government can be used beneficially and correctly, and they will look for a reason to not believe any officer because he wears a badge. We have attorneys who during *voir dire* ask prospective jurors: "Would you give a greater or lesser weight to the law enforcement officer than you would any other witness?" When you deal with the personality of the jury, I bring the concept that I experienced where I grew up. People on the jury try to do the right thing. I don't see law enforcement as being self-centered in the way portrayed on TV saying and doing anything they have to do to get their way and get this guy convicted. Maybe it is that way in a big city, I don't know, but I don't see it in my community.

To answer your question. Yes, I think the judge will bring to the bench his experience and his philosophy even when he interprets the facts that are provided to him. The same set of facts will be interpreted by one judge as believing the evidence and another judge questioning and disbelieving. Where is your inclination to do that? If I lived in Dade County, I may have an inclination to believe that all law enforcement is dirty, e.g., cops taking cocaine from suspects and selling it. I don't see that in my community and, fortunately, don't have to deal with it. That doesn't mean we haven't prosecuted and convicted deputies who have stolen cocaine.

Do you see discretion coming back?

No. On the local level, I didn't see it. I believe it will happen at some point because in juvenile court I think they have made a serious mistake. They have gone too far by removing discretion from the judge who is sitting there. They don't need a human put it in a grinder and hear the numbers. What do you want me for? "Rubber stamping?" I think that is a mistake in juvenile. I don't see the legislative yet understanding the consequences. I think when the consequences become sufficiently glaring and negative as the results show where people are abused by it repetitively, then they will back off and let the judge use more discretion. But they haven't done that yet and I don't see that in the foreseeable future, I think they will ultimately do it because I think they are going to continue to go too far.

Everybody likes their own power. Everybody believes they're including the legislature; they believe that they know best. And, that's the big problem of powerful big government. They believe they know best and they decide with a sledge hammer what the ultimate consequences are going to be. It's interesting, but it doesn't always make for the best resolution on an individual. I'm not a legislator. I do not decide what is best for all. The legislature makes that decision. I have to take what they give me and apply it to the individual. I look at an individual thinking what tools they have given me. I have to figure out which of those tools that I need to use for this defendant based upon my observations of that defendant. I have gone to the defense bar before and said, "Look, all I have on your client is a 'booking sheet,' a plea. I get to watch him in the courtroom with him immobile. I watch him walk from his seat up here, and I look at him for 45 seconds and I'm supposed to make a judgment call on how to sentence him among all of my quivers, my little arrows in the quiver, and figure out which arrows to pull out to work with your client. That's all I get to know about and why I take these guys (attorneys) and I use them because if I can get them to believe that my objective is to better their client by avoiding them repeating the same process, I may be cutting you out of a future client, but I am protecting your children and community. I will depend on my local private bar that knows the clients better than I do because all I have, literally, is a booking sheet, and 45 seconds, and perceptions of how he walks, wears his hair, how tall he is, what his educational level is, how does he speak, if he is articulate. I have to interpret how to deal with this. I want them to make a recommendation that is going to best serve their client and tell me little things like, you know, "Judge this is an abnormality for this client to be drunk and act out like this. He has been shocked by it as you are, she has immediately within one week got herself into counseling, she is in AA, she has quit drinking, she is doing … ."

You don't need to slap her to get a response from her; she is doing it all and she is doing in on her own. Now, the truth may be known that this counsel here knows what to recommend in the privacy of the office; what the client needs to do in order to get a lenient sentence from me. I really don't care why she quitting counseling because all of our studies tell us that when defendants go to counseling on their own or at the recommendation of their attorney, it is so much more successful than when I order them to do it. I really don't care why she is getting before I get the case, she is getting because the lawyer recommended, suggested it or put it in a contract, it is going to be more beneficial to her and the community.

I'll order counseling to someone who continues to drink and smoke their marijuana until sentencing. I've got a problem and now I have to make a decision to figure out how to deal with something that… I don't care how you get it, but you get it done. If you can get it done, more power to you and your client and you don't need me.

In your practice, have you seen any different types of cases or personalities?

The correct answer is no, I have not. However, let me give you a more appropriate reality. We saw a dramatic change as a result of the Rodney King case, and that is white-collar, upper-level management, upper-level officers, older, conservative jurors, more trusting of law enforcement, and when you charge the defendant before Rodney King with resisting arrest without violence and the officer took the stand and described what happened and the defendant took the stand and denied it, the jury would come back with a guilty verdict.

After Rodney King, with the same set of facts, the jury would return with a not guilty verdict. The state did not believe that a change occurred and thought merely that it was an aberration, and after trying a similar case the jury again came back with a not guilty verdict.

As a consequence of televised cases, the conservative white-collar jury did not believe, without question, the testimony of an officer, and we could not get a guilty jury verdict on resisting arrest.

I think today we could get a guilty on that. But the state finally saw the handwriting on the wall; I haven't seen a difference from 911. Weightlifter body builder in the mall fighting with six officers and his defense was they were hurting him and "I couldn't put my hands behind my back which they told me to do so that's why I took out six officers", the jury came back not guilty.

I believe it is going to happen at some point, like juvenile court, they have made a serious mistake.

What has been the most difficult problem as a county court judge with which you have had to deal?

No courtroom problems that are glaring. The most difficult displeasure is dealing with behind the scenes in the Florida courts; the behind the scene is administrative issues. Primarily dealing with the things that are outside of our control.

Interview of Judge Winston P. Bethel, Retired, Chief Magistrate Judge

12

CATHERINE A. JENKS

Contents

Therapeutic Jurisprudence at the Entry Level of the Criminal Courts

Introduction

Judge Winston P. Bethel is a retired chief magistrate judge of DeKalb County, Georgia, where he served as a judge for 25 years. Judge Bethel holds a Bachelor of Applied Studies from Mercer University, a Master of Arts in Sociology from the University of West Georgia, a Juris Doctor from the John Marshall Law School, and a Master of Laws from the Woodrow Wilson College of Law. During his tenure on the bench, he was instrumental in the development and implementation of several innovative initiatives that were grounded in the philosophy of therapeutic jurisprudence. He has given over 20 professional presentations directly related to this judicial philosophy and served as a grant peer reviewer for several Substance Abuse and Mental Health Services Administration (SAMHSA) grant applications on jail diversion and reentry.

The United States has a dual court system, which means that there is a court system in each of the 50 states and there is one federal court system. Violations of federal law are heard in the federal system, while infractions against state laws are heard in the state systems. Criminal cases begin at the magistrate court level in many states. The magistrate court system in the State of Georgia was created by an Act of the Georgia Legislature that became effective in 1983. All counties in the state were required to have a chief magistrate. This court is the entry level court for all criminal cases. The court is responsible for issuing private or individual warrants for misdemeanor offenses, holding initial appearance and preliminary hearings in all felony and misdemeanor cases, making decisions related to pretrial release, and issuing protective orders. No criminal trials are held in these courts of limited jurisdiction. The trial court of general jurisdiction, which has exclusive jurisdiction over felony criminal cases, is Superior Court. The appellate jurisdiction courts are the Court of Appeals and the Supreme Court, with the latter serving as the court of last resort. While the magistrate courts are the lowest level courts, they deal with a large number of criminal matters considering the fact that most offenders in the United States commit petty crimes, which are classified as misdemeanors. In effect, these judges are the front line of entry into the court system.

My interview with Judge Bethel took place in 2012. Due to our conflicting schedules, we were unable to do the interview in person. We agreed to improvise and to video conference via Skype. The interview lasted for two and one-half hours and was recorded with an audio/video recording software program, Evaer. Judge Bethel was a model respondent whose passion for serving as a judge and for promoting therapeutic jurisprudence came through in what could be characterized as a most pleasant interview.

Career Background and Judicial Philosophy

Winston P. Bethel obtained an Associate of Arts in Design Technology and Engineering from Miami-Dade Community College in Miami, Florida, in 1966 during the Vietnam War. He spent the early part of his career working for several different corporations as a design engineer. He relocated to Atlanta in 1973 to attend Georgia State University to obtain an undergraduate degree. Before actually registering at Georgia State, he was made aware that there were law schools in Georgia where admission could be granted to those who had completed two years of college. He figured that he would give that a try for a semester to see what it was like. Once he started the program, he fell in love with the study of law and legal institutions. In 1974, he was hired by Ebasco Services where he became a personnel representative and legal liaison. He continued in this position until 1978 while attending law school in a night program offered through the John Marshall Law School in Atlanta. Upon graduating, passing the Bar Association examination, and being admitted to the bar in 1977, he attended Woodrow Wilson College of Law in Atlanta and earned a Master of Laws in 1978. That same year, he left Ebasco Services to practice law as a sole practitioner initially and then as partner in the firm of Robinson, Bethel, and Dixon. The law firm engaged in general practice with a concentration in personal injury litigation.

In May 1985, Judge Bethel became a part-time associate magistrate in DeKalb County, Georgia, which is part of the metropolitan statistical area of Atlanta. He had been practicing law for seven to eight years prior. As an associate magistrate, he helped with the docket on weekends and during the evenings. In June 1991, he became the chief judge of the Recorders Court in DeKalb County. He held this position through January 1996 when he was elected a full-time associate magistrate. Judge Bethel served as an associate magistrate for two years before being elected chief magistrate in an uncontested bid for the seat. He served as chief magistrate from June 1998 until May 2010, never once having someone run against him in an election.

The Interview

Judge Bethel's personal judicial philosophy is based on the concepts of therapeutic jurisprudence, behavior modification, and diversion. He was introduced to the concept of therapeutic jurisprudence by his mentor, Wayne Purdom, who currently serves as the chief judge of DeKalb County State Court. Throughout their tenure, they developed a variety of initiatives that promoted therapeutic jurisprudence at the magistrate court level. In talking about the role of the judge in society, as far as criminal law is concerned, Judge Bethel feels that:

> the role of the judge should be to utilize the criminal justice system in a way that is going to be beneficial to all parties involved. Now, of course, that is rather broad, but that is where this whole concept of therapeutic jurisprudence comes in. If there is a way to address a particular issue in a way that is going to satisfy the victims and then also rehabilitate the defendant, then that is the route that one should take, as opposed to just being sort of a "hang him high" judge similar to Judge Roy Bean and as opposed to just taking the position that if you're convicted, then you need to go to jail and serve your time.
>
> There are other ways to modify behavior, but that is only if you accept the premise that incarceration is an intervention that is intended to modify behavior. Why else are you putting someone in jail? Well, to protect the community. Yes, well for how long? So, you are going to protect the community for two to three years and then release the individual right back out into the community? That is firmly what I believe at this point. When I started off as a judge, that was not my philosophy. I sort of felt that while I was on the bench

sentencing people or whatever I still felt something inside that there had to be a better way to address these issues. And that is when I started off into alternative sentencing. I never got into any trouble with all of that because I was dealing with low-level misdemeanor offenders. But, you could very well see that that philosophy would not play out in Superior Court where you are dealing with far more serious situations.

Most of what Judge Bethel did during his career was administrative. From an administrative point of view, he was able to take a good look at how things were operating with regard to the response of the criminal justice system to the actual individuals who became entrapped in it. For example, in DeKalb County when someone wants to obtain a warrant that is not obtained by the police but is from the general public, he or she would have to go to the magistrate court and fill out an application for a warrant. If the judge feels that there is enough information, then he will go ahead and issue a warrant. What Judge Wayne Purdom did was have the parties sit down to discuss the application for the warrant so that the judge would have an opportunity to hear from the other side; Judge Bethel adopted this strategy.

> This would diffuse a lot of the issues before it actually became a warrant and … before someone actually ended up getting arrested, especially someone who shouldn't have been arrested.

This concept was later adopted by the State of Georgia. One of the legislators in DeKalb County drafted a bill and presented it to the legislature that was based on the application hearing calendar in DeKalb County. This was Judge Bethel's introduction to the concept of therapeutic jurisprudence, a concept that he maintained an interest in promoting his entire career as a judge and continues in retirement.

During this time, the two men developed a variety of initiatives to keep things that would be better resolved in a different way, such as not issuing a warrant and getting someone entangled in the system, out of the criminal justice system. They developed domestic violence calendars and child abandonment calendars that were directly related to child support. These calendars helped keep the official caseload down in regard to the actual prosecution of criminal offenses. This is something that he has "looked at" his entire career.

Some of the interventions that Judge Bethel is most proud of revolve around the development of specialized accountability courts in the State of Georgia.

> We called them accountability courts; some places call them specialty courts or diversion courts.

Georgia has a group of accountability courts that falls under this umbrella that covers drug courts, mental health courts, family courts, and DUI courts. He became involved with the National Alliance on Mental Illness (NAMI), which is an organization dedicated to improving the lives of those with mental illnesses. He attended SAMHSA's GAINS* Center for Behavioral Health and Justice Transformation national co-occurring disorders conference in Miami, Florida, in 1998. It was through these associations that Judge Bethel became an advocate for the development of a mental health court.

> They call it the jail diversion treatment court. The mental health court was the primary initiative to come to fruition. In May of 2001, we opened our doors and were one of the first mental health courts in the state. It did not take a long time between the stakeholder meeting to the actual opening of the mental health court due to the fact that the structure and plan the stakeholders envisioned was that of resource realignment, not the creation of a new free-standing court. Therefore, the legislature did not need to be involved. We rearranged one of our calendars to deal with only those individuals who had some sort of an issue with mental health problems. By being able to bypass the legislature, we were able to speed the process along. Everything we did in the mental health court was done on a daily basis, but we refined it to the point where we put more attention on the individual defendants coming in by giving them an option to participate in the mental health court or go the regular route through prosecution. This was the primary initiative during my tenure. There were other initiatives that were under way, but this was the big one.

He states that it seems more like present day the primary focus is on drugs and drug courts. It is getting some structure with regard to these initiatives because once the mental health courts and the drug courts became popular, they were starting to proliferate across this nation with no real guidelines as to how to structure the court.

> Everyone was all off in different directions. And, with the drug courts, there was a lot of manipulated data that appeared to show support for the success of drug courts. However, the data were skewed. Data were manipulated in order to maintain the funding from the grants. The grants are to seed a new idea and to help bring that new idea into existence. However, once the ball gets rolling and clients are being served, it is up to courts to find different methods of support. It has always been a problem, however, depending on how you hire the person who is the director of that court, if they are paid through the grants, then during the first month or two, they are focused on the grant

---

* GAINS: **G**athering information, **A**ssessing what works, **I**nterpreting the facts, **N**etworking, and **S**timulating change.

initiative itself, but the rest of the time the focus is on being able to refund the grant. This is an issue.

For example, [in] the DeKalb County Mental Health Court, the individual who was the director was actually a former prosecutor as opposed to a clinician. It had always [been] my belief that whoever the director of the court is, they need to know how to navigate the criminal justice system. A clinician coming into the system from the outside cannot do that effectively due to their lack of knowledge of and experience in the system. Based upon the sequential intercept model, developed by Policy Research, which could be viewed as the parent of the GAINS Center for co-occurring disorders, Hank Steadman and Patricia Griffin put together an intercept model that could pretty much be used in any jurisdiction to show where to extract individuals from and how to develop a statewide model to provide treatment. And so there's certain intercepts along the criminal justice continuum. The clinician would not understand how to go in and pull a person from the reentry portion of the continuum or to pull someone in from the prebooking portion of the continuum and how to actually structure a program around that.

In addition to maintaining the therapeutic jurisprudence philosophy and maintaining the various calendar initiatives, Judge Bethel embarked on engaging in dialogue with others about therapeutic jurisprudence at international conferences. He made several presentations at GAINS conferences. Taking that same level of energy, he taught and presented this at the police academy to try and get them focused on how to address some of these issues.

One of the other initiatives Judge Bethel was a part of on the state level was crisis intervention teams (CIT). Originally started in Memphis, Tennessee, there is a national CIT, and police departments from municipalities and counties will send the individuals for training to become CIT officers. Georgia was one of the first to implement this statewide, strictly because of a push by Director Vernon Keenan of the Georgia Bureau of Investigation to have it set up in this manner. There is an advisory board of which Judge Bethel is a member for the statewide CIT. It is done in conjunction with NAMI (National Alliance on Mental Illness) Georgia. They provide training throughout the year with the goal of trying to train at least 20% of all of the officers in the state. They are interested in going beyond that; however, it is strictly voluntary on the officer's part. According to Bethel, "Trying to make it mandatory doesn't work because it takes a certain type of individual for the type of training and support that they do." The CIT was developed out of the need for officers to be trained to be more sensitive toward and capable to support the needs of those with mental illness.

These things always seem to develop out of some sort of incident. There was an incident that occurred where an individual who was off of his meds had a psychotic break and officers not knowing how to respond … they ended up shooting the individual who ultimately died from his injuries. The community was in an uproar. Most of the community members were aware that this individual took medication for his mental illness. This is when they first developed the whole CIT initiative. Their model has been used throughout the country. The program here is modeled after the one in Memphis. I am one of the instructors for the program. I do the mental health and the law portion of the training, which is a 40-hour, 1-week program.

Toward the end of his career, Judge Bethel became more involved in teaching by becoming a faculty member for the National Association of Juvenile and Family Court Judges and a part-time instructor with a local public school district. He also developed a program for the Institute for Continuing Judicial Education that is an online jail diversion program for judges.

When asked if he was surprised by the development of his career, Judge Bethel states that he feels that getting involved with the therapeutic jurisprudence philosophy to be surprising even though he leans toward that type of jurisprudence. He was never really able to identify it until talking with Dr. John Randolph Fuller, a criminologist at the University of West Georgia. Fuller made Bethel aware of a Web site developed by David Wexler and Bruce Winick, the co-founders of the therapeutic jurisprudence perspective. When he looked into that, he felt that it had covered everything that he had been talking about. Judge Bethel actually made a trip up to Memphis to a Bar Association meeting to meet with Wexler. Wexler operates out of Puerto Rico and this was a unique opportunity for Bethel to meet him and to discuss the principles of the therapeutic jurisprudence with him. He views these two gentlemen as the gurus insofar as documenting everything related to therapeutic jurisprudence. For him, this was a high point and the more rewarding aspect of his career.

He also notes that his career far exceeded his expectations. He had no idea where it would end up after first becoming a judge. At the beginning of his career as a judge, he was just trying to get acclimated to the position.

You just want to be a part of identifying your role within the criminal justice continuing and how you fit into that role and how you become accepted by your peers and so forth. After a period of time you begin to develop your own personality and the start date in lines the functioning of the courts and start to think in terms of how things might be dead differently in order to make the more efficient ... and to make an impact.

Back when he first became a judge, this type of thinking outside the box in regard to sanctions and how to deal with specific individuals was called alternative sentencing. A lot of people knew Judge Bethel's type of alternative sentencing.

For example, an individual had been brought into Recorders Court for disorderly conduct after having a party. I found out that it was sort of a domestic violence-type of a situation. Not to where they came to blows or anything like that, but it was the conflict between the husband and the wife. In talking with him, I came to find out that his problem was that the two of them never talked to each other. As a part of my sentence, I required him to just take her out to dinner at a nice restaurant and to bring me the receipt. So, okay, that is alternative sentencing. Well, the guy came back a week later [laugh] with some receipts where he had bought his wife these different outfits. And, uh, he said that she said she didn't want to go out to dinner, she just wanted the clothes. And I told him, "Well, you violated the order. Now you are out of $150 here." because I told him he had to spend at least $150. I wanted him to go to a nice restaurant. So, I said now you need to go back out and take her to that restaurant and bring me the receipt where she signed that the two of you went there. [Laughing]... Now whether or not that actually helped, I don't know. But just trying to get them to sit down and talk to each other I thought would've been beneficial. Back then you did not have the dispute resolution places and other counseling and so forth where you could send someone, or at least I wasn't aware of any that weren't charging an arm and a leg. But it was that kind of sentencing that I was doing in recorders court because you're not dealing with as serious an infraction as you would be say in state or superior court.

According to Judge Bethel, the most important changes that happened in the criminal justice system during his tenure would have to be the development of the accountability courts. He thinks that they are being driven by overcrowding in prisons. If not for overcrowding, he does not think there would be as much focus on accountability courts because there would be a place to house people. If they are kept out of sight, then they are out of mind. To him, this has been the biggest change and his biggest concern, especially when you are talking about therapeutic interventions within the prison system. He does not see us having many interventions and behavior modification in the prison system, especially in private prisons, due to the lack of a profit motive in providing these services.

Just trying to develop the interventions throughout the criminal justice system continuum so that you are doing more to benefit, and we're not talking about the serial killers or the hardened criminals ... because when you take a look at the data from the Department of Corrections, what you will end up with is statistics showing that the average individual who is sentenced for a felony stays behind bars anywhere from two to three years. So, you're not talking about your mass murderers. That is not the individual you are talking about.

The only two ways that an incarcerated offender leaves jail or prison are when he or she dies or is released back into the community. Georgia

Department of Corrections statistics, which are readily available online, show that very few, if any, inmates die behind bars. It becomes very important in Judge Bethel's mind to say what we are doing with this individual during those two to three years. Are we doing anything to modify his behavior? Thus, behavior modification has sort of become his banner. The problem, according to him, is that all of that is based on the concept of institutional capture. We just cannot see beyond the discourse of our respective disciplines. Therefore, those who work in the criminal justice system will not see incarceration as a means of behavior modification. He proposes that we have to get these individuals to look at other means of modifying behavior, and that is where we get into the therapeutic jurisprudence aspect of it. However, it is not easy to implement such interventions considering the current state of affairs in the United States.

> You have the combination of the economic crisis and the political arena in Georgia wanting to be tough on crime. With the economic crisis in place, you can see the spike in crime … and a lot of that having to do with, you know, the domestic violence of the situations that have occurred since the economic downturn … you have families struggling financially and the stress that that puts on the family and the domestic violence that ensues has really made it very tough. In conjunction with that, you have different people running for office who want to lock up all the bad guys, which in turn puts even more stress on the criminal justice system because they are facing budget shortfalls and so forth. … it is very hard to try to talk about implementing therapeutic interventions at a time when you have the spike in criminal activity because most politicians are demanding accountability and you still have a group and school of thought out there that these types of courts are not holding criminals accountable for their actions.

Overall, Judge Bethel thinks that it depends on which jurisdiction you are in if you see that the quality of criminal justice over the past 20 years has improved or if it has declined. The different members of the criminal justice continuum will pretty much dictate the quality of what occurs within that jurisdiction. If you have a police chief who is tough on crime and who is totally focused on clearing out the criminal element, then that is going to impact the entire criminal justice continuum because they are at the front end of the continuum. That will impact the courts and the cases they have to handle at a point time when they're being told to cut their budgets. Then you have more individuals going into the prison system. He feels that the entire initiative behind the accountability courts is to try to keep individuals out of the prison system so that we do not have overcrowding in the prisons because that is an enormous portion of every state's budget.

Preferred Priorities and Strategies of the Judiciary

Judge Bethel believes that the judge should be the judicial change agent, or the primary point person with regard to the development of mental health courts. The judge also could be the primary point person on the development of any variety of interventions.

> I just feel that the judiciary at this point can make an impact on how cases flow through the criminal justice system and that is whether or not a case is going to prosecution even though that is the prosecutor's responsibility. But, each of the specialty courts has what they call a "staffing" and this is where the prosecutor and the different clinicians and so forth—the judge is generally excluded from this or should be because [he or she does] not want to influence it or the project director—but they sit down and they actually talk about how best to move forward with a particular defendant. And, I think that it may be time consuming, but over a period of time it could be streamlined. Now you take jurisdictions like New York or California where they have severe over-crowding in the jails and they are looking for different options, they are not going to have time to do this and this is why. A lot of times these kinds of non-violent misdemeanors that diversion courts handle don't work in most juris-dictions because the defense attorneys know that, "hey, my guy is convicted of five days anyways, so why should he be subjected to three to six months of judicial oversight to complete some sort of treatment program?" It is just not going to happen. But, in all of your more serious offenders, you look at their background and you see that they had all of the small offenses first before they became a major offender.

Effective Policies and Programs

While some of the judges in magistrate court, including Judge Bethel, tried to implement many different policies and programs, the perception of the effectiveness of these programs was not ascertained due to the fact that there was no way for the judge to monitor or assess the impacts of the decisions that were being made.

> When I was a Recorders Court judge, there was no way for me to monitor the impact of any decision that I made because we didn't have anyone, no probation or anything like that, where they could actually monitor individu-als. The only time you knew whether or not something did not work is when you see the individual rearrested for the same offense. And, it was mostly the offense of public drunkenness or things of that nature. Some of the programs that we implemented in magistrate court where we had grants, we had the results because the research that was done. With the mental health court, the research was done by Dr. Peter Ash at Emory University. So, we got all the data from that to show the recidivism rates and things of that nature. When

you start talking about things like a preliminary hearing calendar or an application hearing calendar, there was no monitoring of those individuals once they left the court. There was a general feeling amongst us judges that the individuals were satisfied with being able to have a day in court and as long as they had the day in court it was not that important that they have a warrant issued because you're talking about neighbor disputes and things of that nature where someone wants to obtain a warrant.

Once the law was passed with regard to the issuing of protective orders in domestic violence cases, there was a flood of individuals coming in to obtain protective orders for either stalking or domestic violence. So, in DeKalb County, as with many other major urban areas, they have designated the magistrate court judges to handle that because of the volume and superior court judges can't just stop what they are doing to address protective orders every 10 or 15 minutes. So, we have started doing that and we were tracking the data and what was going on there with the volume of individuals that were coming in, the number of cases that ended up being dismissed, and so forth. So, we were able to track pretty much a lot of that. We found that the majority of cases, as long as a protective order is issued right away, by the time the individual is to come to court everything has calmed down and the victim doesn't bother to come to court because he or she is of the opinion that the situation between them has pretty much been resolved. This caused an enormous decrease in caseloads and anticipated caseloads for superior court judges.

Judge Bethel could not recall any initiative that he would have considered "a complete bust." Many of the initiatives that were developed sort of evolved into their current states by way of a process where the judges were doing something and simply trying to do a better job, which eventually became an intervention. Judge Bethel thought a fair description of the process was that it was more of an evolution. Being an evolutionary process is one of the reasons why the interventions worked well. It was not a full-blown implementation, it was more of a start here, tweak it a little bit, keep going, and tweak it a little bit, and so forth until you have something that is sustainable and you have data to back it up to say that it works. Judge Bethel noted that they never had anything that was dumped in their laps that they were mandated to implement without it having some sort of background or something to draw from in order to structure it the way it needed to be structured in order for it to be effective. One exception might have been the protective orders.

When the superior court judges requested the magistrates to handle the protective orders, and people around the courthouse knew Judge Bethel not for doing "off-the-wall stuff," but for doing things differently, he conducted his own ethnographic investigation of the process.

I went down and applied for a protective order just to see what steps the person went through. And then I conducted interviews of all the people that I had encountered with that and I presented that to the superior court judge to show them what was occurring. They were shocked because things were not happening the way they thought they were and it was making victims really jumping through hoops in order to get a protective order. So after that, we restructured the protective order process because we knew what the judges wanted and what was required and how to blend it in with the clerk's office. We put our program together for a protective order process. Thus, this particular process was dumped on the magistrate judges; however, there is still enough out there to draw from and then especially walk you through the steps of say a victim and then eliciting for how well-trained the staff in the clerk's office was and how much they were lacking in knowledge about a particular thing. But this exposed a lot [about] the process.

When asked if the protective order was a mandate that was external or if it was developed from within, he responded that it was external in the sense that the legislature said, "Boom! This is what is going to happen."

Legislation was enacted regarding the protective order process. While not completed abreast of the history of the law, Judge Bethel indicated that, through the Office of Violence Against Women, the legislation was enacted and passed down from the national level and was going to affect funding unless the states implemented it.

So the states, you know, put together the whole protective order process and dumped that on the judges. Then the judges were infuriated that they would have to stop in the middle of a trial because a female came in and made a protective order because she is being beaten by her husband.

[Bethel had noted earlier in the interview that the timeliness of the issuance of this order was paramount. It was an imposition for superior court judges to drop everything that they're doing in order to issue the protective order on the spot.]

If an individual comes into the court for the protective order, the order will be issued that day and then the sheriffs go out and remove the individual from the house that evening. That is a sign of the kind of timeliness you are talking about. Or, if a victim is really threatened, then they would be able to remove the victim to a safe haven, such as an emergency shelter, immediately.

The Greatest Problem Facing Criminal Courts

While conceding that pinpointing one problem facing courts was a difficult task, Judge Bethel chose the lack of trust of the community and how it views courts as one of the things that stood out the most. I probed to see if he felt that was a jurisdiction specific issue or if it was a general issue.

> I think that it is a general issue. Anytime you have, say, something on the news media about a judge letting an individual out of jail or giving him a bond when he shouldn't be out of jail and then that individual goes out and commits another crime that, you know, pretty much destroys that degree of trust that the general public should have with the court system. I think many efforts are being made for judges to get more out in the community to talk with … different groups and so forth and to explain the criminal justice system to people. … and you are always going to have a chief of police saying, "I don't know why the judge did that, but you know they let them out; we do our best to capture them and put them in jail and all they do is let them back out." The police and the prosecutors have the liberty to go out and talk with the media, whereas the judges do not.

Judge Bethel conceded that there were several other problems that the courts are facing. One of those issues is in the administration of therapeutic jurisprudence. The current district attorney in DeKalb County, Robert Jenkins, has been trying to implement a variety of initiatives in order to redirect individuals prior to actually going through the whole criminal justice continuum. Judge Bethel has heard of the same thing being attempted in other jurisdictions. But, his concern there was that they were charging a fee for this type of diversion program. Attaching a fee always concerns him.

> This is similar to what is going on with DUI courts. These courts charge an enormous fee to individuals in order for them to be diverted from DUI prosecution. And that, to him, presents the problem. Because now you're not dealing with everyone, you're not dealing equally with everyone who is coming before the court because if you have money, then you get the intervention. If you do not have money, then you go ahead and serve your time. This is inequitable and adversely affects the poor and minorities. They don't have the option to be able to pay. It is my belief that they do it this way because they feel that individuals are going to pay that amount of money in order to keep their driver licenses or stay out of jail.

In his opinion, the problem that is the most difficult for a judge to deal with is staff that have not been properly trained. The court staff is separate from the judge's staff. They are assigned from the clerk's office to a particular court. The bailiffs come from the sheriff's department, while the clerks come from the clerk's office, and the judge has his or her particular staff, which would be a secretary and the law clerk. He also notes that inadequate facilities are problematic.

> Having staff within the courtroom who are not adequately trained, to me, creates a real problem. Not being able to get proper files and so forth that would be needed for a particular court session. Back when I first started judging, you would have an arraignment in the afternoon with 200 people on the calendar.

In the court that we were in at that time, the facilities were not adequate to accommodate that number of people. It always presented a fire hazard. So, you had those kinds of issues. They built a new courthouse some time ago, around 2000. They do have a new courthouse, but that has cut down the number of people that you could take up for arraignment. So, courts can only bring 18 to 30 people into the courthouse. When you have maybe 100+ that actually need to go through arraignment, the logistics becomes somewhat confused They will house some downstairs in a holding area and then take them upstairs to the correct courtroom via elevator. The county really needs to have a new courthouse ... where they have a means of getting individuals in and out in a secure area.

One of the things that I was trying to implement before I retired was to have them to be able to conduct that hearing at the jail and teleconference with the judge in the court. It was a real security issue because the jail is like maybe a block and a half away from the actual court. It is a little, small court over there that we have for those hearings. Across the sidewalk is recorder's court. The deputies would have to pick up an individual from the jail, bring them around and parked alongside the road and escort the individual to court. There were days when the recorder's court had so many people backed up they just had a mass of people out there in front of their court. And, so there would be no way that one deputy bringing over maybe two inmates could ever protect himself or secure inmates if there were gang members waiting out there for a particular individual. I put together a presentation and presented this to the Sheriff's and Jailer's Association to make them aware that this was an extreme hazard and that we needed to get funding in order to get this remote teleconferencing in place. So, I was just informed about two months ago that they finally got it in place.

Although he was not there to see the program come to fruition, Judge Bethel notes that there was an enormous amount of information that the judge has to put into the computer system. The sitting judges pushed back stating that they could not get through all of the hearings due to the time-consuming nature of the data entry. Depending on what happens on a particular evening, there could be 20 defendants present for hearings. If the judges had to do all of the paperwork for each individual person, even if it only took five to ten minutes per case, it would lengthen the time per hearing to two to three hours due to multiple warrants and other considerations, which he concedes is a very long time for an individual hearing.

The Relationship between Theory and Practice

In considering the role that theory plays in the practice of therapeutic jurisprudence, Judge Bethel, as noted earlier in the interview, decided to take it upon himself to experience what persons coming to magistrate court experience in order to ascertain areas that were in need of improvement.

I think I have conducted about three ethnographic investigations out there where I would walk through to see what was supposed to occur. Not considering it an actual theory, but what people believed was occurring, and what was actually occurring in those investigations was markedly different, which leads one to believe that staff will take the course of least resistance. No matter what discipline you are, you are going to find a way to move people through that system with the least amount of resistance. That is where I think it pretty much breaks down with regard to theory compared to what is actually happening. No one takes the time to go back through and take a real solid look at it and say, "Okay, this is where we are having issues and now let's try and work on that so we can modify theory to what's happening, or change what's happening to get it close to theory."

When prompted with the idea that not enough research is done on the process itself and what can be done to improve it, Judge Bethel provided an actual example that occurred in his courtroom. He recalled this particular situation was very upsetting to him. He did not identify the actual court that it took place in, so as not to "cast aspersions on anyone." He recalled the development of a DUI court, which have been popular. He recalled that not many people were being sentenced to DUI courts in the beginning. They tried to attract individuals because it was voluntary to divert to this particular problem solving court.

It was on a voluntary basis because of the cost associated with it. In the report that I read, in this one particular jurisdiction, their numbers were really down. So, the request, the innuendo, the word that was trying to be put out was to have the other judges in that court start sentencing heavier on their DUI cases in order to encourage individuals to opt out to the DUI court intervention. So, the end result, theoretically, was that you are now having the judges collectively sentencing people more. Then, one of the individuals would say, "Well, I don't want to go to trial" or whatever or enter a plea; "I would rather go into the DUI court."

According to Bethel, if the above situation were not the case, then likely the individual would have gone ahead with the sentence and received 10 days in jail and a steep fine or another combination sentence. If the defendant knew a more severe sentence was probable, which the judges have the option to mete out, then other alternatives to spending time in jail would be sought out. Of those, the top-rated alternative would be DUI court. Judge Bethel believes that there is no alternative for some.

Well, now you can see the effect that that has on the individuals who could not afford the DUI court. That is where the problem lies. The end result is that certain minorities and people of color were not able to avail themselves of that option. Therefore, they were stuck with the more severe sentence.

When probed about the presence of a class and minority bias, Judge Bethel stated that there was indeed a minority and class bias and that is not the way it should work.

> If you have some sort of an intervention, then it should be available to all of the individuals who are within that population. I am expecting at some point that some lawyer is going to come up with an equal protection argument with regard to several of these specialty courts.

In regard to the relationship between theory and practice in the criminal justice system, Judge Bethel believes that there needs to be more follow-up as to how theory is being applied, implemented, and he does not see that happening as much as it should.

> Yes, not as much as it should because you end up with a theory ... All of the different disciplines that are within that continuum are made aware of the theory, what it is you want to do, and then each discipline gets their piece of it and they take the path of least resistance in order to get that through their particular discipline because, granted, a majority of the courts and everybody all feel that we are understaffed. They do not have enough people and they are still looking at budget cuts. I think it is going to be very detrimental in DeKalb County this year. So, how do you address that? If you continue to do what has been structured with less people and with less resources, then there will be repercussions.

I asked Judge Bethel how he would characterize the relationship. Did there seem to be collaboration between those who developed the theories and those who practice about how to best approach specific types of offenders? Or is it more of a dictatorial relationship with mandates and the recipients of those mandates trying to find the path of least resistance to do what they are told to do when it is really not collaborative?

> I hear from clinicians that this is a lot of what happens in their staffing the different drug courts. They do not feel as if they are equal members at the table, so to speak. I know that we never had that problem because that is not the way that we structured our Diversion Treatment Court. Everybody has equal input and it is interesting that you talk about the collaboration. That was one of my big points when I presented at the GAINS conference back in 2002. This is what needed to happen. You cannot bring people to the table to discuss any sort of an initiative when everyone does not feel that they have an equal voice. That can be a problem because there are still, even now, many initiatives out there where the judges quite frankly are dictatorial in how they want the court run. And there are those judges who say, "I'm the guy in the hot seat and if anything happens, it is going to be on me, therefore I need to be the one to

call shots." However, a lot of feedback that I have been getting from the ICJE course online is that they keep saying that judges are not supposed to be a therapist or treatment provider. Judges do not know that kind of stuff. And my response is: "So why are you not listening to the treatment providers or the therapists?" It kind of makes sense, but still some of them in their responses will say things like: "How was the judge supposed to diagnose an individual who was in court?" And they are not. That is what the collaboration is all about; that is what staffing is all about. It is not about you becoming a doctor or psychiatrist. That is not your role. Several of them don't seem to get that point, which I find to be interesting. There is still this big rift between using specialty courts or just tough love and go ahead and put the guy in jail and he or she will learn. I don't know how you get beyond that.

In regard to therapeutic jurisprudence research, Judge Bethel thought that there were questions that could be researched that would be most useful for practice.

Really in trying to convince other judges that these therapeutic interventions work, if you had research that would follow, and that would be the expensive part, really follow some of the participants in the specialty courts, which is what they're supposed to be doing now anyway. I still kind of had my questions about the validity of the research strictly because of what I mentioned earlier about individuals working to continue the grant as opposed to focusing on the subject of the research. But, there has to be data to show not only that the interventions work, but to show that the interventions are cost-saving because legislatures don't want to hear anything about how well you're treating criminals. All they want to know is if it's going to save a dollar. That, to me, is sad because I would think that you are going to have an enormous savings especially when you're dealing with mental health because you've got to have the medications for the individuals anyway. If the lion's share of what the jail is spending is on these medications, then is there really going to be a cost savings there? I think that there is a big struggle going on now to be able to show that there is a cost savings with a lot of these interventions. But nobody wants to talk about the improvement of the quality of life for a particular defendant who was on drugs and who is now not on drugs and has also become a member of the factor market. Here you have a guy who has a job and is paying taxes and nobody seems to work that into the equation. I do not know of any research that I have seen where they tried to factor that into the cost-savings analysis.

He thinks that this type of cost benefit analysis research would be most beneficial to the cause. For him, the goal is trying to convince the lawmakers because of the initial capital outlays of millions of dollars, whether it is by way of a grant or other means. He commented that Governor Nathan Deal just signed a bill for $10 million for the accountability courts in the State of Georgia. This is a large sum of money that will be distributed to these courts.

One of the other things that I wanted to mention, the initial grants for drug courts did not allow them to take in individuals who had a mental illness. The initial grants back when they first started, mental health courts did not allow them to take in any participants who also were using drugs. Two thirds of all of the mental health individuals out there are self-medicating with illegal drugs. And then, what was it about four to five years ago, the rage became co-occurring disorders. Every court out there was addressing co-occurring because that's what the funding stream was.

On the future, he states:

Trying to see where therapeutic jurisprudence is going to go is somewhat difficult because now it seems that everyone is interested in it. If there is a funding stream amount there, then every court is going to say that they are doing whatever is required in order to get the money. The big topic now (what is in the forefront) is veteran's courts. You hear a lot of talk about veteran's courts. Many people are trying to start veteran's courts. In my opinion, this is occurring solely because there is money out there available to fund these types of courts.

When asked if this is more of "how can we get funds because there isn't much money out there right now with the recession and lower tax revenues," Bethel responded that his view on grants runs counter to the more popular view of grant money. He views these funding streams as a means to "test the hypothesis" to see if a new, innovative idea is worth the cost and would be effective.

Once you have tested that hypothesis and you have received your data, then you decide whether or not you're going to make that a line item in the county's budget, or somebody's budget somewhere, so that you do not have to continue trying to get grants every year. If it is something that is functional and it is working, which a lot of these courts are, the drug courts, the mental health courts, like ours in DeKalb County, our recidivism rate is between five and seven percent. … Just based on that, the last grant that we received was one of two grants that were given by SAMHSA. These are federal dollars. The funding streams are not meant as a way to continually support an existing program.

What Judge Bethel sees happening around the country is everyone applying for grants to continue their particular initiatives. Sustainability is supposed to be a part of every grant application. Even though there is talk of sustainability, to him it just seems like every year the same courts are getting funded without the local jurisdiction taking ownership of the initiative. He firmly believes in the notion of ownership.

If nothing has changed, then now you are taking the money and using it to the benefit of that particular jurisdiction, as opposed to you have already done it here, you see that it works, now it's time for you all to take some ownership over that initiative and let's try it elsewhere.

In this vein, more dollars would be available to start initiatives in jurisdictions that currently did not have any financial support to start them.

In Judge Bethel's view, in order for problem-solving courts to maintain their existing funding streams, the focus of the court will be broadened to include new subpopulations of interest, such as veterans.

This is what I was saying about keeping an eye on what is happening now. The funding stream is going to be veteran's courts. So, now you watch—every drug court or every mental health court out there is going to say, "Oh, yes, we address veterans." We have a separate calendar for veterans and so forth and so on.

Judge Bethel supports this assertion with evidence from a conversation he had with the Veteran's Administration (VA).

They had indicated to me, a couple of individuals at the VA, that there was one particular judge in the State of Georgia who was going to develop this veterans court and was well on the way and had never even attempted to talk to anyone at the VA about it. See, the collaboration is the most important thing. Before you put anything together, you sit down and talk with all the stakeholders. That is one thing I [have] learned—you have to have the stakeholders at the table so that when you begin to structure your intervention everybody understands what you are doing and know how they can participate. That is when you come up with this realignment of resources instead of trying to get a whole bunch of additional funding. From a collaborative standpoint, you're bringing in people who are experts in that area who might have pertinent information that you are not privy to that would help the cause to be effective. No one should expect the judge to know everything. That is not possible.

Academic Research Informing Court Processes

In regard to consulting research conducted by academics in order to inform court processes, Judge Bethel indicated that he most definitely engaged in this practice. He stated that he did this frequently as a judge and was able to use research findings from different organizations, such as the National Association for Juvenile and Family Courts Judges, which produces readings specifically structured for judges. However, in his opinion, a judge must go beyond that type of reading, especially if you want to understand some of the other disciplines that are involved in judicial decision making, problem-solving courts, and therapeutic jurisprudence. According to Judge Bethel, "It is multidisciplinary."

Impact of International Events on Magistrate Courts

When asked if he felt that events on a global scale and those happening internationally had an impact on magistrate courts, Judge Bethel responded, "Not really." He recalled that they had groups from other countries come and visit their court, but were not very influential on the court and its processes. He recalled a group that visited some years ago.

> We have had groups from other countries come to visit our court. Some years ago a contingent from Russia came. They were interested in what we were doing. The connection there came through the clinicians because they were coming to visit with the clinicians here at the DeKalb Community Service Board. We, in turn, told them about the initiative that we had in conjunction with the development of the mental health court. They definitely wanted to see that. We had a visitor from Barbados who I've met through the therapeutic jurisprudence blog who was traveling through here and wanted to see what our court was doing. And I think just about a month or two ago there was a contingent from France that was touring this country to look at the different initiatives that were going on.
>
> I thought it was beneficial to see how other countries dealt with say some issues. One of the things that really stood out for me was with the Russian contingent and talking with them about driving under the influence. I thought it to be quite interesting that they did not have all of these different requirements and stringent laws. If you want to drive under the influence, then you could, but if you have an accident or if you hit somebody, then you're going to jail, period. It is that kind of, I guess, enforcement that makes people adhere to the law. It is kind of self-policing because they do not want to end up going to jail. I guess Russian jails are not all that great, whereas here we seem to go overboard trying to keep people from driving. I don't know how to explain this, but it is just that the atmosphere is different. In other words, my position is that, okay if I'm drunk, then I am not going to drive because there is all this bad stuff that is going to happen to me, but I'm drunk; I think I can make it home, which kind of gives the impression that we're soft on crime. We are not really implementing the full measure of the law for that particular offense. That just seemed to be a marked difference. Over here [we will] arrest an individual for sleeping on a park bench, whereas over in Russia you can go ahead and sleep on a park bench, but everybody's going to talk about you. There is a social stigma attached to those behaviors over there, whereas here there is not.

How have developments post-September 11, 2001, affected what you do at the magistrate court level?

> I don't think it has affected us that much. I don't recall. I mean, there have been changes within the courthouse that were implemented by the sheriff especially after the shooting that was in the Fulton County Courthouse—Brian Nichols.

But, insofar as anything dealing with September 11, I don't recall any specific changes that would've occurred immediately following that.

Are you basically satisfied or dissatisfied with the developments in criminal law and criminal procedure in your system? What are the developments that you have seen happening and would like to see happening?

The whole accountability courts thing? I am totally satisfied with that. I have been satisfied with the role that many of the court systems have been playing, but I think that the magistrate court could play a bigger role in that. In some of the jurisdictions within Georgia, the magistrate court does not have the same degree of respect as say a magistrate court in the urban areas have. Of course, you know that in Georgia and in many of the rural areas, a lot of the magistrates are not lawyers. They definitely would not have the same degree of respect from the lawyer judges who are in Superior Court and, therefore, many of the duties that, say, the judges in the magistrate courts in urban areas would have would not be the same as those in rural areas. There is some history to this because all it took to become a judge in some areas in rural Georgia was to have a family name. If you were the wife of the sheriff or the son of the mayor, then your name on the ballot you will get elected.

Then there came this whole issue of training. Back when I first became magistrate, there was no training counsel for magistrate court judges. Through the efforts of Wayne Purdom for one and the development of the bench book for magistrates to get everyone on the same page, the Magistrate Court Council was developed and as part of that you had training within that organization. But, you still have issues in trying to enforce a lot of the training with regard to the judges. It is at a point now where if you do not comply with a certain number of hours of training per year, then you end up going before the Judicial Qualifications Commission for not complying with the requirements and you could be removed from office by the Supreme Court.

What you think is most needed now to improve the system?

I honestly think that at some point in the future we will be moving toward the unified court system. There are so many different courts around with so many different things that it's hard to get one umbrella over everything and then just try to really address the issue of how do you deal with crime as it is occurring. Everybody's got their own little system everywhere. And so even though you may have the Supreme Court indicating that one thing should occur, everybody's probably implementing it differently. I think they are undertaking an initiative now to develop standards for accountability courts. Back when the drug courts and the mental health courts first started, everybody was trying to get their name in the newspaper as having developed one of these types of courts. Now the drug court was way far ahead of everyone else and they developed the drug court standards in an effort to make sure that everyone was on the same page. Now that is happening with the mental health courts, but all of the jurisdictions are different and one of the things I have always said is that what works over here is not necessarily going to work elsewhere. So, you have to be able to look at any sort of rules or codes in a very broad perspective until we actually get a handle on how to treat this.

Standardization of Processes

Some judicial scholars argue for the standardization of much of the judicial process. The underlying thinking is that such alignment would be fairer in terms of justice. When asked if he thought that a move to standardization would limit a currently sitting judge who thinks the way he did and wants to see the same types of policies implemented as he did when he was sitting on the bench, he replied that moving to a very highly structured and standardized system would inhibit the magistrate judge from being innovative in coming up with new ideas for new types of courts that have yet to be established. Indeed, he felt that it would limit the judge's thinking and restrict him or her in what could be done.

> It is all based on the fact that you are going to have this particular outcome, but if you are not dealing with a population that is similar to what was previously dealt with in order to achieve that outcome, then it is not going to happen. So, there has to be leeway; the judge has to be able to incorporate things that are peculiar to his or her particular jurisdiction. No two jurisdictions are identical. Each of these groups of courts, the municipal court judges and their counsel, and the probate court judges and their counsel, or magistrate court judges, they're going to fight vigorously to hold onto their particular status. As for the whole mental health court initiative some years ago when I presented to probate court judges, I told them that Georgia already has 159 mental health courts and that we call them probate courts. But, probate courts still cannot do anything in regard to a criminal case. It is very confusing. One of the things that I used to tell all of the magistrates in the early 2000s was that I felt that the magistrate court was at the entry level of the criminal justice system because that is where somebody is coming to take out a warrant. That being the case, the magistrate court could do far more about identifying individuals and planning therapeutic interventions right at the outset to sort of dictate what path that particular defendant would take. … I firmly believe that to still be the case. … if you are in a jurisdiction where the Superior Court judge or State Court judge has no respect for the magistrate court judge, then your hands are going to be tied because you are not going to really be able to do much. Or, if you have a prosecutor or district attorney who does not buy into the concept, then you still have problems. But I do think that the municipal court and magistrate court are really pretty much on the frontline. They could do a lot to diffuse situations before they actually end up becoming more serious.

In Judge Bethel's opinion, if we do not address the underlying problems via accountability or problem-solving courts, then offenders will just be incapacitated for two to three years and then be forced to reintegrate back into the exact same environment. He noted that when we release an individual back into the exact same environment, then they will go back to what they know and do the exact same things. One of the goals that accountability courts try to accomplish is to make a strong effort to try and empower individuals to manage their own problems and to get them to take ownership of their situation to where they can manage their own issues. He concludes that he believes that is why these types of courts have such good recidivism rates.

Conclusion

Judge Bethel truly believes in the role of accountability courts in Georgia to provide diversionary and therapeutic interventions to offenders in order to prevent them from progressing through the criminal justice continuum. He is passionate about the role that therapeutic jurisprudence plays in dealing with criminal behavior and believes that magistrate court judges play an integral role in this judicial philosophy because they are the frontline of entry to the criminal courts. However, he concedes that these interventions need to be tested more thoroughly in order to provide accurate data on their effectiveness. While this philosophy is being applied in many of these lower level courts, there is not sufficient data to currently support their cost-benefit effectiveness to lawmakers. Moreover, he sees a discrepancy in funding of the initiatives. In his opinion, grant-funded initiatives should only be used to test new programs, not to sustain them. Judge Bethel believes that the current economic crisis in the United States will only exacerbate the issue of limited resources for courts.

Glossary

Accountability Courts: Courts such as drug court, mental health court, or DUI court that seek to address a specific problem. Georgia currently has nine types of accountability courts that attempt to address specific types of criminal behaviors and their underlying causes—adult drug, adult mental health, juvenile drug, juvenile mental health, DUI, family dependency treatment, veterans issues, domestic violence, child support, and some hybrid courts (e.g., drug/mental health and DUI/drug). These courts adopt a therapeutic component by way of integrating treatment services into the case processing. For example, drug court mandates that participants undergo drug testing, treatment, and counseling.

Alternative Sentencing: Sentencing that avoids traditional sanctions of the penal system, such as rehabilitation programs.

Arraignment: Appearance in court before a judge in which charges are read and a plea is entered.

Defendant: The individual accused in a criminal proceeding.

Ethnographic Investigation: Investigation of a group of individuals through their experiences.

Gubernatorial Appointment: Appointment by the state governor for a position that becomes open, such as a judge, in the middle of a term without an election.

Initial Appearance: Appearance before a judge to determine if a crime has been committed, if it occurred within the jurisdiction, and if there is probable cause that the defendant committed the crime.

Jurisprudence: The science or philosophy of law.

Magistrate Court: A court with limited jurisdiction over minor civil and criminal matters, such as traffic violations, misdemeanors, or preliminary hearings, for those who will move to other courts for trial.

Merit Selection: The process for selecting state court judges by nomination to appointing authority for final appointment. This selection process may require legislative confirmation.

Misdemeanor: Criminal offense less serious than a felony; a crime in which the penalty is incarceration for one year or less.

Problem-Solving Court: A court that is an alternative to the traditional criminal court model. These courts are outcomes focused and based on a team approach that provides support, treatment, and education while individualizing justice and holding the offender accountable all at the same time. Due to the emphasis on offender accountability, some states refer to these problem solving courts as "accountability courts."

Recidivism: The relapse to a previous behavior or condition, such as the repetition of criminal activity.

Recorder's Court: Court of limited jurisdiction, similar to traffic court.

Therapeutic Jurisprudence: Holistic, interdisciplinary approach to studying the effects of law and the legal system on the behavior, emotions, and mental health of people.

Conclusion

The 12 magistrates, justices, and judges interviewed for this volume offer their views on the most significant legal developments and issues in criminal and procedural law facing their respective nations. They also discuss their professional development and accomplishments, opening a window into their personal lives and providing a context for understanding their experiences and opinions. These experienced judicial officers offer a unique insiders' perspective of their countries' legal and judicial systems. They also provide insight into career development of legal and judicial professionals in their respective nations. The judges and justices interviewed represent a diverse array of nations and cultures ranging from Canada and the United States in North America to Austria, Bosnia-Herzegovina, and Slovenia on the European Continent to India in Asia to Australia. They serve on trial and appellate courts at the local, provincial, regional, state, and national levels.

The judges and justices interviewed include: Judge Hilmo Vucinic, State Court Justice for Bosnia and Herzegovina; Judge Aleksander Karakaš, Criminal Judiciary Department of Maribor District Court, Slovenia; Mag. Friedrich Forsthuber, president of the Vienna Criminal Court; Judge Wally Oppal, Queens Council (Q.C), Supreme Court of British Columbia and former attorney general of British Columbia, Canada; Stephen N. Limbaugh, Jr., District Judge, United States District Court, Eastern District of Missouri; Judge Robert Bell of the Maryland Court of Appeals (State Supreme Court); Judge Eugene C. Turner, Collier County Court, State of Florida; Chief Judge Wilson Rambo, 4th Judicial, State of Louisiana; Judge Winston P. Bethel, Retired, Chief Magistrate Judge DeKalb County Georgia; Judge Manmohan Singh, Delhi High Court, India; Magistrate Gregory Andrew Benn, regional magistrate, Kalgoorlie-Boulder, Western Australia, and Senior Judge Stephen McEwen, The Youth Court of Australia.

The main goal of the interviews was to present the justices' views and interpretations of legal developments and current issues in the criminal law and procedure in their nations. Each of the judges had extensive legal and judicial experience in his national legal system. Based upon their extensive experience and knowledge of the legal and judicial system, we set out to determine how these judges evaluated and interpreted the developments they saw in the legal profession and criminal courts of their countries.

The interviews also were designed to provide insight into the legal profession, the judges' careers, and their personal and professional development. We began the interviews by asking the judges about their career, their legal education, occupational history, areas of specialization, and the factors that influenced their career decisions and professional development. Their answers to these questions provided insight into the legal and judicial professions in their respective nations. We inquired into whether any surprises occurred during the course of their career development and whether their work had proved as interesting and rewarding as they thought it would. These questions elicited valuable background information that provided unique insight into the human dimension of judicial officials.

Judges typically began their careers as lawyers, either in the private sector or government. In general, entrance to the legal profession required completion of secondary or high school, followed by a university education, and, in the United States, three years postbaccalaureate legal study. Some European countries, such as Slovenia, require apprenticeships or internships in addition to formal classroom education. Major differences exist between the European and U.S. models of legal education. The European model typically involves study at the university under the Law Faculty. The U.S. and Australian model requires four years undergraduate study at the university, followed by three years of law school. Many of the judges had to move from their hometowns to attend the university or law school and returned home for varying lengths of time following completion of their studies. For example, Hilmo Vucinic moved from Gorazde to Sarajevo to attend the university and returned to Gorazde to begin his legal career, Aleksander Karakas moved from Maribor to Ljubljana to attend the university and returned to Maribor to begin his legal career. They also were required to move from one city to another during their judicial careers. Judge Bell of the Maryland Court of Appeals began his university education in his hometown of Baltimore, Maryland, moved to Boston for law school and returned to Maryland to begin his career. These moves reflect a commitment to their careers and contributed to a broader perspective than those who remained in their hometowns for their education and careers.

Most of the judges interviewed entered the legal profession not intending to be judges. Some were truly surprised by their career paths and the fact that they ultimately joined the bench. It was not always easy for judges to articulate why they entered the legal profession. For example, Judge Robert Bell indicated that, although he did not know precisely why he entered the legal profession, he knew he wanted to be a lawyer for a long time. He was intrigued by author Erle Stanley Gardner's portrayal of lawyers in his *Perry Mason* series, the good that lawyers did, and the excitement of the profession. Similarly, Judge Eugene Turner's interest in the legal profession began at an early age. Ironically, his aunt told him at age 10 that he "would make a good judge." He began visiting the courthouse and watching the proceedings not long after. For other judges, such as Stephen Limbaugh, the legal profession was a family tradition. Judge Limbaugh's father and grandfather were lawyers. He practiced with both at the family firm for a number of years and indicated that they were "the best mentors imaginable."

The decision to apply for a judicial position or run for judge arose relatively early in the legal careers of those interviewed. Upon graduation from law school and successful completion of the bar exam or its equivalent, the newly admitted attorneys either went into private practice or took a variety of government positions. Several, including Judge Limbaugh, ran for office and were elected state's attorney or prosecutor. Others were hired by state's attorney's or prosecutor's offices and served as trial prosecutors. The decision to enter the judiciary was a professional and personal decision. As Judge Hilmo Vucinic explains, "I was not an idealist; this job is a responsible job, it is unique, complex, requiring a lot of time and effort." Many of the judges interviewed were engaged in a variety of civic activities prior to being appointed or elected judge. Some were able to continue these activities upon entering the judiciary, while others had to give them up to comply with judicial canons of ethics and avoid potential conflicts of interest.

The judges appeared to be content with their career choices. They indicated that the job was demanding, involved working long hours in and out of the courthouse, and required dedication and commitment. Nevertheless, they indicated that the job was fulfilling, and that they were satisfied. Several expressed gratitude for spouses and family who supported their career choices and understood that the demands of the job meant certain personal sacrifices.

We then inquired about what the judges considered to be the most important changes that had occurred in their nations' criminal justice system over the course of their careers. We explored changes in philosophical approaches, organizational arrangements, policies and programs, technology, personnel issues, and other areas. We also examined external environmental changes: community support, judicial relations with minority communities, political influences, changes in legal powers, and resource provision. Finally, we asked whether the overall quality of the criminal justice system improved or declined. Several key themes emerged from the judges' responses to these questions. These include the impact of political change on the courts, diversity on the bench and in the community, trends in sentencing philosophies and the development of problem-solving courts, judicial integrity as a core philosophy, the relationship of legal and social science theories to judicial practice, the effects of technological innovation on the administration of justice, and the influence of transnational legal matters on judicial decision making.

All of the judges experienced changes during their careers. However, some of the changes were more profound than others. The nature and extent of the changes varied greatly. Not surprisingly, those judges in transitional democracies experienced the most change in a relatively short period of time. However, even in established democracies, such as the United States, Canada, and Australia, major changes occurred during the professional lives of those interviewed.

First, with regard to transitional democracies, Bosnia–Herzegovina and Slovenia were in the midst of democratization shortly before and during the interviews. Both countries passed new constitutions and created new courts. All three branches of government—executive, legislative, and judicial—were undergoing a profound transformation. As Judge Vucinic explained, under the former continental approach, the court led the entire process from investigation through sentencing. The new legal and judicial system is based on an Anglo-Saxon adversarial approach in which the prosecution and defense are separate elements of the adjudication process. Judge Vucinic of Bosnia–Herzegovina also experienced the transition from military to civilian courts. He first served as a judge on the military court in Gorazde and later on the civilian Cantonal Court, before his subsequent appointment to the Cantonal Court in Sarajevo and eventually the Court of Bosnia–Herzegovina that has jurisdiction over war crimes, organized crime, corruption, and election complaints. Judge Karakaš of Slovenia experienced so many constitutional amendments and statutory changes while serving on the bench that it made his job far more difficult than it otherwise might have been. As he put it, "The current path toward a correct decision, which has to be made in a reasonable time, is longer and more complicated than it once was."

There have also been profound changes in the United States. Maryland Chief Justice Robert Bell came of age during the civil rights revolution of the 1960s. His first experience with the courts was as a criminal defendant during his high school years in Baltimore, when he was arrested for participation in a lunch counter sit-in, part of the African American struggle for civil rights. Ironically, Judge Bell would eventually replace the attorney and former Maryland Chief Justice who argued against his case on appeal. Judge Rambo of the 4th Judicial District of Louisiana noted the increasing diversity of the Louisiana courts, as well as the judiciary, nationally, both with regard to African Americans and women. While the percentage of African Americans and women holding judicial office is not representative of their percentage of the population, it is growing. Chief Magistrate Bethel of DeKalb County, Georgia, also raised the issue of diversity and judicial relations with minorities and the poor.

Diversity and minority relations were not just issues in the United States. Judge Wally Oppal, former Supreme Court Judge and Attorney General of British Columbia indicated that 40% of the population of Vancouver, British Columbia, were "visible" minorities and that 25% were foreign born. He argued that greater representation of minorities on the judiciary was important and that the bench should reflect the makeup of society. Regional Magistrate Gregory Benn of Kalgoorlie-Boulder, Western Australia, discussed the overrepresentation of Aboriginals in the Australian criminal justice system. Delhi High Court Judge Manmohan Singh addressed diversity on the Delhi High Court Bench and indicated that 8 of 48 judges on the court were women. He also discussed the multicultural nature of Indian society. Interestingly, Magistrate Friedrich Forsthuber of Austria revealed that, while women comprised one third of the judiciary in 1991, that number had grown to two thirds in 2012. The reasons for the dramatic growth in the number of women serving on the judiciary are not clear. Magistrate Forsthuber believes that a contributing factor is the fact that many young professionals find the judiciary much more family friendly than in the past.

Judge Bell highlighted another major philosophical change in the United States that has taken place with regard to constitutional protections afforded to criminal defendants. The U.S. Supreme Court under Chief Justice Earl Warren, often referred to as the Warren Court, vastly expanded defendants' constitutional rights in the 1960s and early 1970s. These rights included the exclusionary rule set forth in *Mapp v. Ohio* 367 U.S. 643 (1961), the requirement that defendants be advised of their right to remain silent prior to a custodial interrogation in *Miranda v. Arizona* 384 U.S. 436 (1966), and the right of indigent defendants to representation by counsel at trial in *Gideon v. Wainwright* 372 U.S. 335 (1963), among others. Defendants' rights reached their zenith in the 1970s and have been reduced or moderated ever since. Not coincidentally, parallel to the decline in the rights of criminal defendants has been a rise in jurisprudence concerning victims' rights. Magistrate Friedrich Forsthuber confirmed a similar increase in attention to victims' rights in Austria.

Canada underwent a similar expansion of the rights of criminal defendants with the passage of the Charter of Human Rights and Freedom in 1982. Judge Wally Oppal explained that illegally obtained evidence would no longer be admissible in criminal prosecutions. One of the reasons for this was to prevent wrongful convictions. Judge Limbaugh of the U.S. District also mentioned the importance of preventing wrongful convictions.

India is also undergoing major philosophical changes driven in part by external conditions. Public attitudes toward the death penalty in India have shifted dramatically in recent decades. "Capital punishment is now only awarded in the rarest of rare cases," remarked Judge Singh. Even more remarkable is the changing concept of family and marriage in India. In 2010, the Supreme Court of India dramatically changed the legal landscape and ruled that it is no longer a criminal offense for unmarried couples to live together. Finally, sodomy was decriminalized as a result of an Indian Supreme Court decision in 2009, which held that homosexual relations between two consenting adults was a fundamental right protected by the Indian Constitution.

The U.S. Supreme Court decriminalized sodomy in 2003 in the case of *Lawrence v. Texas* 539 U.S. 558 (2003) and ruled favorably on certain aspects of gay marriage in 2013. Judge Bell discussed political efforts to interfere with the judiciary in Iowa, following the Iowa State Supreme Court's decision to legalize gay marriage.

Another area where major changes have occurred is criminal sentencing. All of the American judges mentioned changes in sentencing and were opposed to mandatory sentencing guidelines. Lengthy sentences, especially for nonviolent offenses were one of the major contributing factors to the explosion of the U.S. prison population between 1980 and 2010. At the federal level, Judge Limbaugh indicated that the sentencing guidelines for drug offenses were generally far too severe. Despite recent reductions in sentencing for crack cocaine, methamphetamine sentences remain as harsh as ever. Judge Limbaugh commented that these drugs were generally abused by those in the lower socioeconomic classes, with African Americans leaning strongly toward abusing crack, and Caucasians leaning toward methamphetamine. On the other hand, Judge Limbaugh felt that sentencing guidelines for other crimes, such as Medicaid fraud, were too lenient and considered two to three years imprisonment an inadequate punishment for a $100,000 theft. Judge Turner of Collier County, Florida, denounced Florida's mandatory sentencing guidelines and indicated that the Florida legislature had removed discretion from the judiciary. He felt that the courts were becoming more academic and sterile, and that they were more interested in statistics than individuals. Judge Turner prided himself on individualized sentencing and did his best to get to know defendants in the brief period that they appeared before him. He also relied upon defense counsel to know their clients and recommend appropriate treatment.

Judge Rambo of Louisiana was particularly interested in the shift in emphasis from incarceration to reintegration, which he believed was critical given that most inmates return to the community in two to three years. He strongly approved of the Louisiana Department of Public Safety and Corrections movement in this direction. Judge Rambo approached sentencing in the context of theory and practice, believing that sentencing should be guided by theoretical underpinnings.

Judge Bethel of Georgia was also interested in the theoretical underpinnings of sentencing, particularly therapeutic jurisprudence. In fact, he had attended conferences with key proponents of the theory and served as grant reviewer for the Substance Abuse and Mental Health Service Administration (SAMHSA). Accountability and problem-solving courts, sometimes called diversion courts, are central aspects of therapeutic jurisprudence. Judge Bethel cited the financial crisis and high costs of incarceration for the focus on reintegration and problem-solving courts. The problem-solving courts discussed by Judge Bethel include drug courts, mental heath courts, family courts, and DUI courts.

Judge Bell of the Maryland Court of Appeals indicates that the problem-solving courts are another way of trying to deal with the problems that society is facing on a broader scale than it ever has before. He states, "We've got drug courts, we've got drunken driving courts, we're on the verge of doing veteran's courts, we have mental health courts. All of these courts are supposed to deal with an issue that is of some concern to the public and has a disproportionate impact on members of the public. … We have approximately 40 of those courts now across the state …"

Judge Bell suggests that juvenile courts, which have always been specialized courts, are precursors to the problem-solving courts. He indicates that the Maryland judiciary has supplemented juvenile courts with a family, holistic approach. "That's another thing, family courts, that's something we didn't have. What we tried to do is fashion a remedy so that people are dealt with more as a group, as a family, as opposed to individuals separated from each other even though all of their problems interconnected. So we have all of those things that we have put into place in the last fifteen years."

Judge Bell's discussion of the juvenile court raises issues related to those of Senior Judge McEwen of the Youth Court of South Australia. Judge McEwen counters criticism "that despite their humanitarian ideals, children's courts have been transformed from their original model as a social service agency into a deficient, second-rate criminal court that provides people with neither positive treatment nor criminal procedural justice." Judge McEwen argues "that the Youth Court of South Australia is more timely, more efficient, more responsive and ultimately more effective" than the adult courts. This argument has profound implications for the future of problem-solving courts.

Most of the U.S. judges supported problem-solving courts. However, this sentiment was not universal. For example, Judge Limbaugh indicated that he believed that drug courts were not cost-effective. He argued that they "cherry picked" clients most likely to succeed. Interestingly, Judge Bethel, a strong supporter of problem-solving courts, also indicated that he had problems with the data. As a grant reviewer for SAMHSA, he had strong suspicions that data were being manipulated and skewed to make programs look more successful than they were to facilitate grant awards. Judge Bethel also argued that it was essential to gather more data so that programs could be properly evaluated.

Related to sentencing is the issue of plea bargaining. While plea bargaining is a generally accepted practice in many jurisdictions, Judge Singh of the Delhi High Court explained that plea bargaining was first introduced into the Indian Criminal Procedure Code in 2005 and implemented in 2006. It applies only to offenses that can be punished by up to seven years in prison and excludes certain offenses. Plea bargaining has been remarkably helpful clearing Indian court dockets and reducing delays.

Several judges also discussed technological changes. Judge Limbaugh cited advances in DNA testing and fingerprinting as key technological improvements in recent years. He felt that DNA evidence has and will continue to prevent wrongful convictions and indicated that most judges found wrongful convictions "sickening." Technological advances cited by other interviewees included Judge Bell's statement that the courts were moving to a system-wide case management software, which would facilitate tracking of case file information and communication between the different courts and later law enforcement, parole, and probation and treatment professionals. Judge Rambo cited e-signing of warrants and other documents and Judge Singh cited Indian e-courts and online filing of documents. It was also clear from many of the judges that electronic legal research was a valuable tool being employed across the globe. Legal resources included a vast array of proprietary databases and open source information.

On a broader note, we inquired into their personal judicial philosophy. What should the role and function of the judiciary be in society? What should be left to other branches of government and institutions? All of the judges who addressed the issue, believed in a separation of powers approach. The legislature has the power to make laws, the executive enforces these laws and the judiciary interprets them. The judges were unanimous with regard to the importance of judicial independence and integrity. The role of the courts is to provide justice to those who seek it. For trial judges, this function is accomplished through rulings in individual cases. Aleksander Karakaš explained that Slovenian judges need to take responsibility for making the correct decision. The correct decision is reached by following the appropriate process and procedures, as well as properly interpreting and applying substantive law to the facts and parties before the court.

For appellate judges, particularly Supreme Courts or courts of last resort, reaching the correct decision is achieved through constitutional and statutory interpretation, following established judicial procedures and standards for review. For example, Judge Bell indicates that with regard to statutory interpretation, he is a strict constructionist, believing "that judges ought not be bringing to the table their personal views. ..." All of the judges call for an independent judiciary and concur that politics and political pressure should not play a role in deciding cases before the court.

However, the judges also recognize that an independent judiciary relies upon the legislative branch for funding and the executive branch for enforcement. Adequate budgets and funding for the courts are critical issues in both newly emerging and old established democracies alike.

The appointment process for judges varies and involves a variety of political considerations. Trial judges in many U.S. states, including Maryland and Louisiana are elected. Maryland, for instance, provides for election of judges to the Circuit Court, its court of general jurisdiction. Maryland appellate judges are appointed by the state governor and face "retention" votes every 10 years. U.S. District Court judges, such as Judge Limbaugh, are appointed by the president of the United States, confirmed by the U.S. Senate, and pursuant to Article III of the U.S. Constitution, serve for life. Judicial appointments at the state level are often made by the governor, the state's chief executive officer. It is hard to say whether election or appointment does more to prevent political interference. Both are political in different ways. European judicial and/or high prosecutorial commissions are probably the least likely to permit undue political interference. Judge Karakaš's discussion of Slovenian reform recounted how legislative review and reappointment every four years posed a real threat to an independent judiciary and how the new judicial councils are far better.

The judges and justices indicated that the greatest problem facing the criminal courts at this time were increasing caseloads and limited resources. They indicate that there are not enough judges and support staff to handle already substantial and growing case loads. This was a common refrain of judges in the United States and Europe. In India, the lack of resources was so severe and the caseload so high, trial delays often averaged 10 to 15 years. The advent of plea bargaining in 2006 helped the Indian judiciary to substantially reduce delays to period of one to two years. Other major problems cited by U.S. and European judges were implicit or explicit legislative threats to reduce court funding. Judge Bell of Maryland viewed the increasing use of the power of referendum as an effort to weaken the court's protection of civil and human rights.

Judges explored issues of theory and practice and research from very different perspectives. For some who focused on legal theory, the distinction was largely artificial. Judge Bell indicated that judges learn legal theory and then apply it at either the trial or appellate level. It then ceases to be theory and becomes practice which, in turn, informs theory. Other justices viewed theory in terms of social science, criminological, and management theories. The most extensive discussion of theory and practice concerned sentencing criminal defendants. Application of the four sentencing theories (punishment, deterrence, incapacitation, and rehabilitation) appeared to have the greatest potential to influence judicial decision making. Several judges mentioned one or more of the sentencing theories. Judge Bethel of Georgia discussed the theoretical underpinnings of problem-solving courts and therapeutic jurisprudence.

Another type of research involved evaluation of court administrative structures and functions that was discussed by several judges. Finally, little was discussed concerning the potential impact of social science theory on the courts, such as that which was introduced in *Brown vs. Board of Education* 347 U.S. 483 (1954) to argue that separate but equal was inherently unequal in the context of school segregation.

The extent to which transnational relations influence the courts varies substantially between the nations. Countries, such as Bosnia–Herzegovina and Slovenia, which border Western Europe and aspire to be members of the European Union (EU) are subject to extensive international influences far beyond that of the United States and Canada. For example, Judge Vucinic of Bosnia–Herzegovina, Judge Aleksander Karakaš of Slovenia, and Mag. Friedrich Forsthuber of Austria cited extensive international contacts and the need to comply with EU mandates and European Conventions on Human Rights. Most of the U.S. judges indicated that international law and transnational issues have little impact on judicial practice. However, several discussed immigration and drug trafficking problems from Mexico. Somewhat surprisingly, the U.S. judges indicated that 9/11 did not have much impact on the courts, other than increased security.

In summary, the key themes discussed by the justices: the impact of political change on the courts, diversity on the bench and in the community, trends in sentencing philosophies and the development of problem-solving courts, judicial integrity as a core philosophy, the relationship of legal and social science theories to judicial practice, the effects of technological innovation on the administration of justice, and the influence of transnational legal matters on judicial decision-making offer much to reflect upon and explore further.

Michael M. Berlin
Dilip K. Das

Suggested Guidelines
for Interviewers

Thank you for agreeing to help with this book project and agreeing to interview a judge. The following are guidelines to help you know what it is we are looking for and to keep a degree of consistency in the chapters. If you have any questions, please contact one of the editors David Lowe (D.Lowe@ljmu.ac.uk) or Dilip Das (dilipkd@aol.com).

Main Aim of the Interviews (and the Book):
Suggested Guidelines for Interviewers

We have listed a number of topics that should be covered in the interview. Please try to cover the topics mentioned below, acknowledging that the conduct and flow of the interview will dictate this. Also, feel free to add, elaborate, follow up as you see fit and necessary to clarify points, expand on ideas, or pursue an insight offered.

All the topical areas should be asked, but the specific questions listed below for each topic area are suggestions. Interviews have their own dynamics. Follow them down their most fruitful avenues, using questions that cover the topic and fit the interview. Because each of you will be interviewing justices or judges from different world legal systems, the list and sequence of questions may be adjusted in any case.

The wording of questions is, of course, your own. In follow-up questions, try to get specific examples or details of generalizations made. (Examples are *probably* among the most useful pieces of information to readers.)

General Themes to Be Covered in the Interview

The main goal of the interviews is to present the views and interpretations of legal developments and current issues in the criminal law and procedural field by experienced justices and judges. What do they see happening in the criminal courts and legal profession in their countries and internationally, and how do they evaluate or interpret developments? There are many interpretations of legal issues by scholars and policy makers who are not justices or judges, or from outside the organization. What we would like to have are interpretations from within the organization and by the individuals making the judicial decisions. We also are seeking to build personal profiles of the judges interviewed: their careers, backgrounds, influences that shaped their personality, their successes, failures, joys, temptations, and frustrations in their career, in their job.

We are looking to obtain responses on the general themes of:

1. What do justices and judges see happening in criminal law and procedure?
2. What are the issues they consider important?
3. What changes do they see as successes or failures; what are likely lasting futures or passing fads?

The reason for the interviews is that justices and judges do not get time to write and reflect on their experiences, views, opinions, and perspectives. We are requesting researchers like you to record their views and make them meaningful contributions to our understanding of criminal law and procedural problems of today. This may involve the interviewer going beyond simple questions and answers to allow the interviewee to analyze and reflect on the issues discussed. The interviewer needs also to bear in mind that the core elements of the personal profile of the interviewee should be brought out as well.

Role of the Interviewer

The basic goal of the interviews is to capture the views of the justices or judges, not those of the interviewers. Your role should not be too critical or to interpret what they meant to say, but to write as accurately as possible what they did say. When we said above, "reflect," we hope you reflect on what the official said, not on what your views are of the issues discussed. It is the judges' views, based on their career, experience, and thinking, that we are interested in. We know what scholars think about legal issues, but we know less what the people who do the judging think about and how they evaluate trends, developments, and issues in criminal justice. That is the important goal.

Having said that, by not being too critical, we do not mean to suggest that you should not challenge and draw out what it is that the justices or judges tell you. We do not want the official rhetoric that high-level people sometimes fall back on during interviews; we want their personal views and thinking. If you have the sense that you are getting the formal language, see if you can get the justices or judges to go beyond that and push them for their own views. The basic reason for doing the interviews in the first place is our firm belief that justices and judges know a lot; it is that knowledge and their judgments of the legal issues we are after.

What to Do Before the Interview

Get a sense of how much time you are likely to have and what questions you can get to during that time. In no interview will you be able to ask all the questions you want. And, when you write up the interview, you will have space for about 6,000 to 8,000 words. Choose your priorities. The top priorities for us are the reflections by the judges or justices interviewed on changes experienced and the interrelations of theory and practice as well as the insights into the person. These are high priorities for this book.

Topic Areas That Should Be Covered in the Interview

Section 1: Career

- Q1. Tell us a little bit about your career? (Try and include here the length of service as a judge, organizations worked in, movements, specializations, etc.)
- Q2. As your career as a judge has developed, what has surprised you?
- Q3. Has your work as a judge proved as interesting or rewarding as you thought it would when you first started?

Section 2: Personal Judicial Philosophy

- Q1. What do you think should be the role of the judiciary in society?
- Q2. What should be their job, functions, and responsibilities? What should be left to others?
- Q3. What organizational arrangements work and which do not?
- Q4. What policies on relations with the community, with political groups, with other criminal justice organizations work well? What hampers cooperation with other agencies and groups?
- Q5. How difficult is it for judges to relate to the living and social conditions of those from economically deprived backgrounds who appear before them?
- Q6. How can a judge develop empathy for those from the lower rungs of the social division in society from which they can derive a degree of understanding why that person before them did what is alleged?
- Q7. How should the criminal legal system in your country be performing? What should be the preferred priorities and strategies; hard-edged crime control, prevention, services, order work, what mix for which types of problems, etc.?

Section 3: Problems and Successes Experienced

Q1. In your experience, what policies or programs have worked well and which have not? And, can you speculate for what reasons?

Q2. What would you consider to be the greatest problem facing the criminal courts at this time?

Q3. What problems in courts do you find are the most difficult with which to deal?

Q4. What would be easy to change? Internal problems (culture of the organization, managerial deficiencies, allegations of corruption, or gender-related problems, etc.) or externally generated problems (resources, community support, etc.)? Is anything easy?

Section 4: Theory and Practice

Q1. What should be the relationship between theory and practice?

Q2. What can practitioners learn from theory, and what can theory builders learn from practitioners?

Q3. What is the relationship right now? Does it exist? Does it work?

Q4. What holds collaboration or interactions back?

Q5. What kind of research, in what form, on what questions would you find most useful for practice? If not very useful, what could or should theory builders do to make their products more useful to you?

Q6. Where do you find theory-based information? Where do you look? What journals, books, publications, reports?

Q7. Does the judiciary carry supplementary research outside the research required with pending cases? If so, what are the areas, issues, or questions of law researched?

Section 5: Transnational Relations

Q1. Have you been affected by, and how, in the work of your organization by developments outside the country (human rights demands, universal codes of ethics, practical interactions with judges or justices from other countries, personal experiences outside the country, new crime threats, etc.)?

Q2. Have those interactions been beneficial or harmful? What kind of external international influences are beneficial and which ones less so?

Q3. How have developments post 9/11 in the United States affected your work?

Section 6: General Assessments

Q1. Are you basically satisfied or dissatisfied with developments in criminal law and criminal procedure in your system?

Q2. What are the most likely developments you see happening and which would you like to see happening?

Q3. What is most needed now to improve the system?

After the Interview

1. Please write a short introduction to the actual interview. The introduction should:
   a. Summarize the highlights of the justices' or judges' careers, some of this information you can get from the interview and other parts from published sources or vitae.
   b. Briefly describe the basic structure of the **legal system** in your country. You have to be the judge of how much an informed reader is likely to know about the country and how much should be explained.
   c. Describe, briefly, the interview itself: where, when, how pleasant or not, etc.

2. You should, if at all possible, tape record the interview. For publication, edit the interview to bring out the most important discussion and answers. Chances are you will have much more information than we will have space for in the proposed book.

3. Write a short conclusion on your impression of the interview. What the major themes were, how well the views expressed accord with known literature, but do not be overly critical on this point, please. Again, keep it brief.

4. Write a glossary of terms or events mentioned in the interview a reader might not be familiar with. For example, if interview is with a German judge and the 'Rechtstaat' is mentioned, describe very briefly what that is, or, if interviewing an American judge and the Miranda Warning is mentioned, describe what the warning is. Just select the most likely items nonexperienced readers might not know.

5. We have had two basic styles in writing up interviews. Both are acceptable, but we prefer the second style. One style is to simply transcribe the interviews: questions asked, answers given. The second style, which requires more work, is to write short statements about the topic of a question and then insert long excerpts from the

interviews. The main point is to have the voice and views of the judge being interviewed, not your own.

6. Send the completed interviews to the editors.

Including the introduction, conclusion, and glossary of terms, the total word length of the interview should be about 6,000 to 8,000 words.

Finally, each interview will be a book chapter that should be useable to teach students in a university class/professional institute or as a book. It should be a source of knowledge and information to readers interested in legal systems including judges, lawyers, prosecutors, and related professionals.

A Call for Authors

Advances in Police Theory and Practice

AIMS AND SCOPE:

This cutting-edge series is designed to promote publication of books on contemporary advances in police theory and practice. We are especially interested in volumes that focus on the nexus between research and practice, with the end goal of disseminating innovations in policing. We will consider collections of expert contributions as well as individually authored works. Books in this series will be marketed internationally to both academic and professional audiences. This series also seeks to —

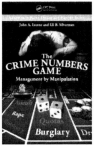

Police Reform in China

- Bridge the gap in knowledge about advances in theory and practice regarding who the police are, what they do, and how they maintain order, administer laws, and serve their communities
- Improve cooperation between those who are active in the field and those who are involved in academic research so as to facilitate the application of innovative advances in theory and practice

Mission-Based Policing

The International Trafficking of Human Organs

A Multidisciplinary Perspective

The series especially encourages the contribution of works coauthored by police practitioners and researchers. We are also interested in works comparing policing approaches and methods globally, examining such areas as the policing of transitional states, democratic policing, policing and minorities, preventive policing, investigation, patrolling and response, terrorism, organized crime and drug enforcement. In fact, every aspect of policing, public safety, and security, as well as public order is relevant for the series. Manuscripts should be between 300 and 600 printed pages. If you have a proposal for an original work or for a contributed volume, please be in touch.

Series Editor
Dilip Das, Ph.D., Ph: 802-598-3680
E-mail: dilipkd@aol.com

Dr. Das is a professor of criminal justice and Human Rights Consultant to the United Nations. He is a former chief of police, and founding president of the International Police Executive Symposium, IPES, www.ipes.info. He is also founding editor-in-chief of *Police Practice and Research: An International Journal* (PPR), (Routledge/Taylor & Francis), www.tandf.co.uk/journals. In addition to editing the *World Police Encyclopedia* (Taylor & Francis, 2006), Dr. Das has published numerous books and articles during his many years of involvement in police practice, research, writing, and education.

Proposals for the series may be submitted to the series editor or directly to –
Carolyn Spence
Senior Editor • CRC Press / Taylor & Francis Group
561-317-9574 • 561-997-7249 (fax)
carolyn.spence@taylorandfrancis.com • www.crcpress.com
6000 Broken Sound Parkway NW, Suite 300, Boca Raton, FL 33487

International
Police Executive
Symposium (IPES)

The International Police Executive Symposium (IPES)* was founded in 1994. The aims and objectives of the IPES are to provide a forum to foster closer relationships among police researchers and practitioners globally, to facilitate cross-cultural, international and interdisciplinary exchanges for the enrichment of the law enforcement profession, and to encourage discussion and published research on challenging and contemporary topics related to the profession.

One of the most important activities of the IPES is the organization of an annual meeting under the auspices of a police agency or an educational institution. Every year, since 1994, annual meetings have been hosted by such agencies and institutions all over the world. Past hosts have included the Canton Police of Geneva, Switzerland; the International Institute of the Sociology of Law, Onati, Spain; Kanagawa University, Yokohama, Japan; the Federal Police, Vienna, Austria; the Dutch Police and Europol, The Hague, The Netherlands; the Andhra Pradesh Police, India; the Center for Public Safety, Northwestern University, United States; the Polish Police Academy, Szczytno, Poland; the Police of Turkey (twice); the Kingdom of Bahrain Police; a group of institutions in Canada (consisting of the University of the Fraser Valley, Abbotsford Police Department, Royal Canadian Mounted Police, the Vancouver Police Department, the Justice Institute of British Columbia,

* www.ipes.info

Canadian Police College, and the International Centre for Criminal Law Reform and Criminal Justice Policy); the Czech Police Academy, Prague; the Dubai Police; the Ohio Association of Chiefs of Police and the Cincinnati Police Department, Ohio, United States; the Republic of Macedonia and the Police of Malta.

The 2011 Annual Meeting on the theme of "Policing Violence, Crime, Disorder and Discontent: International Perspectives" was hosted in Buenos Aires, Argentina, on June 26–30, 2011. The 2012 annual meeting was hosted at United Nations in New York on the theme of "Economic Development, Armed Violence and Public Safety" on August 5–10. The 2013 Annual Meeting on the theme of "Global Issues in Contemporary Policing" was hosted by the Ministry of Interior of Hungary and the Hungarian National Police on August 4–9, 2013.

There also have been occasional special meetings of IPES. A special meeting was co-hosted by the Bavarian Police Academy of Continuing Education in Ainring, Germany, University of Passau, Germany, and State University of New York, Plattsburgh, in 2000. The second special meeting was hosted by the police in the Indian state of Kerala. The third special meeting on the theme of "Contemporary Issues in Public Safety and Security" was hosted by the commissioner of police of the Blekinge Region of Sweden and the president of the University of Technology on August 10–14, 2011.

The majority of participants of the annual meetings are usually directly involved in the police profession. In addition, scholars and researchers in the field also participate. The meetings comprise both structured and informal sessions to maximize dialogue and exchange of views and information. The executive summary of each meeting is distributed to participants as well as to a wide range of other interested police professionals and scholars. In addition, a book of selected papers from each annual meeting is published through CRC Press/Taylor & Francis Group, Prentice Hall, Lexington Books, and other reputed publishers. A special issue of *Police Practice and Research: An International Journal* also is published with the most thematically relevant papers after the usual blind review process.

IPES Institutional Supporters

Australian Institute of Police Management, Collins Beach Road Manly NSW 2095, Australia, (contact Connie Coniglio). +612 9934 4800; Fax: +612 9934 4780; email: cconiglio@aipm.gov.au

APCOF, The African Policing Civilian Oversight Forum, (contact Sean Tait), 2nd floor, The Armoury, Buchanan Square, 160 Sir Lowry Road, Woodstock Cape Town, 8000 South Africa. 27 21 461 7211; Fax: 27 21 461 7213; email: sean@apcof.org.za

Baker College of Jackson, 2800 Springport Road, Jackson, MI 49202, U.S. (contact: Blaine Goodrich) 517-841-4522; email: blaine. goodrich@baker.edu

Cyber Defense & Research Initiatives (contact James Lewis), LLC, PO Box 86, Leslie, MI 49251, U.S. 517-242-6730; email: lewisja@ cyberdefenseresearch.com

Defendology Center for Security, Sociology and Criminology Research (Valibor Lalic), Srpska Street 63,78000 Banja Luka, Bosnia and Herzegovina. 38751-308-914 (phone and fax); email: lalicv@teol.net

Department of Criminal Justice (Dr. Harvey L. McMurray, Chair), North Carolina Central University, 301 Whiting Criminal Justice Bldg., Durham, NC 27707, U.S. 919-530-5204, 919-530-7909; Fax: 919-530-5195; email: hmcmurray@nccu.edu

Cliff Roberson, Professor Emeritus, Washburn University, 16307 Sedona Woods, Houston, TX 77082-1665, U.S. 713-703-6639; Fax: 281-596-8483; email: roberson37@msn.com

De Montfort University, Health and Life Sciences, School of Applied Social Sciences (Dr. Perry Stanislas, Hirsh Sethi), Hawthorn Building, The Gateway, Leicester, LE1 9BH, U.K. 44 (0) 116 257 7146; email: pstanislas@dmu.ac.uk, hsethi@dmu.ac.uk

Department of Psychology (Stephen Perrott), Mount Saint Vincent University, 166 Bedford Highway, Halifax, Nova Scotia, Canada. email: Stephen.perrott@mvsu.ca

Fayetteville State University (Dr. David E. Barlow, Professor and Dean), College of Basic and Applied Sciences, 130 Chick Building, 1200 Murchison Road, Fayetteville, NC, 28301 U.S. 910-672-1659; Fax: 910-672-1083; email: dbarlow@uncfsu.edu

Edmundo Oliveira, PhD, 1 Irving Place University Tower Apt. U 7 A 10003.9723, New York, New York. 407-342-24.73; email: edmundooliveira@cfl.rr.com.

International Council on Security and Development (ICOS) (Andre Souza, Senior Researcher), Visconde de Piraja 577/605, Ipanema, Rio de Janeiro 22410–003, Brazil. 55 21 3186 5444; email: asouza@ icosgroup.net

Justice Studies Department, San Jose State University, 1 Washington Square, San Jose, CA 95192-0050; (Mark E. Correia, PhD, Chair and Associate Professor), mcorreia@casa.sjsu.edu. 408-924-1350; Kerala Police (Shri Balasubramaniyum, Director General of Police), Police Headquarters, Trivandrum, Kerala, India. email: manojabraham05@gmail.com

Law School, John Moores University (David Lowe, LLB Program Leader), Law School, Redmonds Building, Brownlow Hill, Liverpool, L3 5UG, U.K. 44 (0) 151 231 3918; email: D.Lowe@ljmu.ac.uk

Molloy College, The Department of Criminal Justice (contact Dr. John A. Eterno, NYPD Captain Ret.), 1000 Hempstead Avenue, PO Box 5002, Rockville Center, NY 11571-5002, U.S. 516-678-5000, ext. 6135; Fax: 516-256-2289; email: jeterno@molloy.edu

National Institute of Criminology and Forensic Science (Kamalendra Prasad, Inspector General of Police), MHA, Outer Ring Road, Sector 3, Rohini, Delhi 110085, India. 91 11 275 2 5095; Fax: 91 11 275 1 0586; email: director.nicfs@nic.in

National Police Academy, Japan (Naoya Oyaizu, Deputy Director), Police Policy Research Center, 183-8558: 3-12-1 Asahi-cho Fuchu-city, Tokyo, Japan. 8142 354 3550; Fax: 8142 330 3550; email: PPRC@npa.go.jp

Royal Canadian Mounted Police (Craig J. Callens), 657 West 37th Ave., Vancouver, BC V5Z 1K6, Canada. 604-264-2003; Fax: 604-264-3547; email: bcrcmp@rcmp-grc.gc.ca

School of Psychology and Social Science, Head, Social Justice Research Centre (Prof. S. Caroline Taylor, Foundation Chair in Social Justice), Edith Cowan University, 270 Joondalup Drive, Joondalup, WA 6027, Australia. email: c.taylor@ecu.edu.au

South Australia Police (Commissioner Mal Hyde), Office of the Commissioner, South Australia Police, 30 Flinders Street, Adelaide, SA 5000, Australia. email: mal.hyde@police.sa.gov.au

Southeast Missouri State University (Dr. Diana Bruns, Dean), Criminal Justice & Sociology, One University Plaza, Cape Girardeau, MO 63701, U.S. 573-651-2178; email: dbruns@semo.edu

The Faculty of Criminal Justice and Security (Dr. Gorazd Meško), University of Maribor, Kotnikova 8,1000 Ljubljana, Slovenia. 3861 300 83 39; Fax: 3861 2302 687; email: gorazd.mesko@fvv.uni-mb.si

UNISA, Department of Police Practice (Setlhomamaru Dintwe), Florida Campus; Cnr Christiaan DeWet and Pioneer Avenues, Private Bag X6, 1710 South Africa. 011 471 2116; Cell: 083 581 6102; Fax: 011 471 2255; email: Dintwsi@unisa.ac.za

University of Maine at Augusta, College of Natural and Social Sciences (Richard Myers, Prof.), 46 University Drive, Augusta, ME 04330-9410, U.S. email: rmyers@maine.edu

University of New Haven (Dr. Mario Gaboury, School of Criminal Justice and Forensic Science), 300 Boston Post Road, West Haven, CT 06516, U.S. 203-932-7260; email: rward@newhaven.edu

University of South Africa, College of Law (Professor Kris Pillay, School of Criminal Justice, Director), Preller Street, Muckleneuk, Pretoria. email: cpillay@unisa.ac.za

University of the Fraser Valley (Dr. Darryl Plecas), Department of Criminology & Criminal Justice, 33844 King Road, Abbotsford, British Columbia V2S7M9, Canada. 604-853-7441; Fax: 604-853-9990; email: Darryl. plecas@ufv.ca

University of West Georgia (David A. Jenks, PhD), Pafford Building 2309, 1601 Maple Street, Carrollton, GA 30118, U.S. 678-839-6327; email: djenks@westga.edu

Index